Rand McNally StreetFinder®
Lake County

Contents

Lake County Major Communities   2

Lake County Municipal Offices   2

Lake County Quick Reference Guide   3

How to Use the StreetFinder®   4

Map Legend   4

Lake County Locator Map   5

Lake County StreetFinder® Maps   6

StreetFinder® Index   54

Rand McNally & Company
Chicago • New York • San Francisco

© 1986 Rand McNally & Company

Lake County Major Communities

Lake County Population: 470,500
County Seat: Waukegan
Principal City: Waukegan

Towns and populations for Lake County are based on the 1980 United States *Census of Population* and the latest available estimates for unincorporated places not listed in the 1980 census.

Towns	Population
Antioch	4,419
Aptakisic	200
Bannockburn	1,316
Barrington	9,029
Barrington Highlands	350
Beach	4,650
Big Hollow	100
Brookhill	150
Bull Creek	150
Cedar Island	100
Channel Lake	1,613
Countryside Lake	250
Countryside Manor	900
Crocketts Estates	350
Crooked Lake	300
Crooked Lake Oats	350
Deep Lake	300
Deerfield	17,432
Deer Park	1,368
Del Mar Woods	300
Diamond Lake	1,500
Druce Lake	250
Duck Lake Woods	250
East Loon Lake	400
Echo Lake	300
Foresthaven	300
Forest Lake	1,148
Fox Lake	6,831
Fox Lake Hills	2,199
Fox Lake Vista	500
Fox River	1,067
Gages Lake	3,814
Glen Arms	150
Grandwood Park	1,600
Grass Lake	2,191
Grayslake	5,260
Green Oaks	1,523
Gurnee	8,695
Hainesville	187
Half Day	400
Harbor Estates	150
Hawthorn Woods	1,658
Highland Lake	400
Highland Park	30,599
Highwood	5,455
Horatio Gardens	400
Indian Creek	236
Indian Point	300
Indian Trail Estates	200
Ingleside	1,676
Island Lake	2,293
Ivanhoe	300

Kildeer	1,609
Klondike	400
Knollwood	1,500
Lake Barrington	2,320
Lake Bluff	4,434
Lake Catherine	1,335
Lake Forest	15,245
Lake Villa	1,913
Lake Zurich	8,225
Liberty Acres	120
Libertyville	16,520
Lincolnshire	4,151
Lindenhurst	6,220
Long Grove	2,013
Long Lake	2,201
Loon Lake	600
Lotus Woods	350
Mettawa	330
Meyers Bay	150
Meyers Bay	1,055
Mundelein	17,053
Mylith Park	250
Nippersink Terrace	200
North Barrington	1,475
North Chicago	38,774
North Hills	400
North Libertyville Estates	700
Oak Spring Woods	250
Old Mill Creek	84
Orchard Valley	150
Park City	3,673
Petite Lake	1,350
Pistakee Bay	900
Pistakee Heights	200
Pistaqua Heights	400
Prairie View	600
River Glen	180
Riverwoods	2,804
Rondout	130
Round Lake	3,175
Round Lake Beach	12,921
Round Lake Heights	1,192
Round Lake Park	4,032
Russell	150
Shaw	1,700
Stanton Point	375
Sylvan Lake	350
Third Lake	222
Timber Lake	600
Tower Lakes	1,177
Venetian Village	2,817
Vernon Hills	9,827
Volo	200
Wadsworth	1,104
Wauconda	5,688
Waukegan	67,653
West Miltmore	1,300
Wildwood	2,034
Wildwood	400
Williams Park	500
Winthrop Harbor	5,431
Wooster Lake	400
Zion	17,861

Lake County Municipal Offices

Office	Grid	Map
Antioch Village Hall 874 Main St; 395-1000	23W-42N	8
Bannockburn Village Hall 2165 Telegraph Rd; 945-6080	11W-22N	52
Deerfield Town Hall 850 Waukegan Rd; 945-5000	10W-21N	52
Fox Lake Village Hall 305 Rt 59; 587-2151	26W-36N	14
Grayslake Village Hall 164 Hawley St; 223-8515	20W-33N	25
Gurnee Village Hall 4573 Grand Ave; 673-7650	14W-35N	19
Hainesville Village Hall 221 E Pine View; 223-2032	22W-33N	24
Highland Park City Hall 1707 St Johns; 432-0800	8W-22N	53
Highwood City Hall 17 Highwood Ave; 432-1924	9W-23N	53
Island Lake Village Hall Rt 176, PO Box 41; 526-8764	29W-28N	30
Lake Bluff City Hall 40 E Center; 234-0774	10W-28N	37
Lake Forest City Hall 220 E Deerpath; 234-2600	10W-26N	45
Lake Villa Village Hall 65 Cedar Ave; 356-6100	22W-38N	16
Lake Zurich Village Hall 61 W Main St; 438-5141	22W-22N	47,48
Libertyville City Hall 200 E Cook; 362-2430	16W-29N	34
Lindenhurst Village Hall 2301 Sand Lake Rd; 356-8252	20W-37N	17
Mundelein Village Hall 440 E Hawley; 566-7070	18W-28N	33,34
North Chicago City Hall 1850 S Lewis Ave; 578-7750	11W-31N	37
Riverwoods Village Hall 2300 Portwine Rd; 945-3990	13W-20N	51
Round Lake Village Hall 322 W Railroad Ave; 546-5400	23W-33N	23,24
Round Lake Beach Village Hall 1212 N Cedar Lake Rd; 546-3466	23W-34N	23,24
Round Lake Heights Village Hall 629 W Pontiac Ct; 546-1206	23W-35N	15,16
Tower Lakes Village Hall 115 South Dr; 526-2226	25W-25N	38
Vernon Hills Village Hall 290 Evergreen Dr; 367-3700	17W-24N	42
Wauconda Village Hall 101 N Main St; 526-8786	26W-27N	39
Waukegan Mun Bldg 106 N Utica St; 360-9000	10W-34N	29
Winthrop Harbor City Hall 830 Sheridan Rd; 872-3846	9W-42N	13
Zion City Hall 2828 Sheridan Rd; 872-4546	10W-40N	13

Lake County Quick Reference Guide

Cemeteries

Angolian Cem	22W-37N	16
Ascension Cem	14W-30N	35
Avon Center Cem	21W-35N	25
Benton Greenwood Cem	12W-39N	12,20
Cemetery	25W-20N	47
Cemetery	25,26W-27N	39
Diamond Lake Cem	18W-25N	42
Druce Cem	19W-34N	25
Fort Hill Cem	24W-32N	23,24
Fox Lake Cem	24W-36N	15,16
Grant Cem	26W-33N	22,23
Home Oaks Cem	21W-39N	9,17
Knopf Cem	18W-20N	50
Lakeside Cem	16W-29N	34
Lake Forest Cem	10W-27N	37,45
Lake Zurich Cem	23W-23N	48
Mooney Cem	9W-21N	52
Mount Oliver Mem Cem	12W-41N	12
Mount Rest Cem	16W-42N	10
Naval Cem	10W-30N	37
Nicholas Dowden Mem Cem	17W-28N	34
North Shore Garden of Mem	12W-32N	29
Oakdale Cem	13W-42N	11
Oakwood Cem	10W-33N	29
Orvis Cem	29W-41N	6
Pineview Cem	10W-38N	21
St Marys Cem	10W-27N	37
St Marys Cem	10W-33N	29,45
St Patrick Cem	12W-24N	44,51
St Patricks Cem	16W-40N	10
Sand Lake Cem	21W-37N	17
Vernon Cem	15W-23N	51
Warren Cem	16W-35N	18,27
White Cem	26W-21N	47

Colleges & Universities

Barat Col	10W-25N	45
Benedictine Col	17W-28N	34
College of Lake County	19W-34N	25
Lake Forest Univ	10W-26N	45
St Marys of the Lake Sem	18W-28N	34
Trinity Sem	12W-22N	53

Forest Preserves

Capt Daniel Wright FP	15,16W-24N	43
Countryside FP	20W-27N	21,33
Forest Preserve	16W-30,31N	35
	15W-39,41N	11
Greenbelt FP	12W-32N	28
Gurnee Woods	14W-36N	19,20
Lake Forest Nature Pres.	9W-25N	25
Lakewood FP	24W-26,27N	32,39,40
MacDonald Woods FP	19W-38N	17
Nature And Conservation Area	9W-38N	21
Old School FP	14W-27N	35,36,43
Riverhill FP	15W-33N	27,28
Ryerson Conservation Area	14W-21N	51
Spring Bluff FP	9W-43N	13
Van Patten Woods FP	15W-42N	11
Wilmont FP	15W-30N	35

Golf & Country Clubs

Antioch CC	24W-40N	7,8
Barrington Hills GC	27W-20N	46
Biltmore CC	25W-23N	47
Bob O Link GC	8W-21N	53
Bonnie Brook Mun GC	11W-36,37N	20,21
Brae Loch CC	19W-33N	25
Briarwood CC	10W-20N	52
Buffalo Grove GC	17W-20N	50
Chevy Chase CC	15W-20N	50,51
Countryside GC	20W-27N	33,41
Deerfield Park Dist GC	12W-21N	51,52
Deerpath Park & GC	11W-26N	44,45
Exmoor CC	9W-22N	53
Four Winds GC	23W-27N	32,39
Fox Lake CC	28W-39N	6
Glen Flora CC	10W-36N	21
Great Lakes GC	10W-30N	37
Greenshire GC	11W-38N	21
Highland Park CC	9W-22N	53
Indian Valley CC	18W-25N	42
Knollwood CC	13W-28N	35,36
Lake Barrington Shores GC	26W-24N	38
Lake Bluff GC	11W-29N	37
Lake Zurich GC	23W-23N	47
Northmoor CC	8W-21N	53
Old Elm GC	10W-24N	45
Orchard Hills GC & CC	12,13W-38N	19,20
Owentsia GC	11W-26N	45

Ravinia Green CC	12W-21N	51,52
Renwood CC	22W-35N	25
Seminary GC	18W-28N	33,34
Shiloh Park GC	10W-40N	13
Shore Acres CC	10W-30N	37
Stonehenge GC	27W-22N	46
Sunset Valley GC	9W-21N	53
Tally Ho CC	17W-24N	42
Thorngate CC	13W-20N	51
Twin Orchard CC	18W-22N	49,51
USN GC	12W-30N	37
Village Green GC	19W-29N	33

Hospitals

American International Hosp	10W-40N	13
Condell Mem Hosp	16W-28N	34
County Hosp	12W-35N	28
Good Shepherd Hosp	28W-22N	46
Great Lakes Training Center Hosps	10W-30N	37
Highland Park Hosp	9W-22N	53
Lake Forest Hosp	11W-26N	44
Round Lake Medical Clinic	24W-33N	24
St Theresa Hosp	12W-34N	29
VA Medical Center	11W-30N	37
Victory Mem Hosp	10W-35N	29

Shopping Centers

Caldwell Corners SC	10W-20N	52
Commons SC	21W-35N	17,25
Deerfield Commons SC	10W-20N	52
Diamond Lake SC	19W-26N	41,42
Fairhaven Plaza	18W-27N	33,34
Lakehurst SC	13W-33N	27,28
Lakeland SC	28W-36N	14
Liberty Mill SC	16W-28N	34
Maple Tree Mall	18W-27N	33,34
Mundelein SC	18W-27N	33,34
Orchard Shopping Plaza	23W-43N	7,8
Round Lake Beach SC	23W-35N	15,16,24
Round Lake SC #1	23W-33N	23,24
Round Lake SC #2	23W-34N	23,24
Zion SC	9W-39N	13

How to Use the StreetFinder®

The Rand McNally *Lake County StreetFinder®* is the comprehensive, easy-to-use atlas and quick reference guide to Lake County communities. Included in the StreetFinder® atlas are **Lake County Communities,** a list of the area's municipalities and their populations; and the **Quick Reference Guide** to cultural attractions, educational institutions, recreation areas, and places of interest. In addition, the StreetFinder® also includes a complete **Map Legend;** the **Lake County Locator Map; StreetFinder® atlas maps** of Lake County; and the **community and street index.** For information on using the legend, locator map, atlas maps, and index, see below.

Map Legend

Much useful information is contained in the map legend. The map scale shown on the legend page is the same for all maps which follow.

Key Locator Map

The area included within the numbered grids on the key **Locator Map** is covered in the StreetFinder® maps. The numbers within each grid area correspond to the map pages on which the area will be found.

StreetFinder® Atlas Maps

Approximately 120 communities are included on the maps. You will notice grids made up of thin red lines on each map page. Within each grid is a set of coordinates made up of two sets of directional number-letter combinations (for instance, 9W-16N). The coordinates refer to a particular geographic area on the map page, and allow you to quickly locate streets listed in the index, and features identified in the Quick Reference Guide.

You can locate adjoining map areas by referring to the "See map" notations provided on each side of the map.

StreetFinder® Community and Street Index

The index to Lake County communities and streets provides easy access to the maps. Communities are listed alphabetically; streets included on the map are also listed alphabetically, below the community in which they are located.

Some communities extend over a county boundary, and are identified within the index with an asterisk (*). The additional county location follows the community name.

The street index identifies the street name; the direction in which it runs; the grid coordinates within which the street will be found; and the appropriate page number or numbers within the county atlas. A particular street may extend into an area not covered by the StreetFinder®, but that fact is *not* indicated in the index.

Map Legend

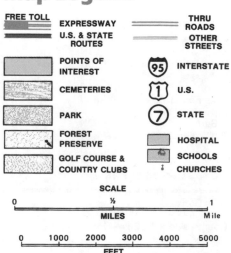

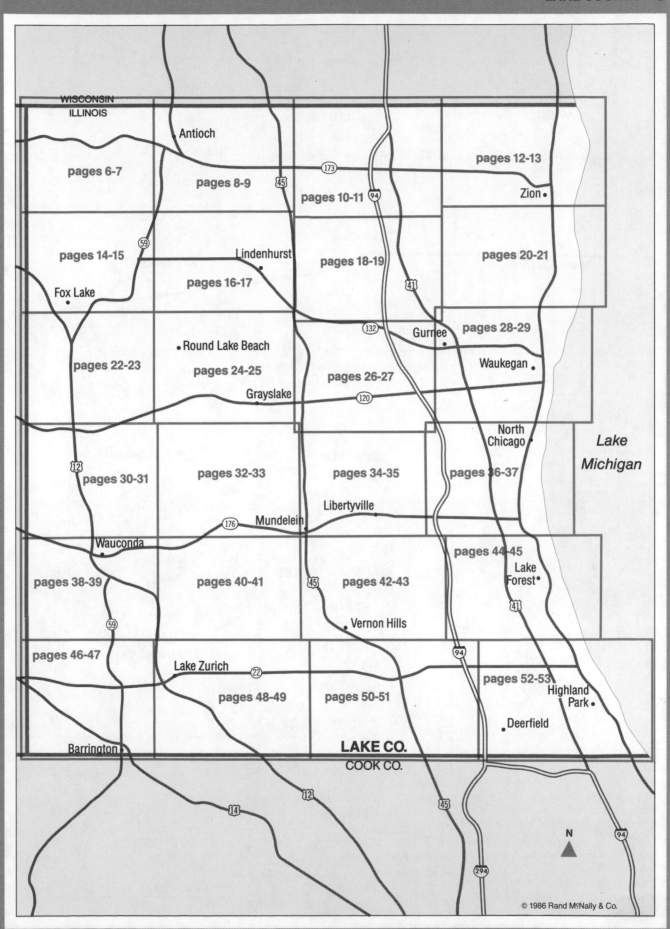

WISCONSIN
ILLINOIS

Antioch

pages 6-7

pages 8-9

(45)

(173)

pages 10-11

(94)

pages 12-13

Zion

(59)

pages 14-15

Lindenhurst

pages 18-19

pages 20-21

Fox Lake

pages 16-17

(41)

(132)

Round Lake Beach

pages 22-23

pages 24-25

Gurnee

pages 26-27

(120)

pages 28-29

Waukegan

Grayslake

North
Chicago

Lake
Michigan

(12)

pages 30-31

pages 32-33

pages 34-35

pages 36-37

Libertyville

(176)

Mundelein

Wauconda

pages 44-45

Lake
Forest

pages 38-39

pages 40-41

(45)

pages 42-43

(41)

Vernon Hills

(59)

pages 46-47

(94)

Lake Zurich

(22)

pages 52-53

Highland
Park

pages 48-49

pages 50-51

Deerfield

LAKE CO.

Barrington

COOK CO.

(12)

(14)

(45)

N

(294)

(94)

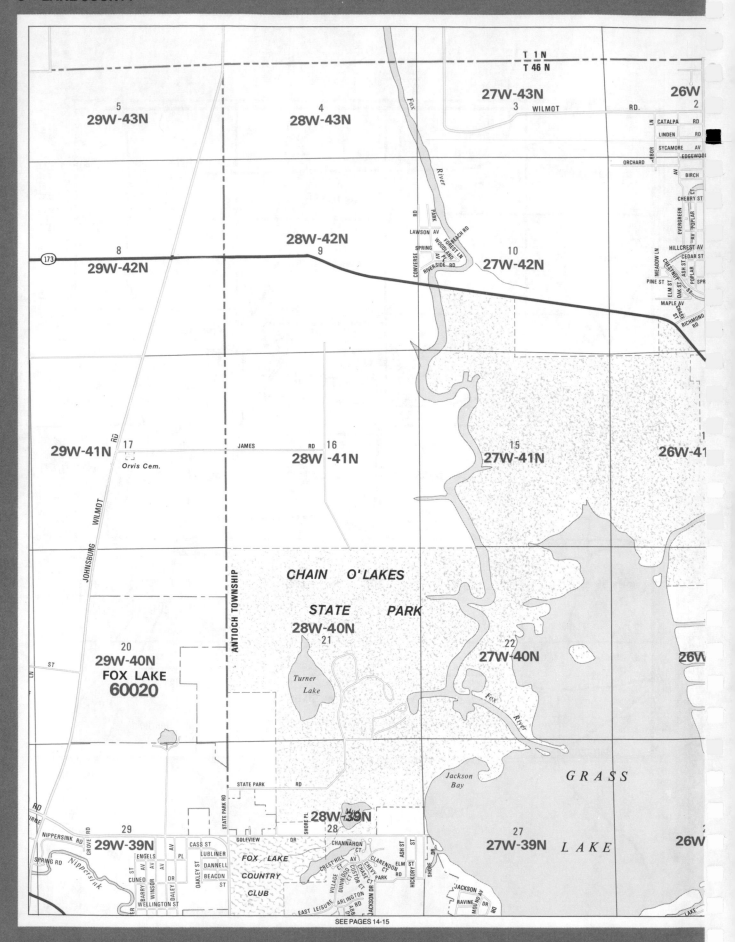

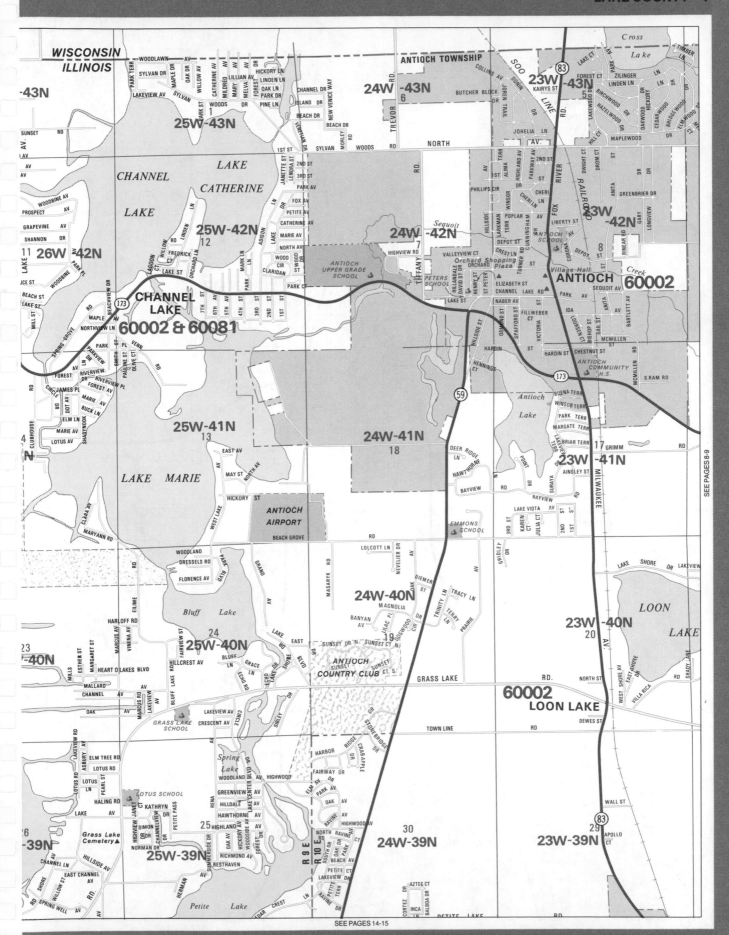

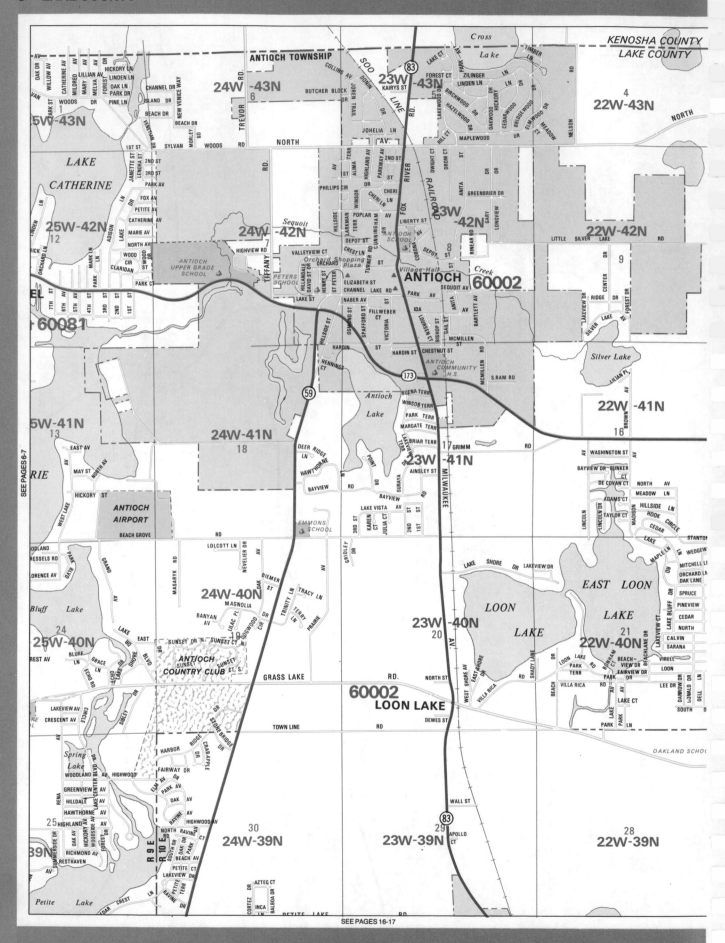

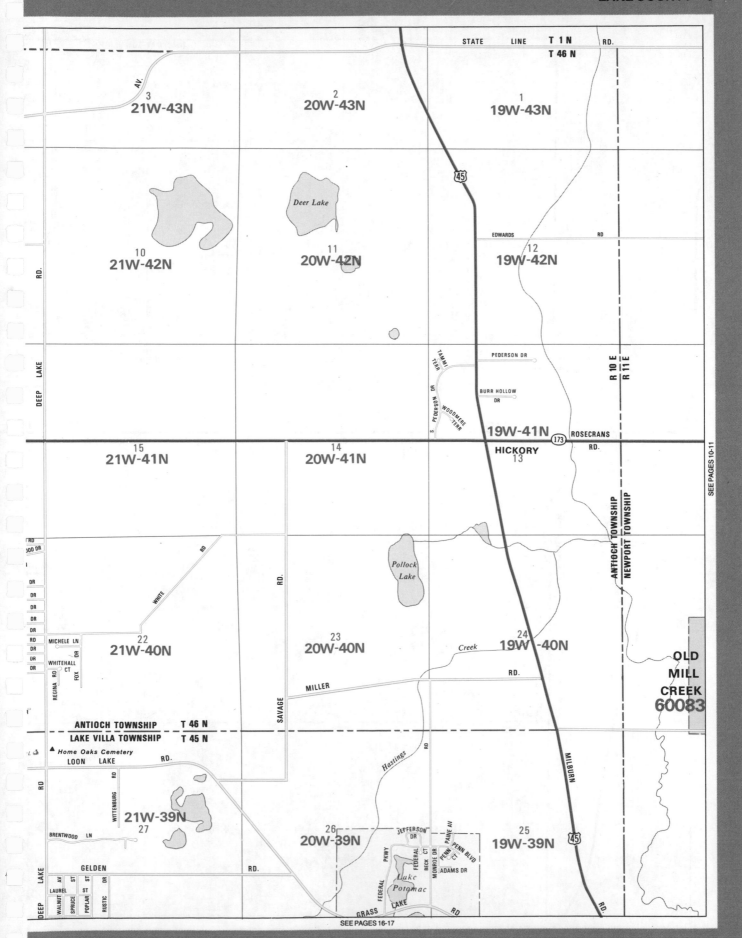

STATE   LINE   **T 1 N**   RD.
T 46 N

AV.
3
21W-43N

2
20W-43N

1
19W-43N

US 45

Deer Lake

EDWARDS   RD.

RD.

10
21W-42N

11
20W-42N

12
19W-42N

DEEP LAKE

PEDERSON DR

TAMMI TERR

S. PEDERSON DR

WOODMERE TERR

BURR HOLLOW DR

R 10 E
R 11E

19W-41N   ROSECRANS
173
HICKORY   RD.
13

15
21W-41N

14
20W-41N

SEE PAGES 10-11

RD.

WHITE

Pollock Lake

ANTIOCH TOWNSHIP
NEWPORT TOWNSHIP

WOOD DR
DR
DR
DR
RD.
MICHELE LN   22   **21W-40N**
FOX DR
WHITEHALL CT
REGINA RD

23
20W-40N

Creek

24
19W -40N

RD.

OLD MILL CREEK 60083

SAVAGE   RD.

MILLER

ANTIOCH TOWNSHIP   **T 46 N**
LAKE VILLA TOWNSHIP   **T 45 N**

RD.

▲ Home Oaks Cemetery
LOON LAKE   RD.

RD.

Hastings

MILBURN

RD.

WITTENBURG RD

21W-39N
27

BRENTWOOD LN

GELDEN   RD.

DEEP LAKE   RD.
LAUREL AV
WALNUT ST
SPRUCE ST
POPLAR ST
RUSTIC DR

26
20W-39N

JEFFERSON DR
FEDERAL PKWY
BECK CT
MONROE DR
FEDERAL CT
ADAMS DR
PENN AV
PAINE AV
PENN CT
PENN BLVD

Lake Potomac

GRASS LAKE   RD.

25
19W-39N

45

SEE PAGES 16-17

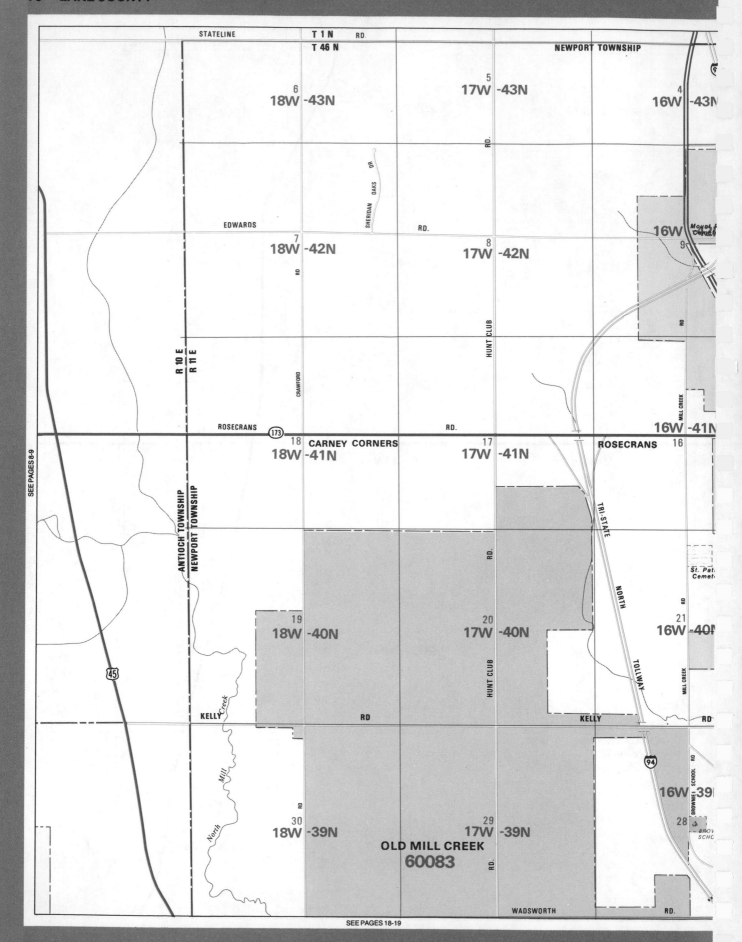

SEE PAGES 8-9

SEE PAGES 18-19

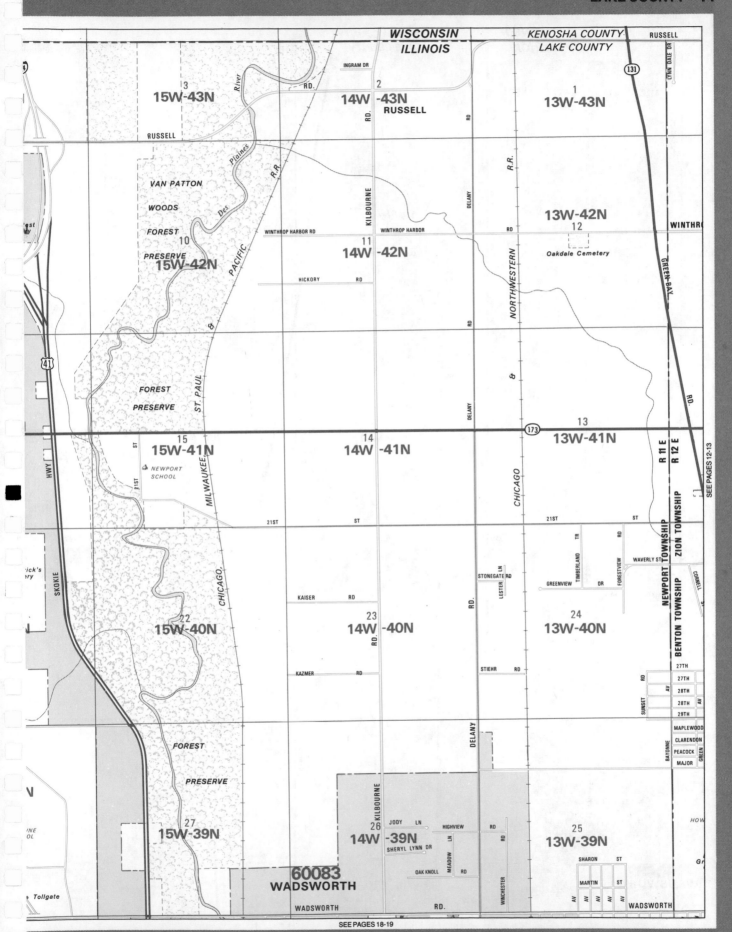

WISCONSIN
ILLINOIS

KENOSHA COUNTY
LAKE COUNTY
RUSSELL

131

INGRAM DR

3
15W-43N

RIVER
RD.

2
14W -43N
RUSSELL

1
13W-43N

LYNN DALE DR

RD.

RD.

RD.

Des
Plaines
River

R.R.

R.R.

KILBOURNE

DELANY

13W-42N
12

WINTHRO

VAN PATTON

WOODS

FOREST

PRESERVE

10
15W-42N

PACIFIC

WINTHROP HARBOR RD

HICKORY

WINTHROP HARBOR

RD

11
14W -42N

RD

NORTHWESTERN

RD

Oakdale Cemetery

GREEN-BAY

RD.

ST. PAUL

&

FOREST

PRESERVE

41 HWY

15
15W-41N

NEWPORT
SCHOOL

21ST

ST

MILWAUKEE

21ST

14
14W -41N

ST

DELANY

173

&

13
13W-41N

CHICAGO

R 11 E
R 12 E

SEE PAGES 12-13

21ST

ST

CHICAGO,

21ST

ST

TIMBERLAND TR

RD

FORESTVIEW

WAVERLY ST

NEWPORT TOWNSHIP
ZION TOWNSHIP

CORNELL ST

SKOKIE

rick's
ery

STONEGATE RD

LESTER

RD

GREENVIEW

DR

KAISER

RD

22
15W-40N

RD.

KAZMER

RD

23
14W -40N

RD.

STIEHR

RD

24
13W-40N

BENTON TOWNSHIP

SUNSET

RD

AV

27TH
27TH
28TH
28TH
29TH

AV

FOREST

PRESERVE

27
15W-39N

INE
OL

DELANY

Tollgate

26
14W -39N

KILBOURNE

JODY

LN

SHERYL LYNN DR

OAK KNOLL

HIGHVIEW

MEADOW LN

RD

RD

WINCHESTER

25
13W-39N

BAYONNE

MAPLEWOOD
CLARENDON
PEACOCK
MAJOR

GREEN

HOW

SHARON

ST

MARTIN

ST

AV AV AV AV

Gr

60083
WADSWORTH

WADSWORTH

RD.

WADSWORTH

SEE PAGES 18-19

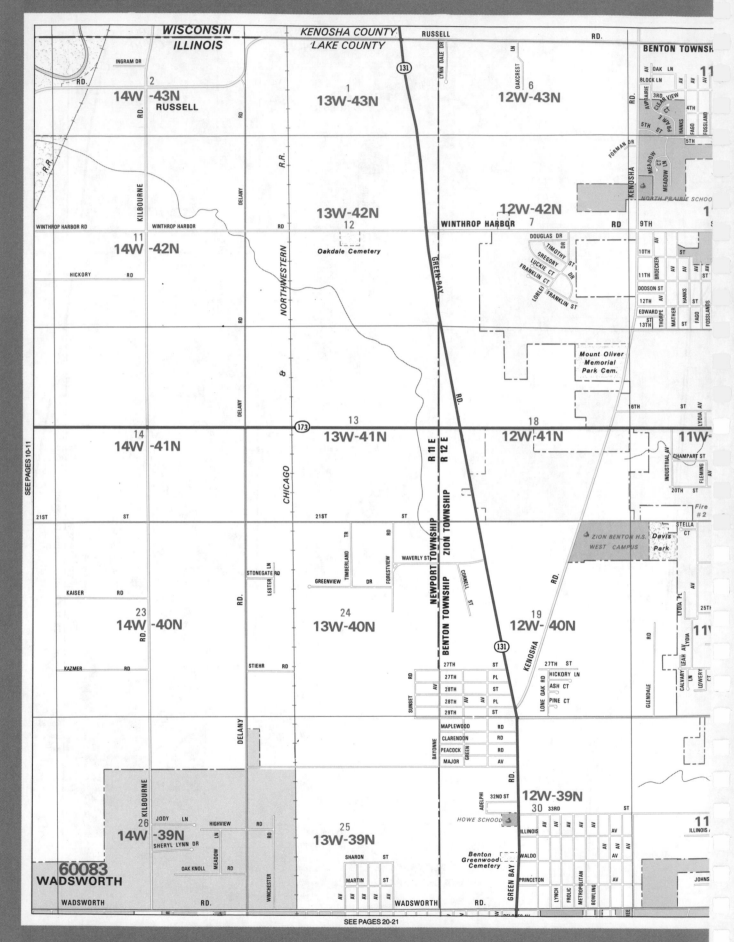

WISCONSIN

ILLINOIS

KENOSHA COUNTY
LAKE COUNTY   RUSSELL   RD.

BENTON TOWNSHIP

INGRAM DR

RD.   2

131

LYNN DALE DR   LN

OAKCREST   6

OAK LN

BLOCK LN   AV

AMPRAIRIE   CLEAR VIEW

3RD   4TH

5TH   ST   PRVD CT

HANKS   FAGO   FOSSLAND

14W -43N
RUSSELL

13W-43N   1

12W-43N

KILBOURNE   DELANY   RD

R.R.

R.R.

FORMAN DR

KENOSHA   MEADOW   CT

MEADOW LN

NORTH PRAIRIE SCHOOL

WINTHROP HARBOR RD   WINTHROP HARBOR   RD

GREEN-BAY

WINTHROP HARBOR   RD   9TH   S

14W -42N   11

13W-42N   12

12W-42N   7

DOUGLAS DR

10TH   AV   ST

HICKORY   RD

Oakdale Cemetery

NORTHWESTERN   &

TIMOTHY ST   GREGORY DR

LUCKIE CT   DR

FRANKLIN CT

LORLEI   FRANKLIN ST

11TH   BROECKER   AV   ST

DODSON ST   AV

12TH   HANKS

EDWARD   ST   FAGO

13TH   THORPE   MATHER   FOSSLANDS

DELANY   RD

Mount Oliver
Memorial
Park Cem.

16TH   ST   AV

LYDIA AV

173

13   **13W-41N**   18   **12W-41N**

R 11 E   R 12 E

11W-

CHAMPART ST

FLEMING ST

14W -41N   14

INDUSTRIAL AV

20TH

Fire
#2

CHICAGO

21ST   ST   21ST   ST

TR   RD

TIMBERLAND   FORESTVIEW

STONEGATE RD   LESTER RD

GREENVIEW   DR

WAVERLY ST

NEWPORT TOWNSHIP   ZION TOWNSHIP

CORNELL ST

ZION BENTON H.S.
WEST CAMPUS   Davis
Park

STELLA CT

KENOSHA   RD.

LYDIA PL   AV

25TH

21ST   ST

KAISER   RD

23   **14W -40N**

RD.

24   **13W-40N**

BENTON TOWNSHIP

19   **12W- 40N**

131

LONE OAK RD   HICKORY LN

27TH   ST   ASH CT

PINE CT

RD

CALVARY   LEAH AV

LYDIA   LN

LOWERY

11W

KAZMER   RD

STIEHR   RD

SUNSET   RD   27TH   PL

AV   27TH   ST

28TH   AV

28TH   PL

29TH   ST   AV

KENOSHA

GLENDALE   RD

DELANY

MAPLEWOOD   RD

CLARENDON   RD

BAYONNE   PEACOCK   GREEN   RD

MAJOR   AV

RD.

12W-39N

ADELPHI   32ND ST   30   33RD   ST

HOWE SCHOOL

ILLINOIS   AV   AV   AV   AV

60083
WADSWORTH

26   JODY   LN

HIGHVIEW

14W   SHERYL LYNN DR

OAK KNOLL   MEADOW LN   RD

KILBOURNE

DELANY   RD

WINCHESTER   RD

25   **13W-39N**

SHARON   ST

MARTIN   ST

AV   AV   AV   AV

Benton
Greenwood
Cemetery

WALDO

PRINCETON

GREEN BAY   RD.

ILLINOIS   AV   AV   AV   AV

LYNCH   FROLIC   METROPOLITAN   BOWLING

JOHNS

11

ILLINOIS

-39N   **14W**

WADSWORTH   RD.   WADSWORTH   RD.

SEE PAGES 10-11

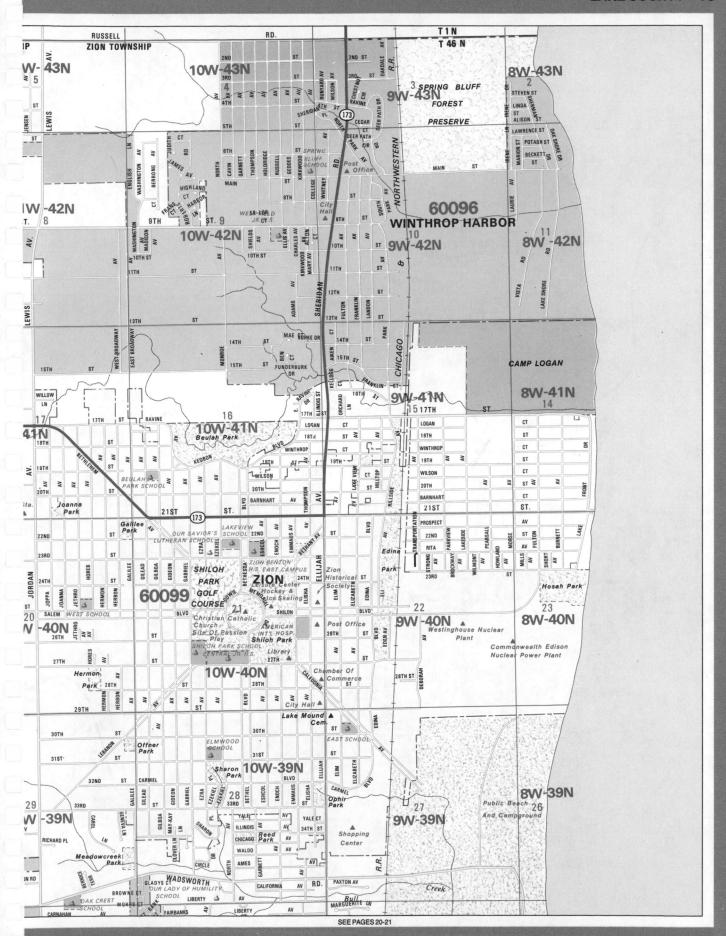

SEE PAGES 6-7

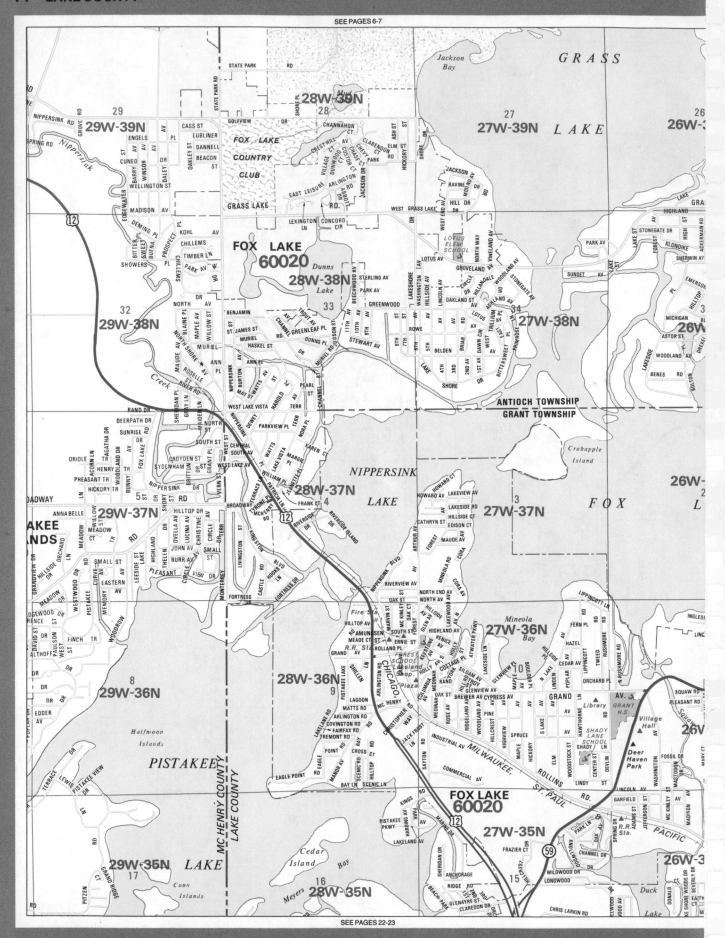

SEE PAGES 22-23

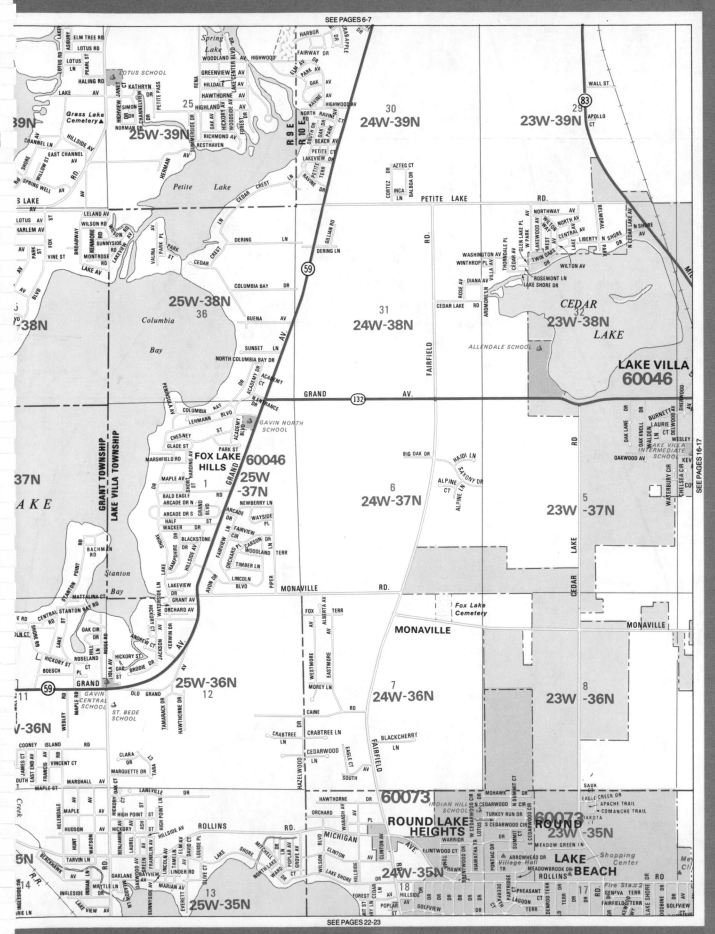

SEE PAGES 6-7

SEE PAGES 16-17

SEE PAGES 8-9

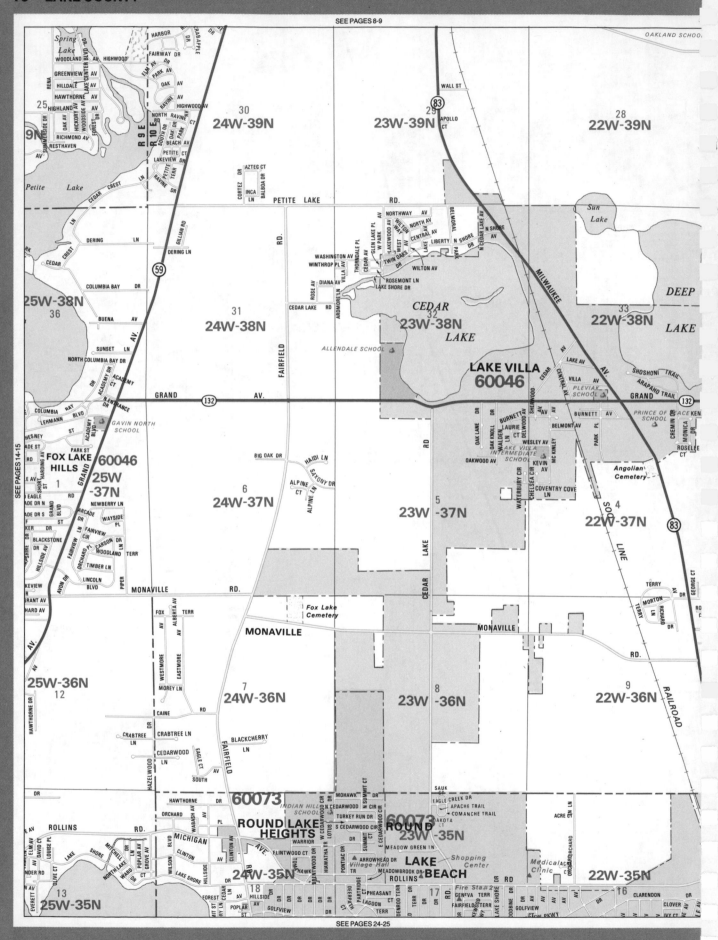

OAKLAND SCHOOL

Spring
Lake

Petite   Lake

25

9N

9N

R 9 E
R 10 E

WALL ST

83
APOLLO CT

30
24W-39N

23W-39N
29
32

22W-39N
28

Sun
Lake

PETITE   LAKE   RD.

DEEP

LAKE

25W-38N
36

31
24W-38N

CEDAR
23W-38N
LAKE

33
22W-38N

FAIRFIELD

ALLENDALE SCHOOL

LAKE VILLA
60046

GRAND   AV.
132

Grand
132

83

FOX LAKE
HILLS   60046
25W
-37N
1

6
24W-37N

23W
-37N
5

4
22W-37N

ANGOLIAN
CEMETERY

SEE PAGES 14-15

GAVIN NORTH
SCHOOL

MONAVILLE   RD.

Fox Lake
Cemetery

MONAVILLE

MONAVILLE   RD.

25W-36N
12

7
24W-36N

23W
-36N
8

9
22W-36N

RAILROAD

60073

ROUND LAKE
HEIGHTS

INDIAN HILLS
SCHOOL

60073
ROUND
23W-35N

ROLLINS   RD.

MICHIGAN

24W-35N

LAKE
BEACH

Shopping
Center

Medical
Clinic

22W-35N

13
25W-35N

18

Fire Sta#2
17

16

SEE PAGES 24-25

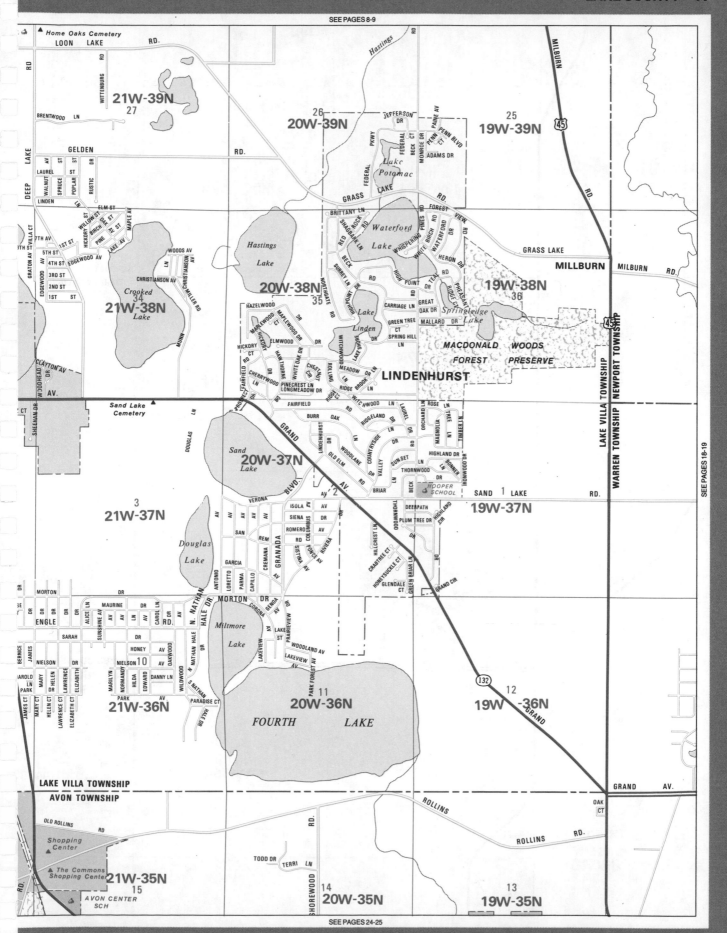

Home Oaks Cemetery
LOON LAKE RD.

WITTENBURG RD

21W-39N
27

BRENTWOOD LN

Hastings

26
20W-39N

JEFFERSON DR

FEDERAL PKWY

PENN PAINE AV
PENN BLVD

MONROE DR
ADAMS DR

25
19W-39N

45
MILBURN

DEEP LAKE RD

GELDEN RD.

LAUREL AV ST
WALNUT ST SPRUCE ST POPLAR ST
RUSTIC DR

LINDEN

RD.

Lake Potomac

GRASS LAKE

BECK CT
FEDERAL

RD.

MILBURN RD

ELM ST
WILLOW ST BIRCH OAK ST
HICKORY PINE ST
MAPLE AV
LAKE AV

GRATON AV VILLA CT
5TH ST 6TH ST
EDGEWOOD AV 4TH ST
3RD ST 2ND ST 1ST ST
EDGEWOOD
CHRISTIANSON AV
CHRISTIANSON RD

WOODS AV
LN
MILLER RD

Crooked Lake

21W-38N
34

Hastings Lake

BRITTANY LN

20W-38N
35

HAZELWOOD
MAPLEWOOD CT MAPLEWOOD DR
HICKORY HICKORY CT ELMWOOD DR
RD HAWTHORNE
CHERRYWOOD PINECREST LN
FAIRFIELD DR LONGMEADOW DR

SHAGBARK LN
RED ROCK RD
BECK
SURREY LN
NORTHGATE RD
HIGH POINT RD

Waterford Lake

WHISPERING PINES RD
WHITE BIRCH
WATERFORD RD
HERON DR

Lake Linden

CARRIAGE LN
GREEN TREE CT
SPRING HILL LN

FOREST VIEW RD

GRASS LAKE
MILLBURN

MILBURN RD.

TEAL DR
PHEASANT RIDGE RD
GREAT OAK DR
MALLARD DR

Springledge Lake

19W-38N
36

**MACDONALD WOODS
FOREST PRESERVE**

WHITE OAK DR CHESTNUT CIR
WITCHWOOD
ROLLING MEADOW DR
RIDGE BROOK DR

LAKE SHORE DR

LINDENHURST

Sand Lake Cemetery

WOODHEAD DR
CLAYTON AV
AV.

SHEEHAN DR
CT

DOUGLAS LN

PROSPECT FAIRFIELD
CHERRYWOOD LN

FAIRFIELD
BURR OAK
LINDENHURST LN
OLD ELM RD

WITCHWOOD LN
RIDGELAND
COUNTRYSIDE LN
WOODLANE RD
VALLEY DR

ORCHARD LN
LAUREL LN
SUN SET LN
THORNWOOD

ROSE LN
TREE LN
MAGNOLIA
HIGHLAND DR
BONNER LN
IRONWOOD DR

TIMBER LN

Sand Lake

20W-37N

3
21W-37N

Douglas Lake

GRAND BLVD

VERONA AV
ISOLA AV
SIENA AV
ROMERO AV
COLUMBUS AV

AV
AV
SAN AV
REM
CREMANA
GARCIA
LORETTO
ANTONIO
PARMA
CAPILLO

GRANADA
TINLISIS AV
PONCE AV
RIVIERA AV

BRIAR
BECK

DEEPATH
HOOPER SCHOOL
ODONNOHU
PLUM TREE DR

HILLCREST CT
CRABTREE CT
HONEYSUCKLE CT
GREEN BRIAR LN
GLENDALE CT

HIGHLAND CIR

SAND 1 LAKE RD.

19W-37N

MORTON DR
N NATHAN HALE DR
ENGLE
MORTON DR MAURINE DR
ALICE LN CAROL LN
SUNSHINE AV RD.
SARAH
JAMES NIELSON
BERNICE DR
HONEY AV OAKWOOD
MARY HELEN
HAROLD LN PARK MARY CT HELEN CT LAWRENCE CT ELIZABETH CT
NORMANDY DR HILDA
MARILYN EDWARD DANNY LN
WILDWOOD
S NATHAN HALE DR
PARK AV
PARADISE CT
HALE DR

Miltmore Lake

LAKEVIEW
LAKE ST
PRAIRIEVIEW DR
WOODLAND AV
LAKEVIEW AV
PARK FOREST AV

GENOA AV
CORONA AV

132
12
19W-36N
GRAND

21W-36N

11
20W-36N

FOURTH LAKE

LAKE VILLA TOWNSHIP
AVON TOWNSHIP

OLD ROLLINS RD
RD.
Shopping Center
The Commons Shopping Center

21W-35N
15

AVON CENTER SCH

TODD DR
TERRI LN

SHOREWOOD

14
20W-35N

ROLLINS RD.

OAK CT

ROLLINS RD.

GRAND AV.

13
19W-35N

LAKE VILLA TOWNSHIP / NEWPORT TOWNSHIP
WARREN TOWNSHIP

SEE PAGES 18-19

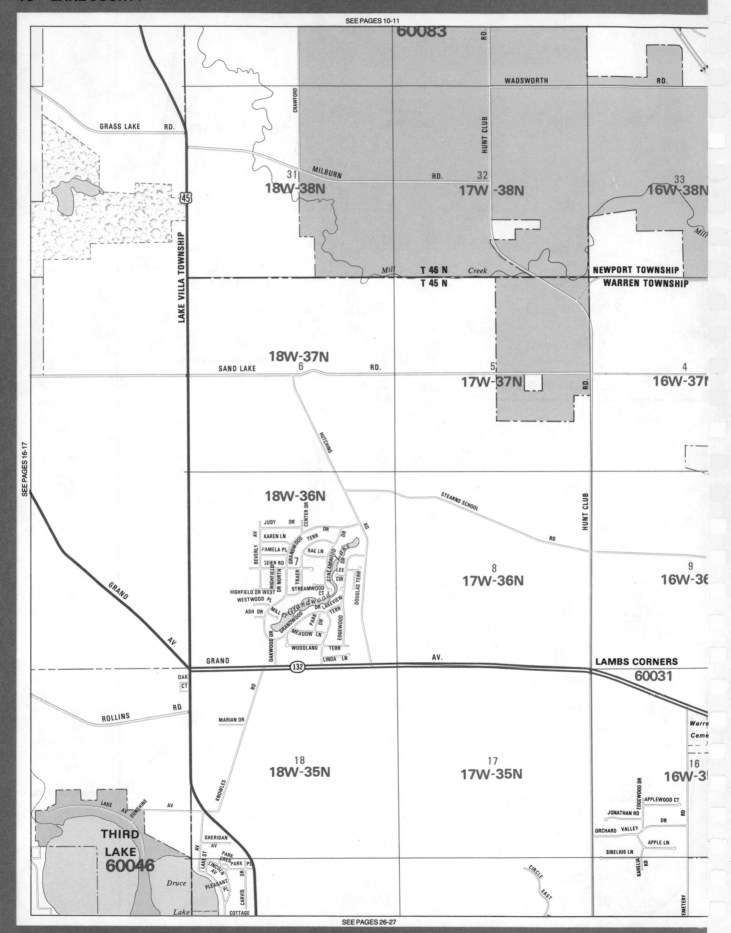

SEE PAGES 10-11

60083

WADSWORTH RD.

CRAWFORD

GRASS LAKE RD.

HUNT CLUB

MILBURN RD.

31

32

18W-38N

17W-38N

33

16W-38N

LAKE VILLA TOWNSHIP

45

Mill T 46 N Creek

NEWPORT TOWNSHIP

T 45 N

WARREN TOWNSHIP

18W-37N

SAND LAKE 6 RD.

5

4

SEE PAGES 16-17

17W-37N

16W-37N

RD.

HUTCHINS

18W-36N

STEARNS SCHOOL

JUDY DR

CENTER DR

KAREN LN

DR

HUNT CLUB

AV

GRANDWOOD DR

TERR

BEVERLY

PAMELA PL

RAE LN

RD

GEIER RD

7

STREAMWOOD

LEE

8

CIR

9

GRAND

HIGHFIELD DR NORTH

TRAER

DR

17W-36N

16W-36

HIGHFIELD DR WEST

STREAMWOOD CT

DOUGLAS TERR

WESTWOOD PL

Grandwood

AV.

ASH DR

MILL

LAKEVIEW

DR

PARK

EDGEWOOD

OAKWOOD DR

GRANDWOOD DR

MEADOW LN

TERR

WOODLAND TERR

GRAND

AV.

LAMBS CORNERS

LINDA LN

132

60031

OAK CT

ROLLINS RD

RD

MARIAN DR

Warre

Ceme

18

17

16

18W-35N

17W-35N

16W-3

KNOWLES

EDGEWOOD DR

APPLEWOOD CT

LAKE AV

SUNSHINE AV

JONATHAN RD

RD

THIRD LAKE 60046

SHERIDAN AV

ORCHARD VALLEY DR

APPLE LN

LAKE ST

PARK CRES

LINCOLN AV

PARK PL

SIBELIUS LN

KARELIA RD

Druce

PLEASANT PL

CIRCLE EAST

CARVIS DR

Lake

COTTAGE

EMETERY

SEE PAGES 26-27

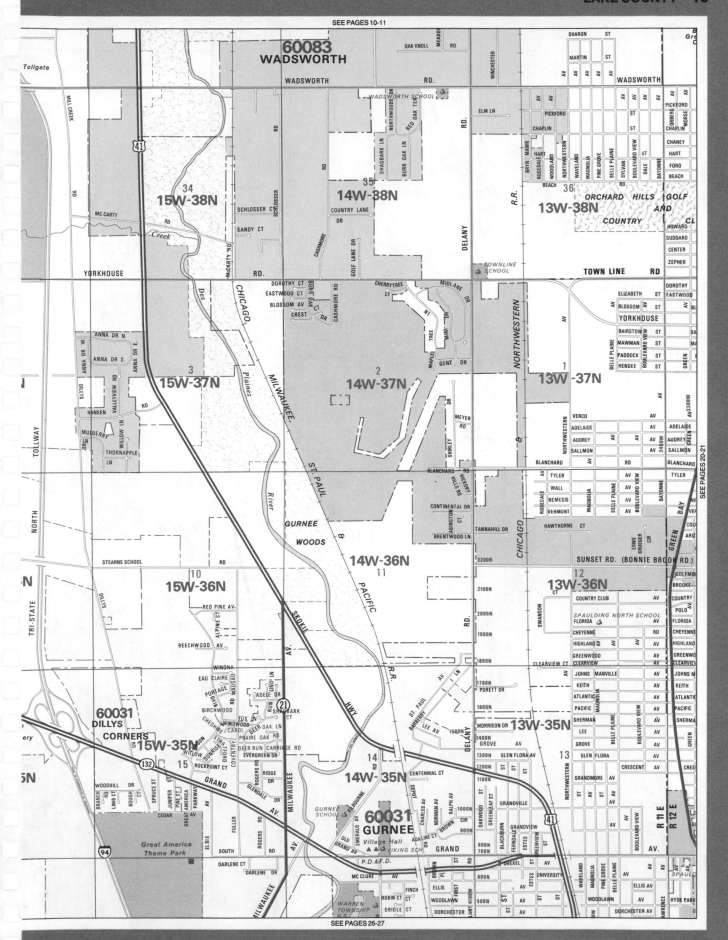

SEE PAGES 12-13

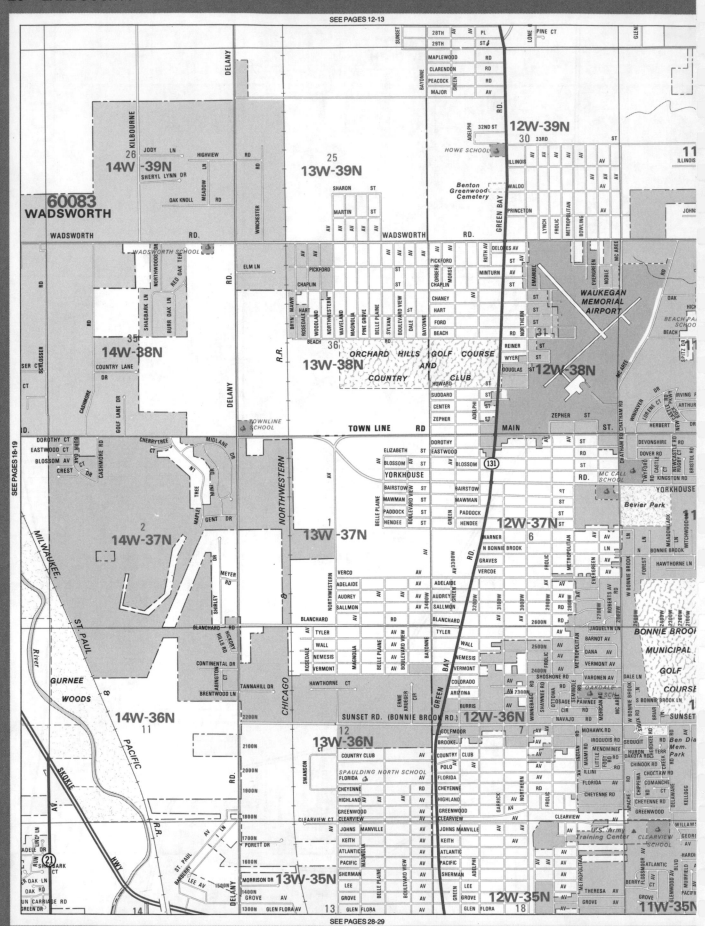

SEE PAGES 18-19

SEE PAGES 12-13

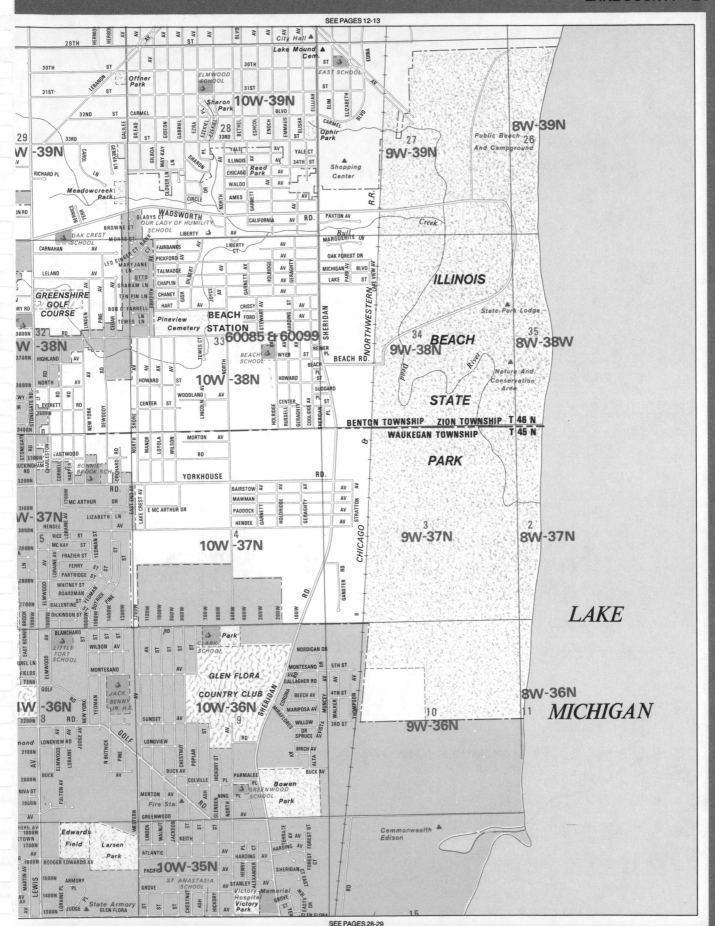

SEE PAGES 28-29

SEE PAGES 14-15

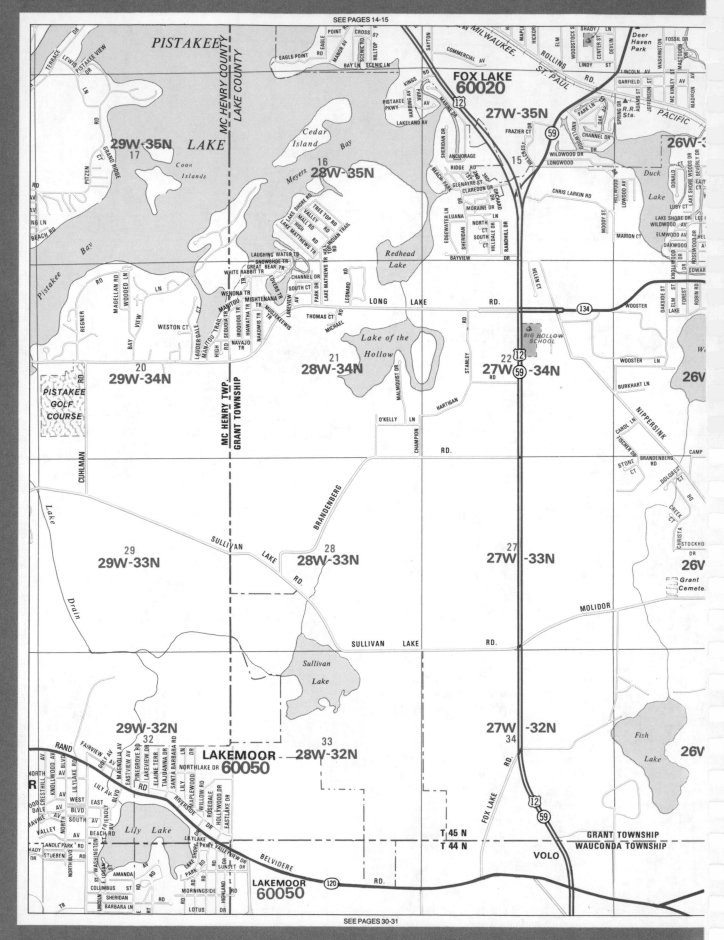

SEE PAGES 30-31

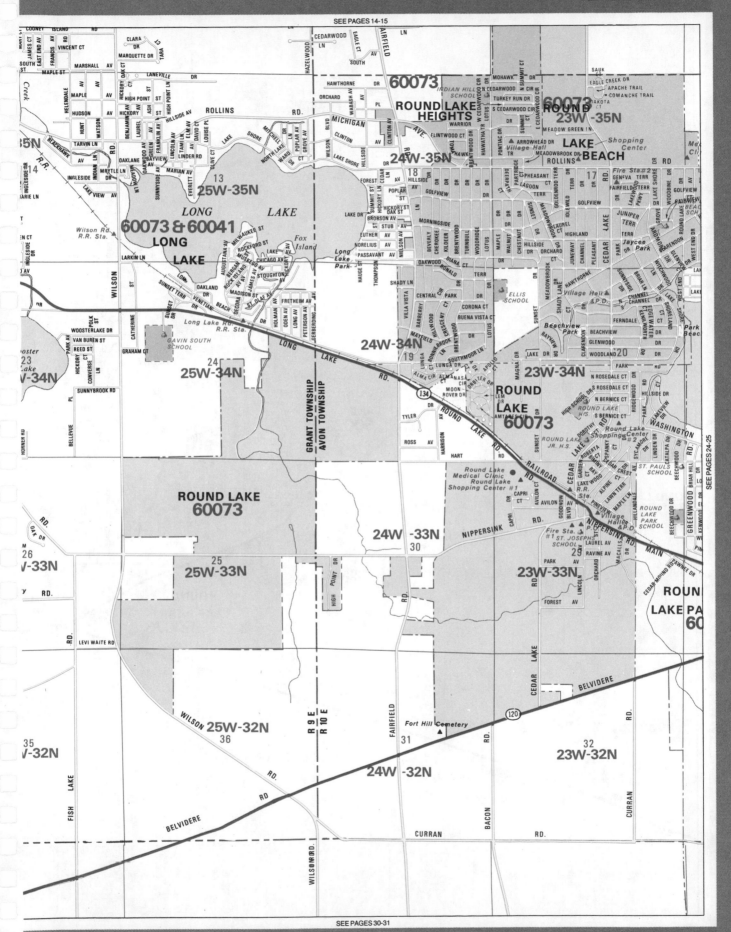

SEE PAGES 14-15

SEE PAGES 24-25

SEE PAGES 16-17

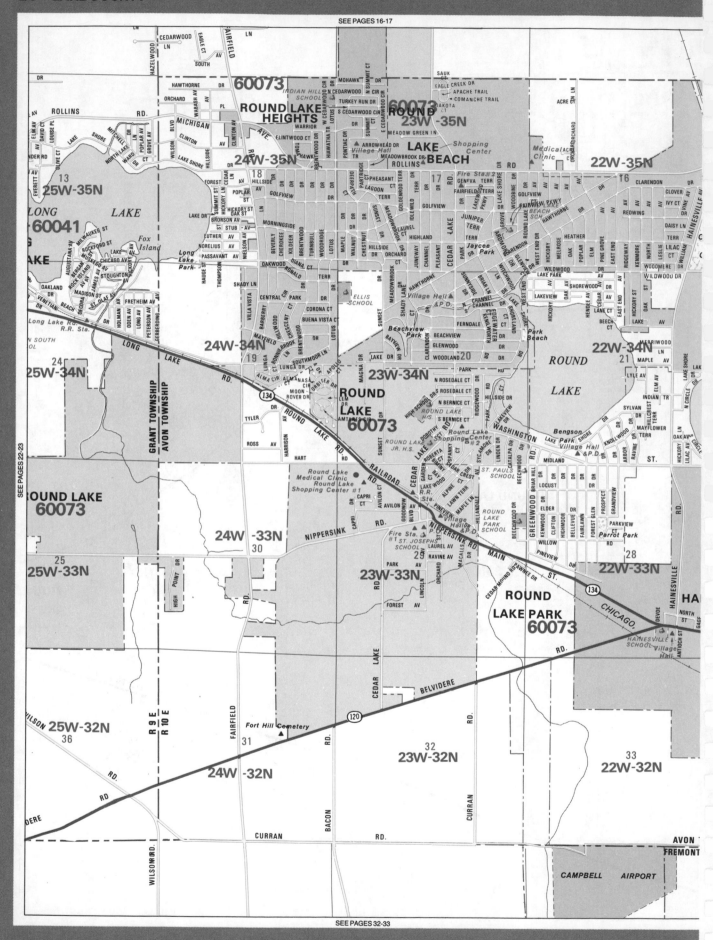

SEE PAGES 22-23

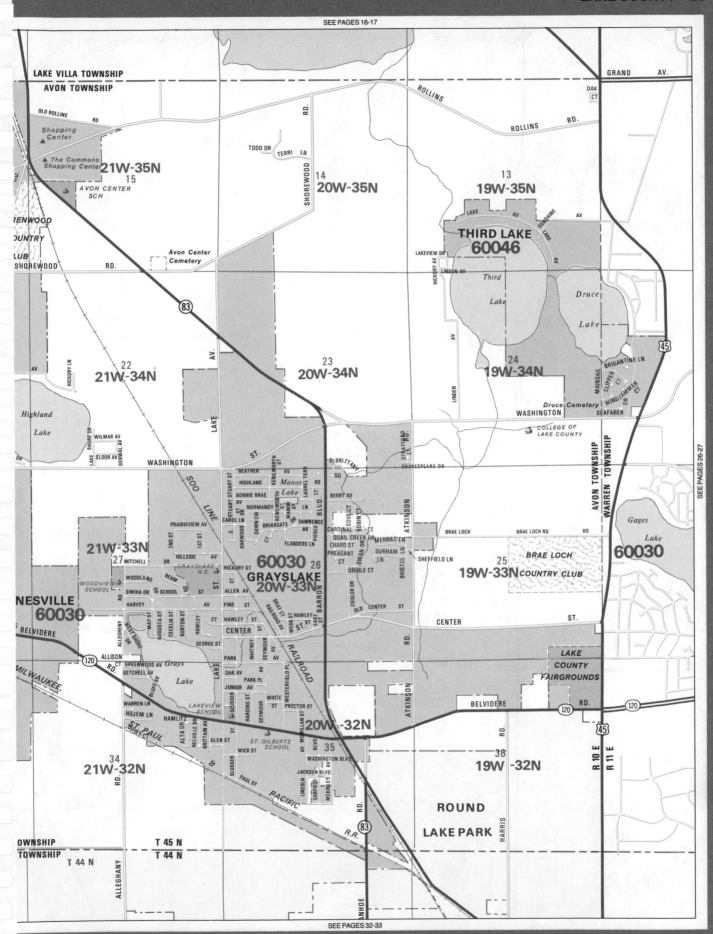

SEE PAGES 16-17

LAKE VILLA TOWNSHIP
AVON TOWNSHIP

GRAND   AV.

OLD ROLLINS   RD.

ROLLINS

ROLLINS   RD.

OAK CT

Shopping
Center

The Commons
Shopping Center

21W-35N
15

AVON CENTER
SCH

TODD DR

TERRI LN

SHOREWOOD   RD.

14
20W-35N

13
19W-35N

LAKE   AV

SUNSHINE   AV

LAKE   AV

THIRD LAKE
60046

LAKEVIEW DR

HICKORY AV

LINDEN AV

*Third
Lake*

*Druce
Lake*

GRENWOOD
COUNTRY
CLUB
SHOREWOOD   RD.

Avon Center
Cemetery

83

22
21W-34N

HICKORY LN

LAKE   AV.

23
20W-34N

AV

LINDEN   AV

24
19W-34N

BRIGANTINE LN

MAINSAIL

CLIPPER CT

WINDJAMMER DR

SEAFARER

45

*Highland
Lake*

LAKE SHORE DR

WILMAR AV

GERWAL AV

ELDOR AV

WASHINGTON

ST.

E. BRITTANY

SQ

SHAKESPEARE DR

STRATFORD CT

Druce Cemetery
WASHINGTON

COLLEGE OF
LAKE COUNTY

AVON TOWNSHIP
WARREN TOWNSHIP

*Gages
Lake*

SOO   LINE

HEATHER ST
HIGHLAND

KENILWORTH AV

*Manor
Lake*

LAUREL TERR

BERRY AV

COVE CT

ROBIN CT

ATKINSON

BRAE LOCH

BRAE LOCH RD

RD

60030

STUART ST
STUART

BONNIE BRAE

NORMANDY

KENILWORTH ST

MANOR DR

LN

LAWRENCE AV

PIERCE

CARDINAL

QUAIL CREEK DR

SWAN DR

DURHAM LN

MERRILL LN

*BRAE LOCH
COUNTRY CLUB*

60030
19W-33N
25

PRAIRIEVIEW AV

2ND ST

1ST ST

CAROL LN

DAWN CIR

BRIARGATE AV

OAKWOOD

FLANDERS LN

ORCHARD ST
PHEASANT CT

ORIOLE CT

BRISTOL LN

SHEFFIELD LN

21W-33N
27 MITCHELL

HILLSIDE AV

GRAYSLAKE H.S.

HICKORY ST

ALLEN ST

GRAY CT

BLVD

60030 26
GRAYSLAKE
20W-33N

ZIEGLER DR

OLD CENTER ST

WOODVIEW
SCHOOL

WOODLAND

BEHM DR

SIWIHA DR

RD

SCHOOL

HARVEY AV

PINE ST

HAWLEY

RAILROAD AV

WEBB ST

HAWLEY ST

EAST BARRON ST

CENTER   ST.

NESVILLE
60030

BELVIDERE

MAY ST

AUGUSTA ST

CECELIA ST

BURTON ST

HAWLEY CT

GEORGE ST

CENTER ST

WHITNEY ST

SEYMOUR

RAILROAD

RD.

ATKINSON

RD.

**LAKE
COUNTY
FAIRGROUNDS**

120

ALLISON RD

ALLEGHENY DR

WEST SHORE DR

GETCHELL AV

GREENWOOD AV

*Grays
Lake*

PARK AV

OAK AV

JUNIOR AV

PARK PL

WHITE ST

WESTERFIELD PL

PROCTOR ST

CENTER   ST.

BELVIDERE   RD.

120

120

MILWAUKEE

WARREN LN

HOJEM LN

HAMLITZ

ST. PAUL

BLUFF AV

LAKEVIEW
SCHOOL

ALTA DR

NELVILLE DR

SLUSSER ST

HARDING AV

SEYMOUR

20W-32N

ATKINSON

45

R 10 E

R 11 E

BRITTAIN AV

GLEN ST

WICK ST

*St. Gilberts
School*

AV MCMILLAN ST

WASHINGTON BLVD

BLVD

35

34
21W-32N

RD.

SLUSSER ST

PAUL ST

PACIFIC

LINCOLN

GARFIELD

JACKSON BLVD

MCKINLEY

RD.

83

R.R.

36
19W -32N

**ROUND
LAKE PARK**

HARRIS

OWNSHIP
TOWNSHIP   T 44 N

T 45 N
T 44 N

ALLEGHANY

ANHOE

SEE PAGES 26-27

SEE PAGES 32-33

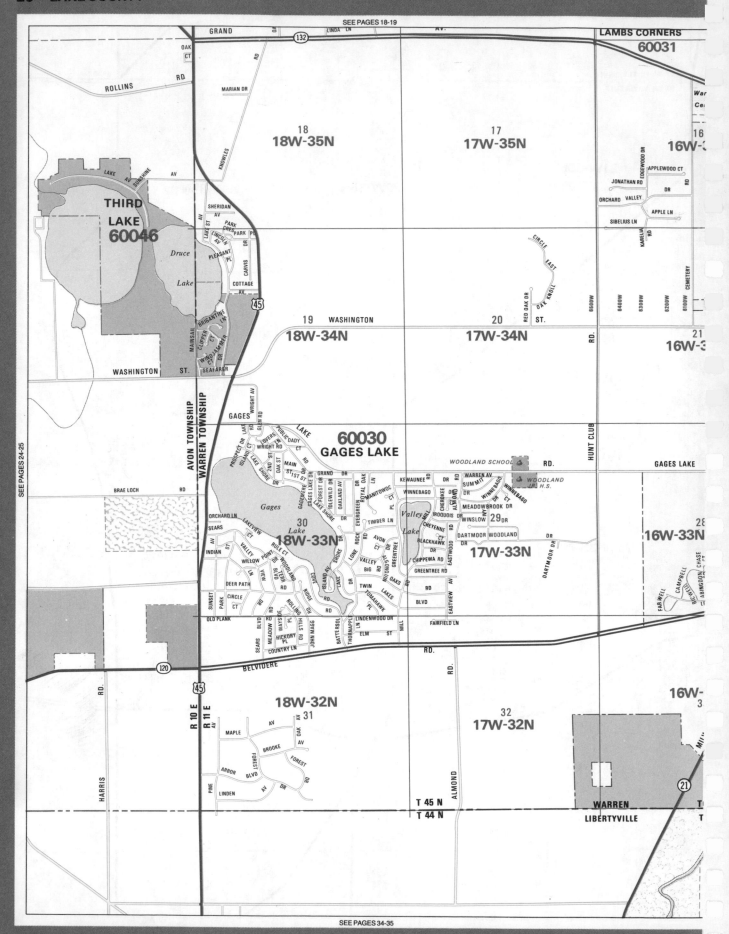

SEE PAGES 18-19

GRAND
LAMBS CORNERS
60031

LINDA LN

132

OAK CT

ROLLINS RD

MARIAN DR

Warren
Cen

18
18W-35N

17
17W-35N

16
16W-3

KNOWLES

EDGEWOOD DR
APPLEWOOD CT

JONATHAN RD

ORCHARD VALLEY

DR

RD

APPLE LN

SIBELIUS LN

KARELIA RD

CEMETERY

LAKE AV
SUNSHINE AV

**THIRD LAKE
60046**

SHERIDAN AV

PARK CRES
PARK RD

LINCOLN AV
PLEASANT PL
LAKE ST

Druce Lake

CARVIS

CIRCLE EAST

RED OAK DR
OAK KNOLL

6500W
6400W
6300W
6200W
6100W

COTTAGE AV

BRIGANTINE LN
MAINSAIL
CLIPPER CT
WINDJAMMER CT DR
SEAFARER DR

19 WASHINGTON
18W-34N

20
17W-34N

ST.

21
16W-3

WASHINGTON ST.

45

AVON TOWNSHIP
WARREN TOWNSHIP

WRIGHT AV

GAGES

GLEN RD

LAKE

HUNT CLUB RD

SEE PAGES 24-25

BRAE LOCH RD

PROSPECT DR
ISLAND CT
LOVERS LN
PUBLIC
DADY CT
WRIGHT RD
LAKE SHORE DR
2ND ST
OAK ST
MAIN
1ST ST

**60030
GAGES LAKE**

GRAND AV
IDLEWILD DR
LAKE FOREST DR
OAKLAND AV
EVERGREEN
ROYAL OAK
MANITOWOC

LN

KEWAUNEE RD

WARREN AV
SUMMIT DR
WINNEBAGO
WINNEBAGO

WOODLAND SCHOOL RD
WOODLAND JR. H.S.

GAGES LAKE

WINNEBAGO RD

MEADOWBROOK DR

GAGEMERE RD
GAGES LAKE DR

Gages Lake

30
Lake
18W-33N

LAKE SHORE DR
TIMBER LN

CHEROKEE RD
IROQUOIS RD
WINSLOW
CHEYENNE

ALMOND DR

29
DR

17W-33N

28
16W-33N

ORCHARD LN
SEARS AV
LAKEVIEW CT
INDIAN ST
VALLEY
RULE CT
WILLOW LN
POINT DR
VIEW
DEER PATH RD
WOODLAND RD
BLVD

LONE ROCK RD

Valley Lake

DARTMOOR WOODLAND DR

DARTMOOR DR

FAR WELL
CAMPBELL
BUCKINGHAM CHASE
ABINGDON

AVON CT
GREENTREE PL
BLACKHAWK
CHIPPEWA RD
GREENTREE RD

EASTWOOD AV

VALLEY BIG RD
MITONGS OAKS RD

SUNSET PARK CIRCLE CT
MEADOW LN
HICKORY PL
COUNTRY LN
WAYSIDE PL
ROLLING RD
STILES RD
JOHN MAGG RD
BATTERSOL RD
THORNAPPLE
RIDGE DR
COVE LN
ISLAND LAKE DR

TWIN LAKES
TOMAHAWK

RD

BLVD

SEARS BLVD
MEADOW

OLD PLANK

LINDENWOOD DR
ELM ST
MILL ST

FAIRFIELD LN

BELVIDERE
RD.

RD.

120

45

R 10 E
R 11 E

AV

18W-32N

31
OAK AV

32
17W-32N

16W-
3

MAPLE AV
BROOKE
FOREST AV
ARBOR BLVD
PINE
LINDEN AV
FOREST DR
FOREST RD

ALMOND RD

WARREN

21

HARRIS RD

T 45 N
T 44 N

LIBERTYVILLE

T

SEE PAGES 34-35

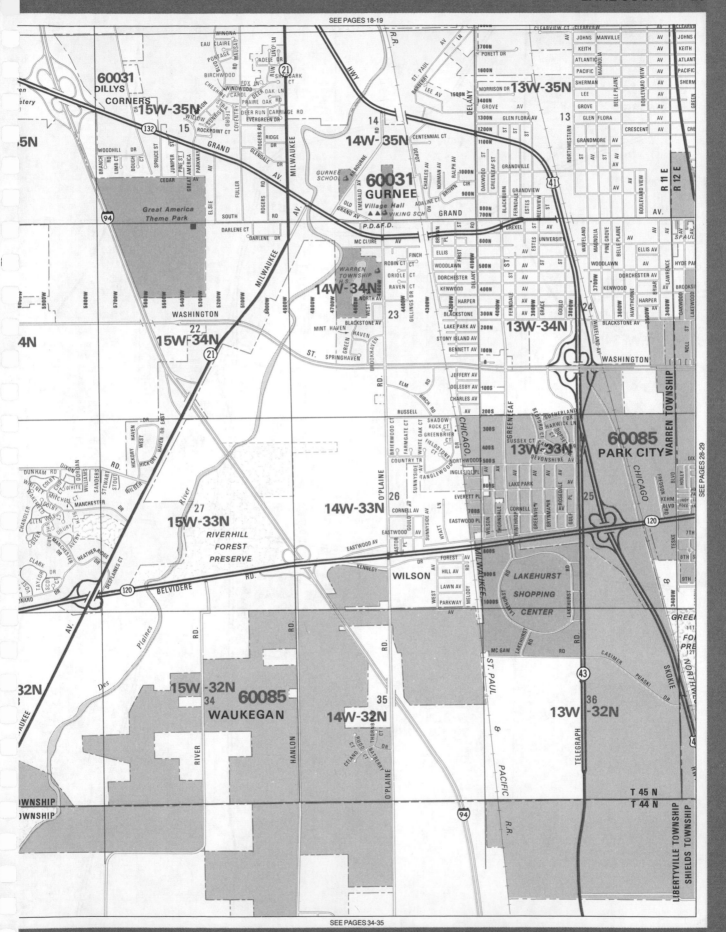

SEE PAGES 18-19

SEE PAGES 28-29

SEE PAGES 34-35

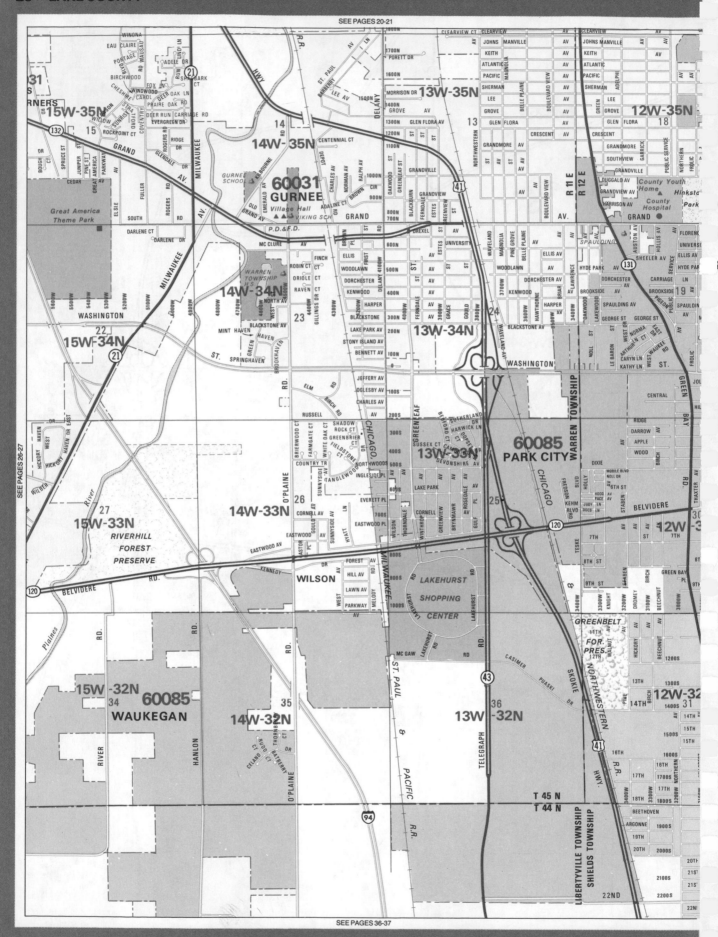

SEE PAGES 20-21

SEE PAGES 26-27

SEE PAGES 36-37

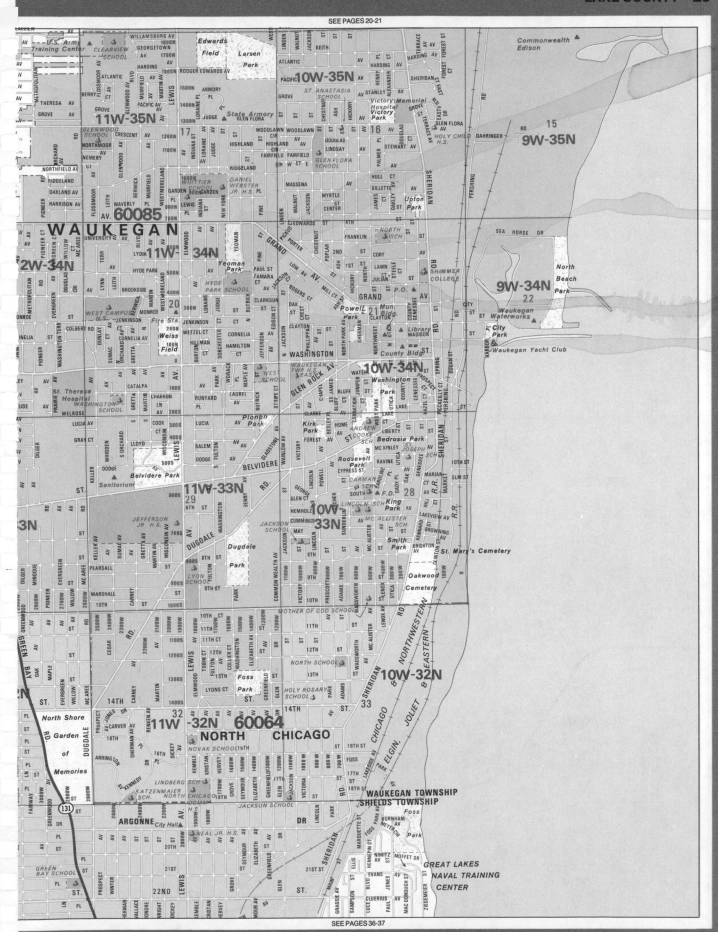

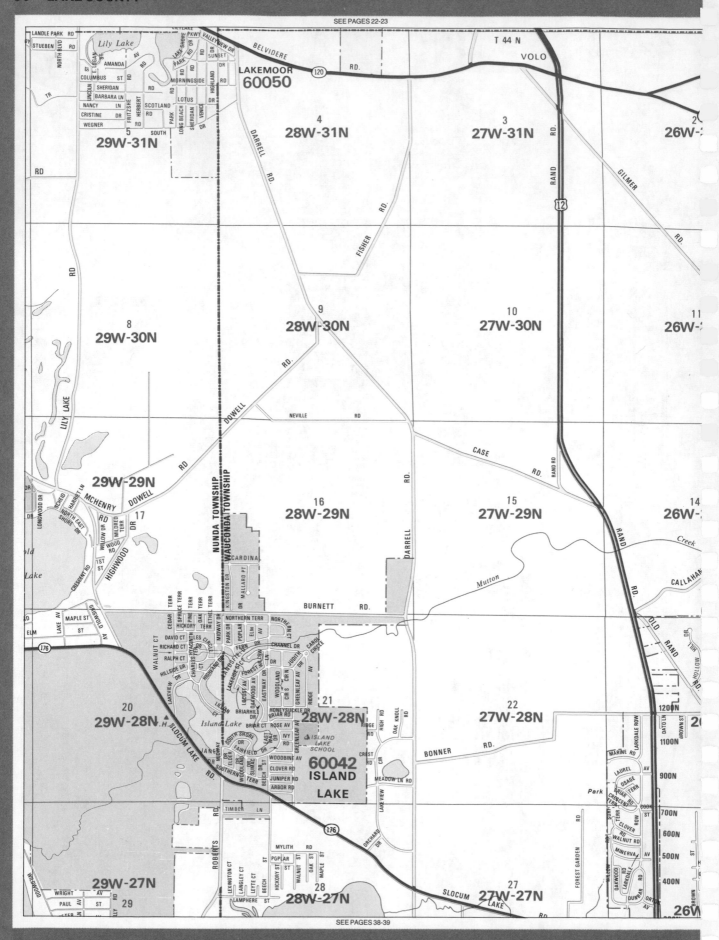

SEE PAGES 22-23

SEE PAGES 38-39

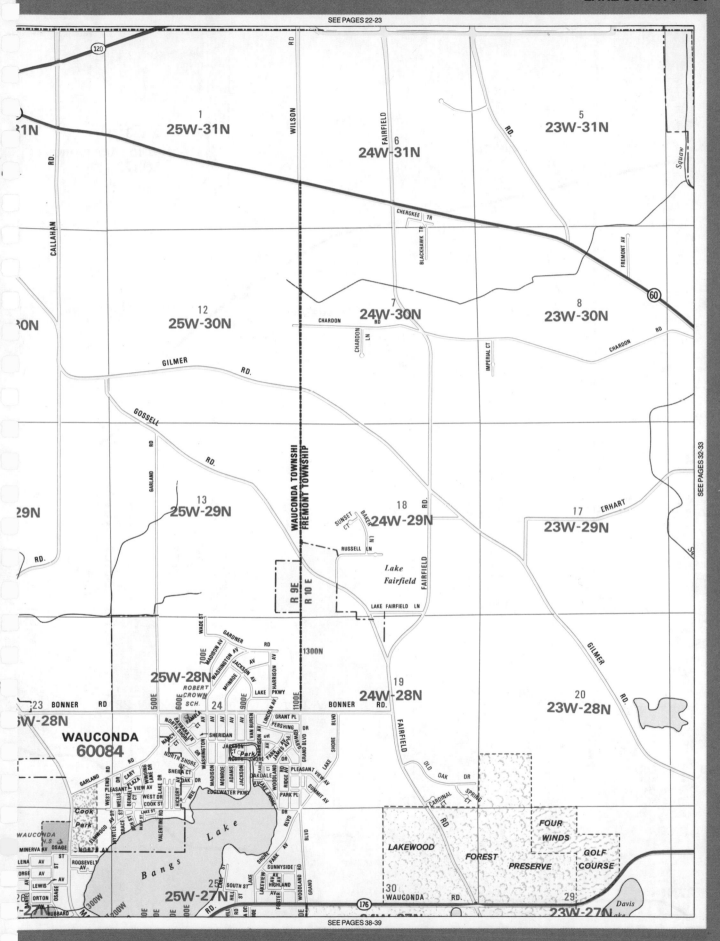

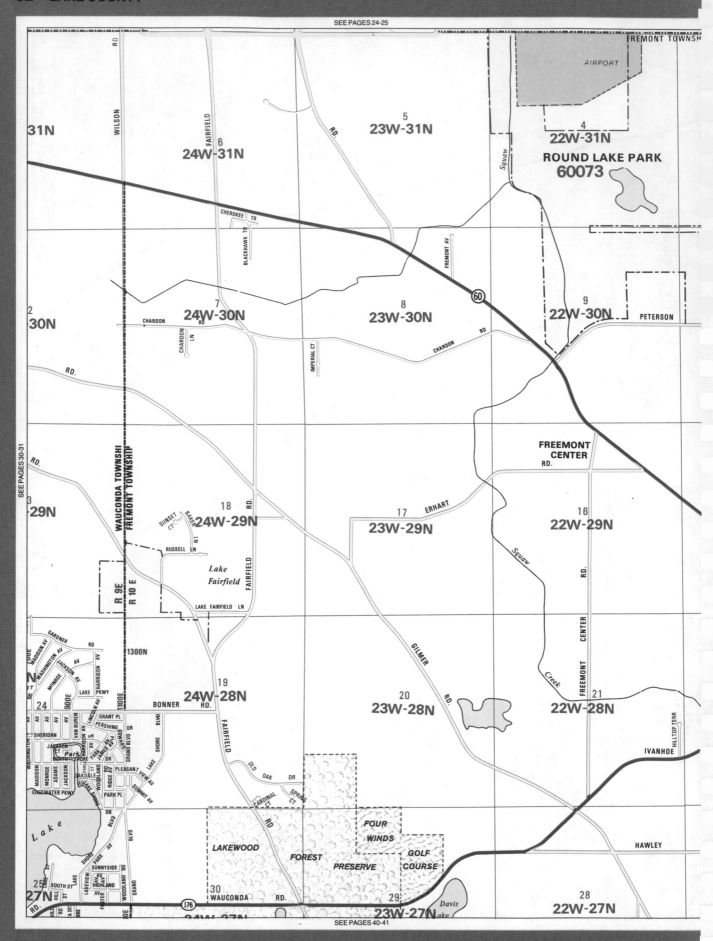

SEE PAGES 24-25

FREMONT TOWNSHI

AIRPORT

31N

5
23W-31N

6
24W-31N

4
22W-31N

**ROUND LAKE PARK
60073**

WILSON RD.

FAIRFIELD

RD.

CHEROKEE TR

BLACKHAWK TR

Squaw

60

FREMONT AV

**2
30N**

7
24W-30N

CHARDON RD.

CHARDON LN

IMPERIAL CT

8
23W-30N

CHARDON RD.

9
22W-30N

PETERSON

RD.

SEE PAGES 30-31

**3
-29N**

RD.

WAUCONDA TOWNSHI
FREMONT TOWNSHIP

R 9E
R 10E

SUNSET CT
BAKER LN
RUSSELL LN

18
24W-29N

Lake Fairfield

LAKE FAIRFIELD LN

FAIRFIELD

17
23W-29N

ERHART

FREMONT
CENTER
RD.

16
22W-29N

Squaw

FREMONT CENTER RD.

Creek

1300N

GARDNER
MADISON AV
WASHINGTON AV
JACKSON AV
MONROE AV
HARRISON AV
LAKE PKWY
RD.

50 E
100 E

24

GILMER RD.

19
24W-28N

BONNER RD.

FAIRFIELD RD.

20
23W-28N

21
22W-28N

GRANT PL
PERSHING
VAN BUREN AV
LINCOLN AV
PARK AV
JAMES AV
GRAND BLVD
LAKE SHORE BLVD

SHERIDAN
JACKSON CT
NORTH
Park
OAKDALE
MADISON
MONROE
ADAMS
JACKSON
EDGEWATER PKWY
LAKE SHORE DR
RIDGE AV
WOODLAND
PLEASANT AV
PARK PL
SUMMIT AV

OLD OAK DR
CARDINAL ST
SPRING CT

IVANHOE

HILLTOP TERR

Lake

SHORE RD
PARK AV
BLVD
SUNNYSIDE AV
LAKEVIEW
HIGHLAND
WOODLAND

**FOUR
WINDS**

LAKEWOOD

FOREST

PRESERVE

**GOLF
COURSE**

HAWLEY

25
27N

SOUTH ST
FOSTER AV
HILL
GRAND

30
24W-27N
WAUCONDA RD.

176

29
23W-27N

Davis Lake

28
22W-27N

SEE PAGES 40-41

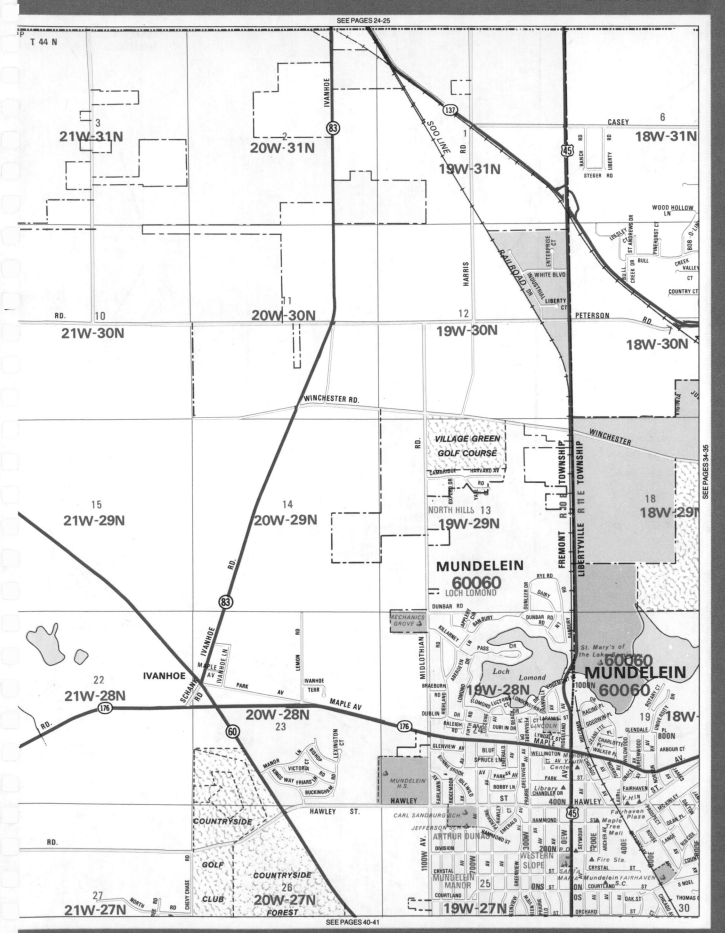

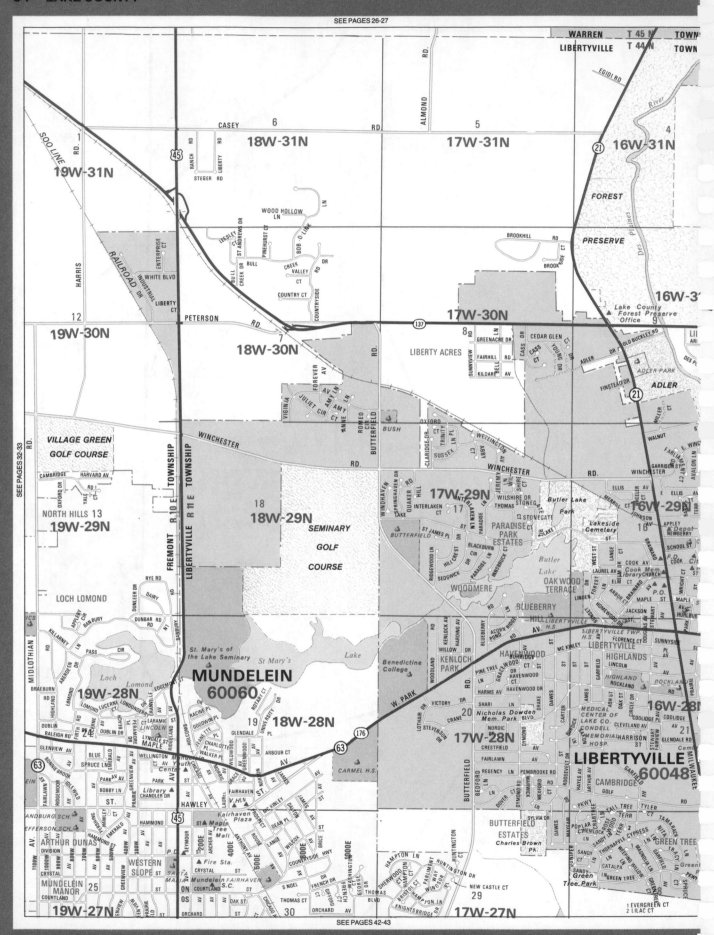

SEE PAGES 26-27

SEE PAGES 32-33

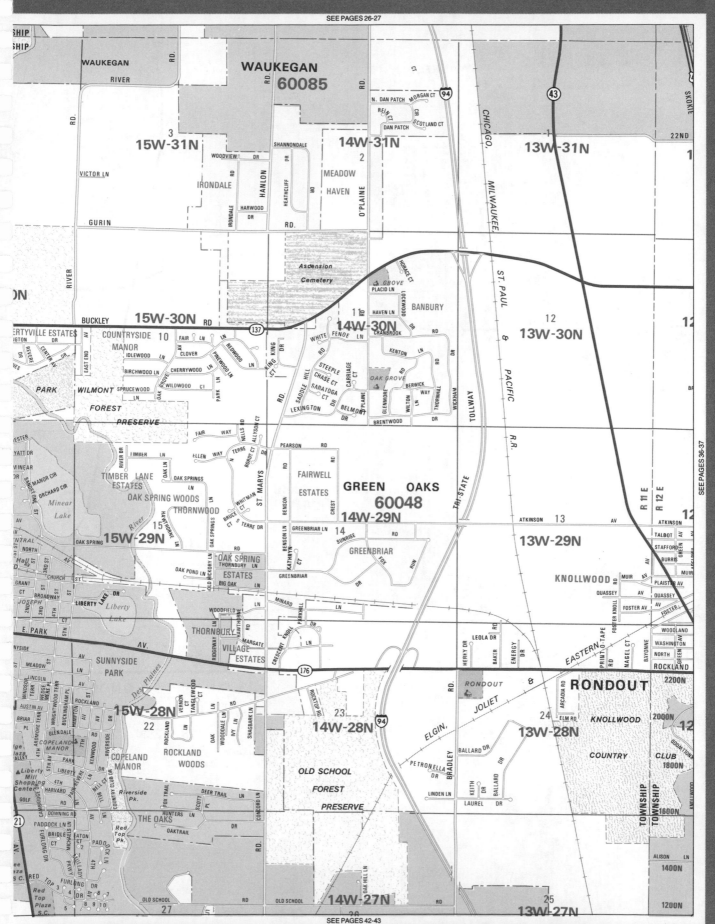

SEE PAGES 36-37

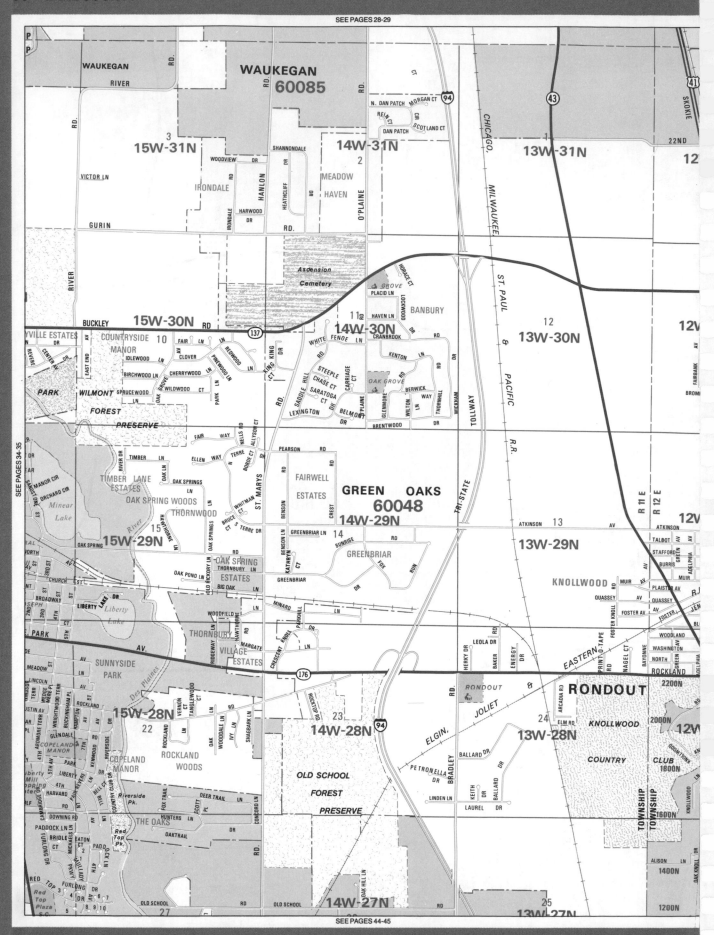

36 LAKE COUNTY

SEE PAGES 28-29

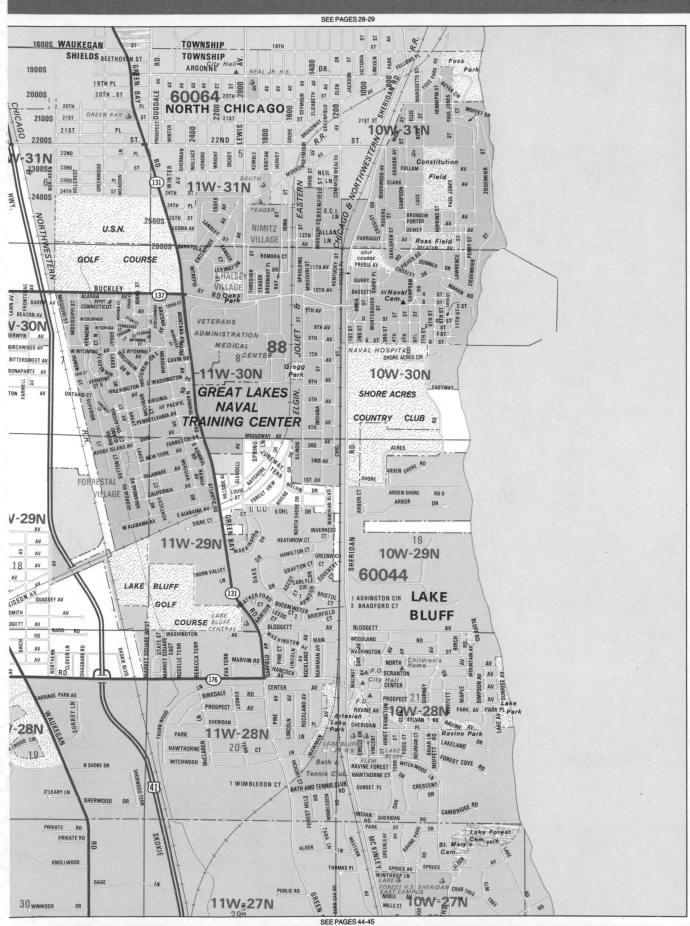

SEE PAGES 44-45

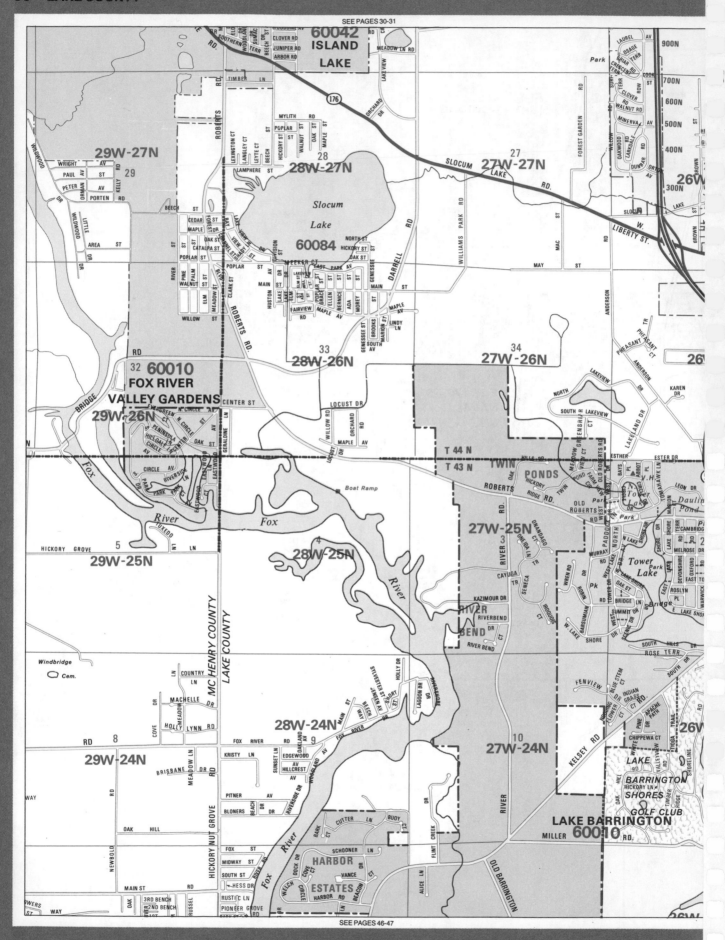

SEE PAGES 30-31

Cook Park

WAUCONDA H.S.

Bangs Lake

LAKEWOOD FOREST PRESERVE

FOUR WINDS

GOLF COURSE

Davis Lake

25W-27N

176

24W-27N

WAUCONDA RD.

23W-27N

Taylor Lake

Schreiber Lake

WAUCONDA

LAKEWOOD FOREST PRESERVE

25W-26N

24W-26N
31

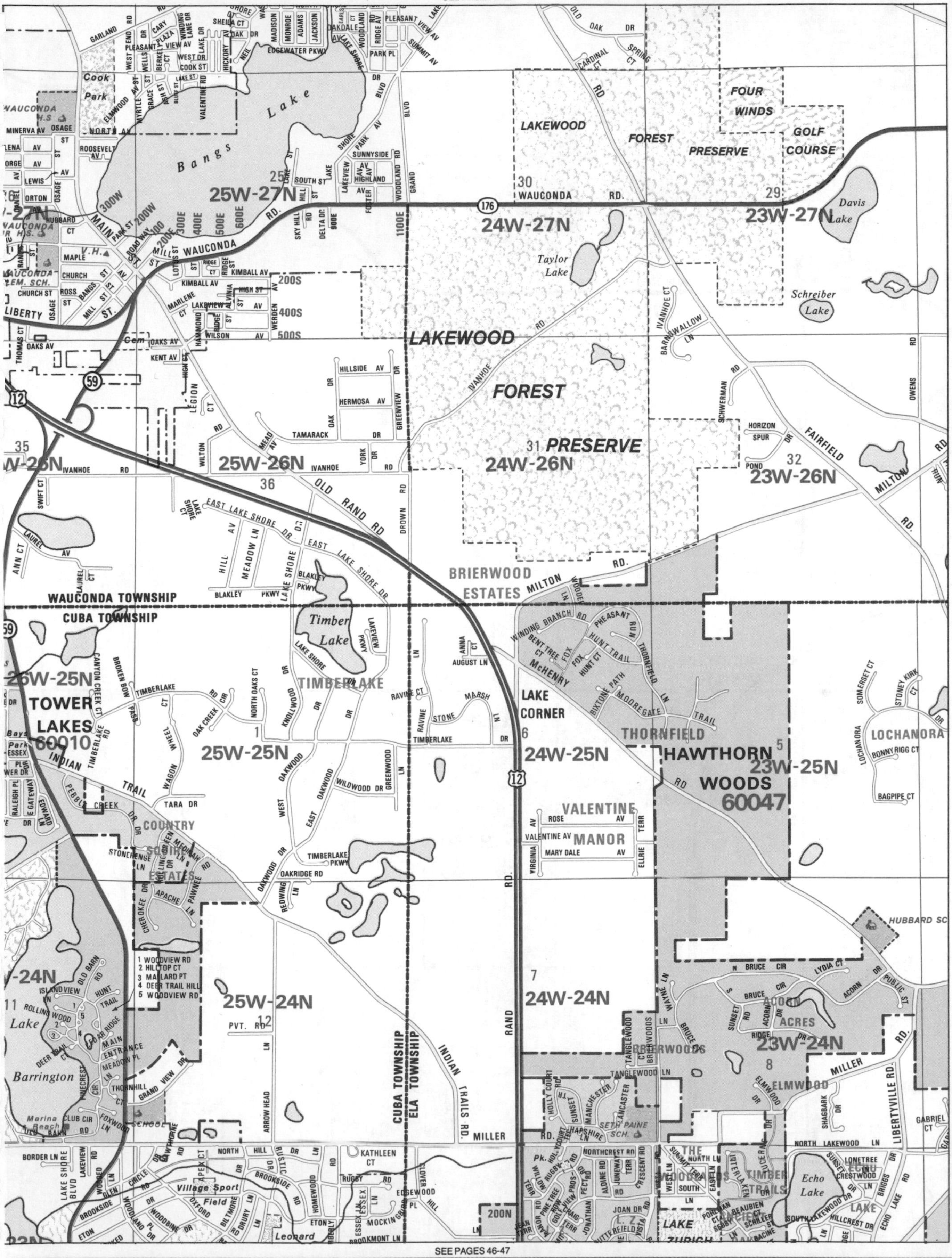

23W-26N
32

OLD RAND RD.

BRIERWOOD ESTATES

MILTON RD.

Timber Lake

WAUCONDA TOWNSHIP

CUBA TOWNSHIP

TIMBERLAKE

LAKE CORNER

THORNFIELD

HAWTHORN WOODS 60047

25W-25N

24W-25N
6

23W-25N
5

LOCHANORA

TOWER LAKES 60010
26W-25N

COUNTRY SQUIRE ESTATES

VALENTINE MANOR

25W-24N

24W-24N
7

23W-24N
8

DEER PARK ACRES

Barrington

HUBBARD SCH.

THE WOODLANDS

TIMBER TRAILS

Echo Lake

CUBA TOWNSHIP
ELA TOWNSHIP

INDIAN TRAILS RD.

LAKE ZURICH

SEE PAGES 32-33

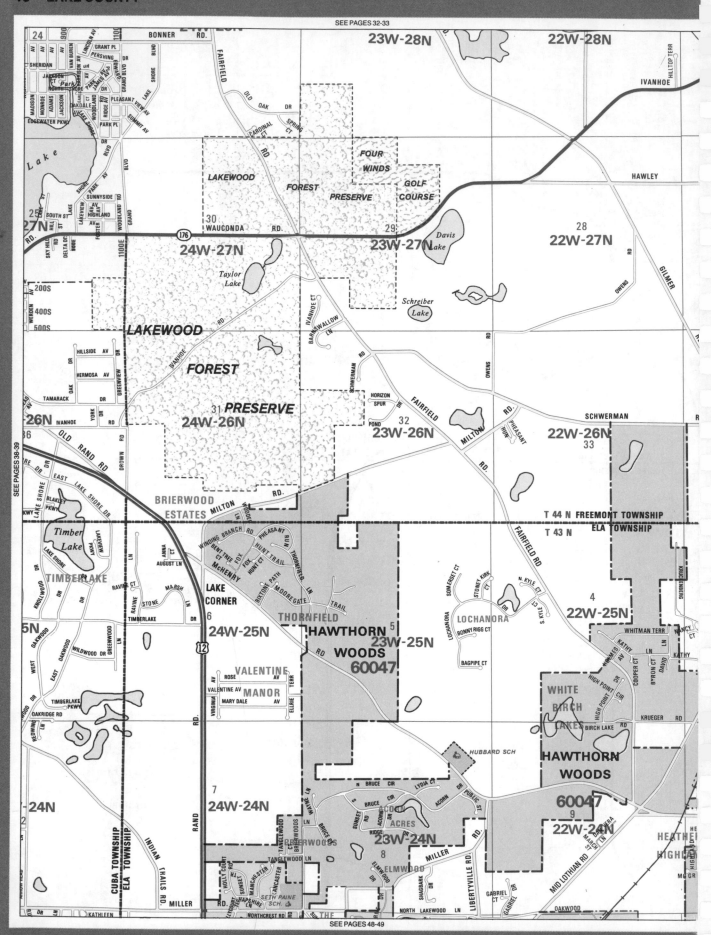

SEE PAGES 38-39

SEE PAGES 48-49

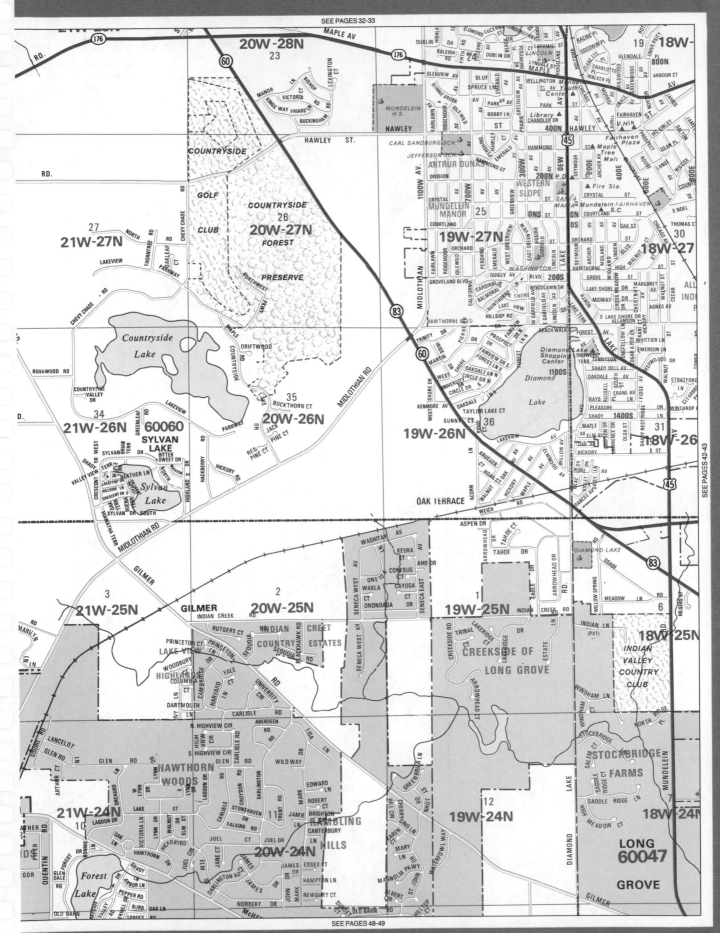

SEE PAGES 32-33
SEE PAGES 42-43

SEE PAGES 34-35

SEE PAGES 40-41

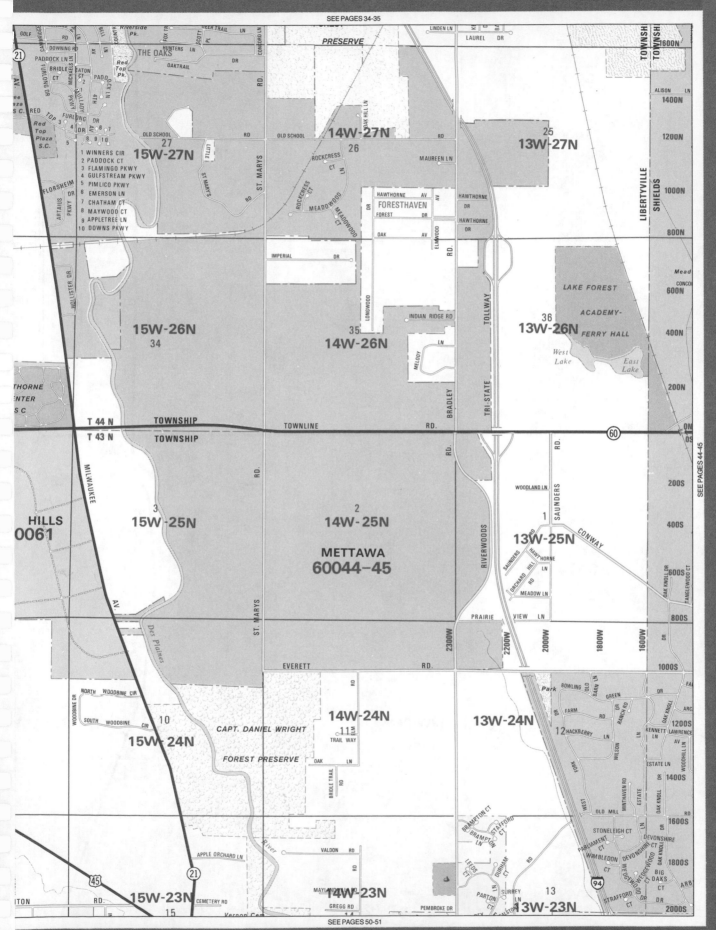

SEE PAGES 34-35

SEE PAGES 44-45

SEE PAGES 50-51

15W-27N
27

14W-27N
26

13W-27N
25

1 WINNERS CIR
2 PADDOCK CT
3 FLAMINGO PKWY
4 GULFSTREAM PKWY
5 PIMLICO PKWY
6 EMERSON LN
7 CHATHAM CT
8 MAYWOOD CT
9 APPLETREE LN
10 DOWNS PKWY

FORESTHAVEN

15W-26N
34

14W-26N
35

13W-26N
36

LAKE FOREST
ACADEMY-
FERRY HALL

West Lake

East Lake

T 44 N
T 43 N
TOWNSHIP
TOWNLINE RD.

HILLS
0061

15W-25N
3

14W-25N
2

METTAWA
60044-45

13W-25N
1

CAPT. DANIEL WRIGHT

FOREST PRESERVE

15W-24N
10

14W-24N
11

13W-24N
12

15W-23N
15

14W-23N

13W-23N
13

CAPT. DANIEL WRIGHT

SEE PAGES 36-37

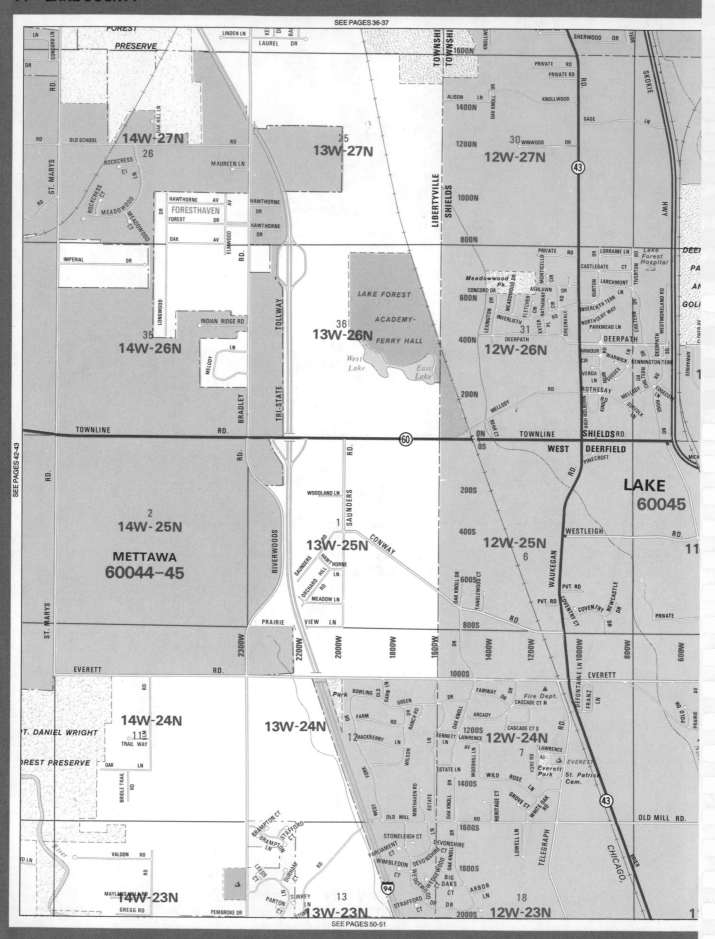

SEE PAGES 42-43

SEE PAGES 50-51

SEE PAGES 36-37

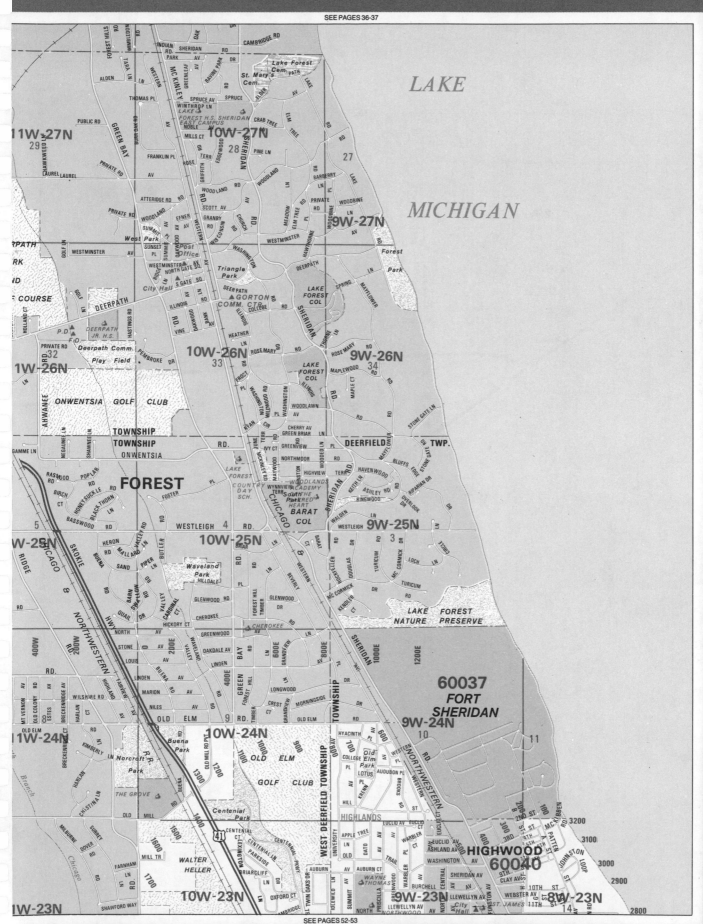

SEE PAGES 52-53

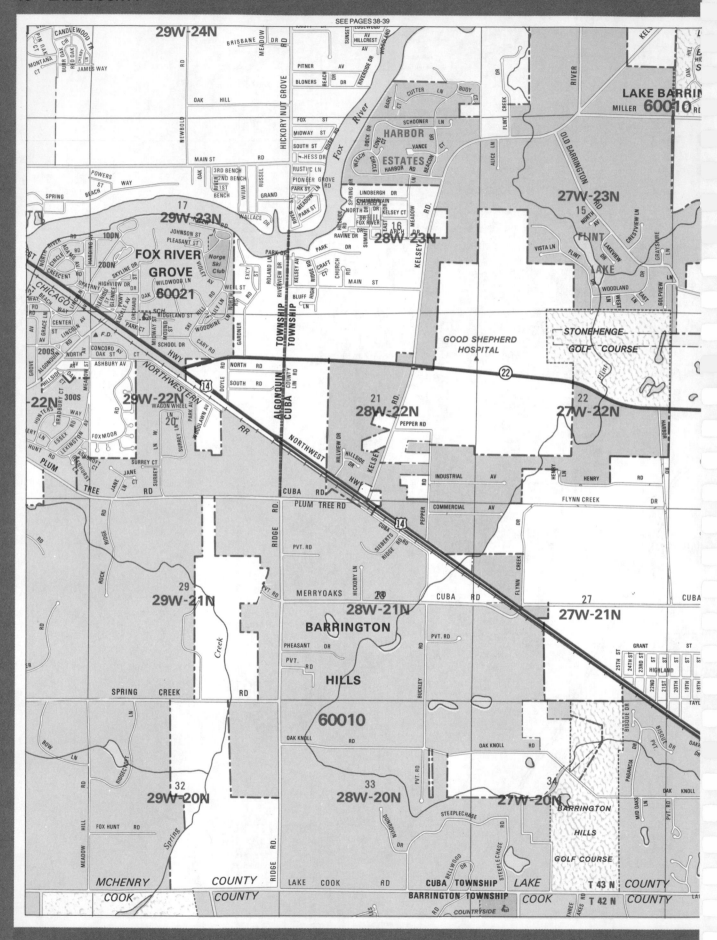

SEE PAGES 38-39

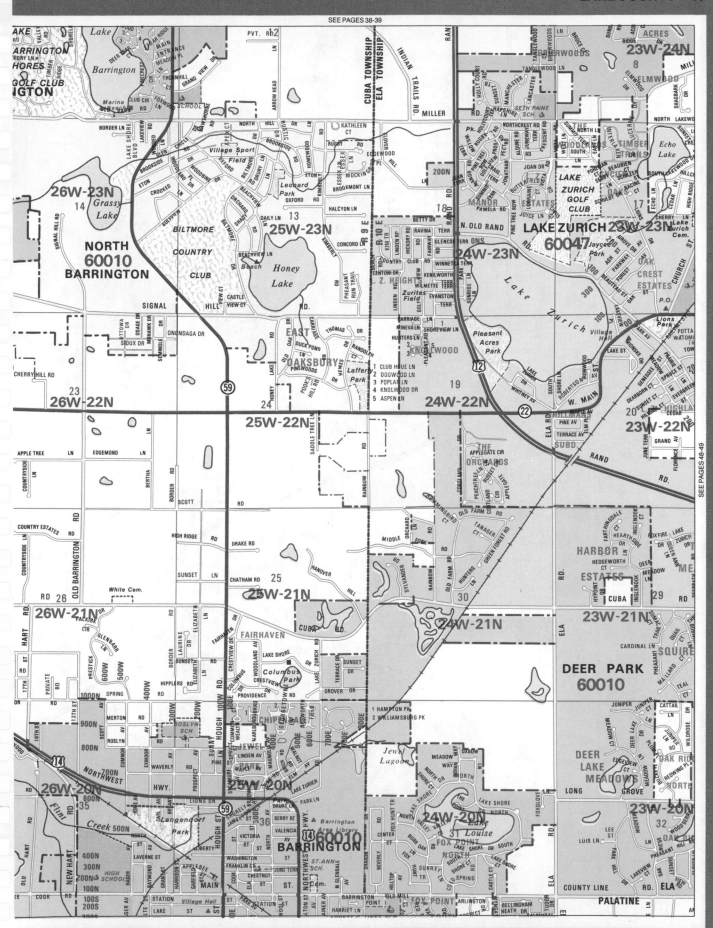

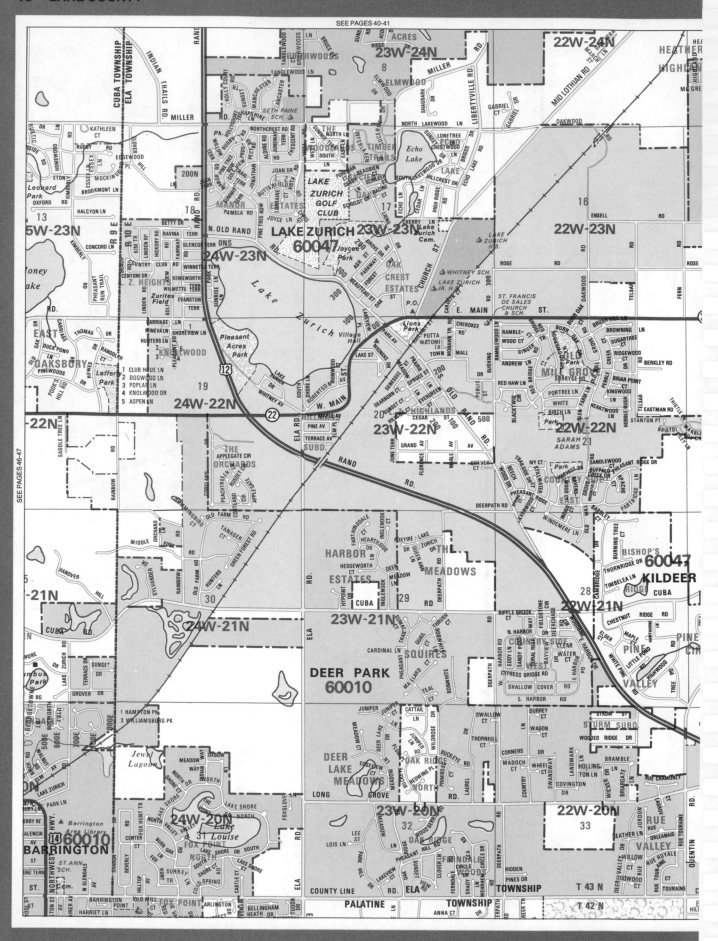

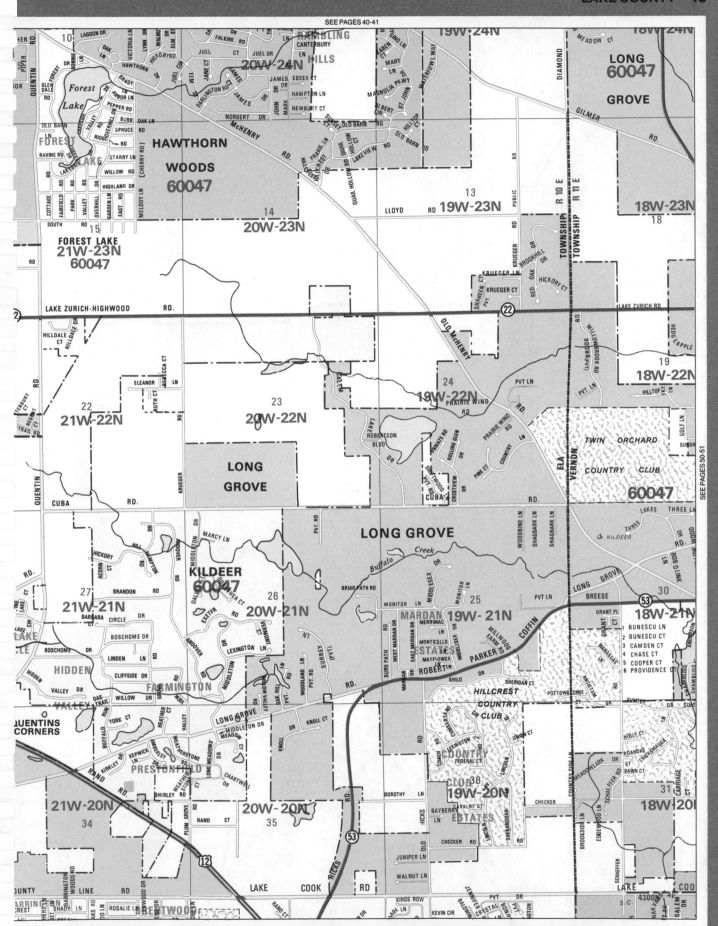

SEE PAGES 50-51

LONG
60047
GROVE

HAWTHORN
WOODS
60047

14
20W-23N

19W-24N

18W-24N

13
19W-23N

18W-23N
18

FOREST LAKE
21W-23N
60047

FOREST
Forest
Lake

Lake Zurich-Highwood RD.

LAKE ZURICH RD.

TOWNSHIP R 10 E
TOWNSHIP R 11 E

HILLDALE
CT

22
21W-22N

23
20W-22N

24
19W-22N

19
18W-22N

LONG
GROVE

TWIN ORCHARD
COUNTRY CLUB
60047

CUBA RD.

LONG GROVE

KILDEER
60047

27
21W-21N

26
20W-21N

25
19W-21N

30
18W-21N

1 BUNESCU LN
2 BUNESCU CT
3 CAMDEN CT
4 CHASE CT
5 COOPER CT
6 PROVIDENCE CT

FARMINGTON

HIDDEN
VALLEY

MARDAN
ESTATES

HILLCREST
COUNTRY
CLUB

QUENTINS
CORNERS

PRESTONFIELD

21W-20N
34

20W-20N
35

COUNTRY
CLUB
ESTATES
19W-20N

18W-20N
31

12

53

LAKE COOK RD.

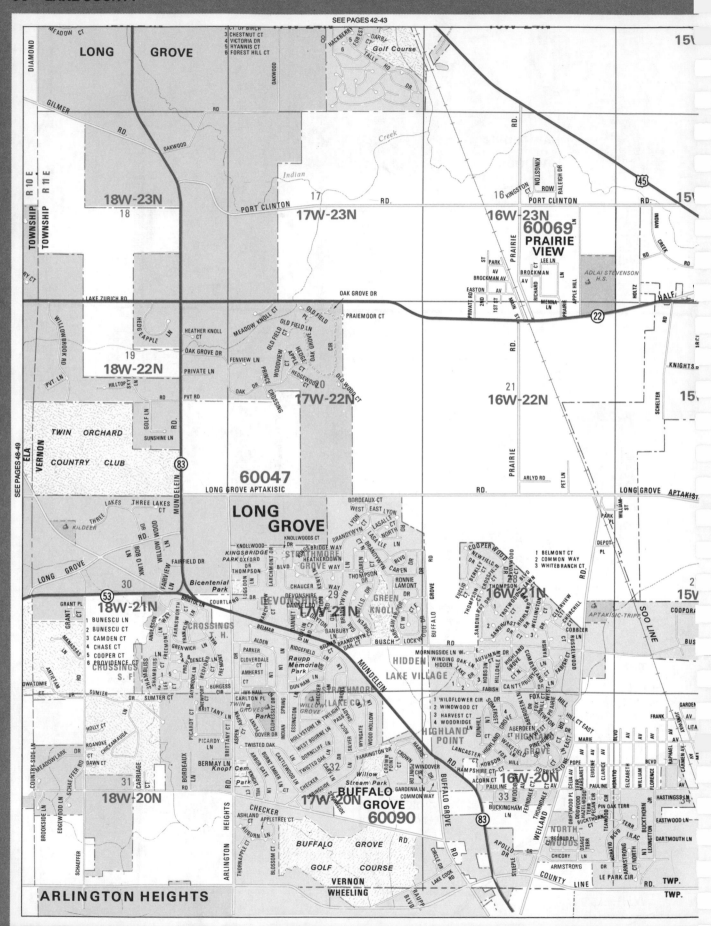

SEE PAGES 42-43

SEE PAGES 42-43

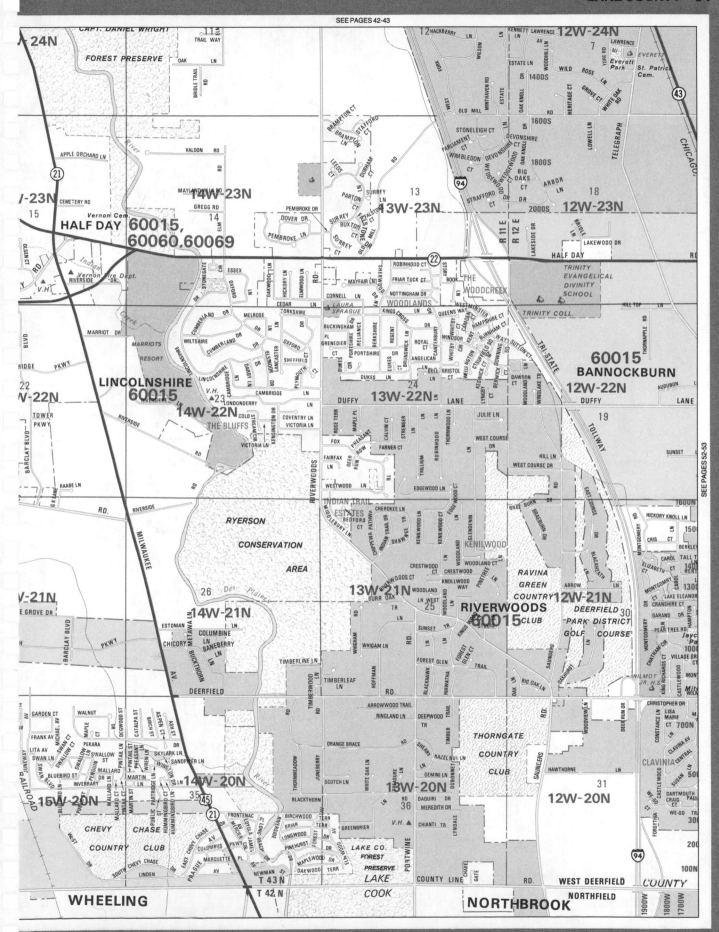

SEE PAGES 52-53

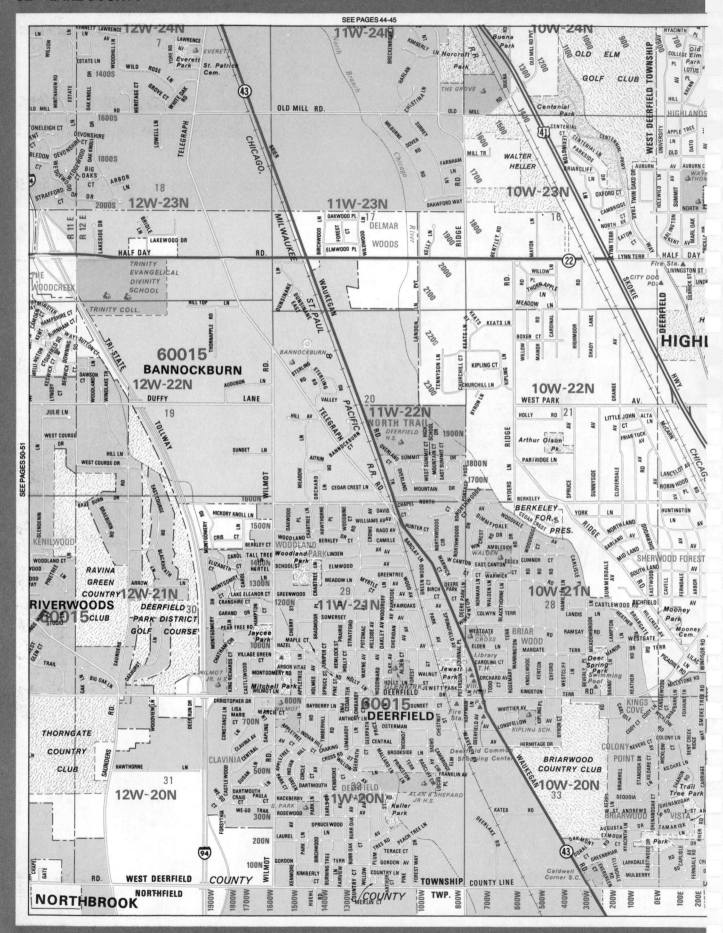

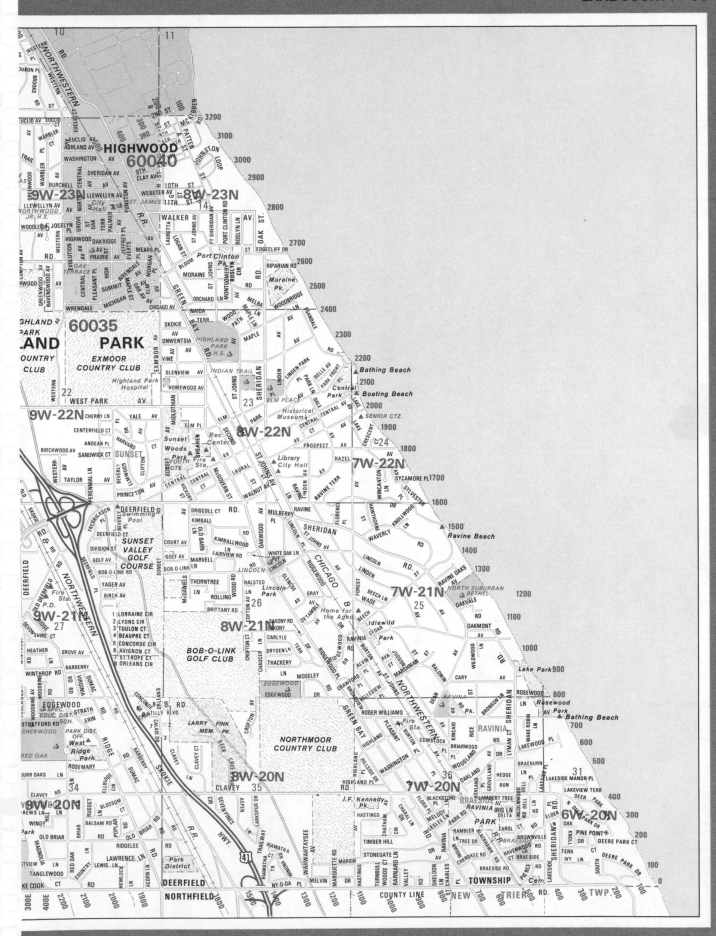

Lake County

Antioch Streets

Page
Alima Terr. N&S ... 23W—42N 7,8
Anita St. N&S ... 23W—42N 7,8
Bartlett Av. N&S ... 23W—42N 7,8
Birchwood Dr. NW-SE ... 23W—43N 7,8
Bridgewood Dr. N&S ... 23W—43N 7,8
Butcher Block Dr E&W ... 23W—43N 7,8
Cedarwood Dr. N&S ... 23W—43N 7,8
Channel Lake Rd E&W ... 23W—42N 7,8
Cheri Ln. E&W ... 23W—42N 7,8
Cheri Ln. NW-SE ... 23W—42N 7,8
Crest Ln. E&W ... 23W—42N 7,8
Cobona Av. N&S ... 23W—42N 7,8
Collins Av. NW-SE 23W—43N 7,8
Cunningham Dr. N&S ... 23W—42N 7,8
Depot St. E&W ... 23W—42N 7,8
Donin Dr. NW-SE ... 23W—43N 7,8
Drom Ct. N&S ... 23W—43N 7,8
Dwight Ct. N&S ... 23W—43N 7,8
Elizabeth St. E&W 23W—42N 7,8
Fillweber Ct. E&W ... 23W—42N 7,8
Forest Ct. E&W ... 23W—43N 7,8
Fox River Rd. N&S 23W—42N 7,8
Gail St. N&S ... 23W—42N 7,8
Gary Dr. N&S ... 23W—42N 7,8
Glenwood Dr. N&S 23W—43N 7,8
Greenbriar Dr. E&W ... 23W—42N 7,8
Hazelwood Dr. NW&SE ... 23W—43N 7,8
Hennings Ct. NW&SE ... 24W—41N 7,8
Hickory Ln. N&S ... 23W—43N 7,8
Highland Av. N&S ... 23W—42N 7,8
Hill Ct. NE&SW ... 23W—43N 7,8
Hillside Av. N&S ... 23W—42N 7,8
Hillside St. NE&SW ... 23W—42N 7,8
Ida Av. E&W ... 23W—42N 7,8
Johelia Ln. N&S,E&W ... 23W—43N 7,8
Joren Trail N&S,E&W ... 23W—43N 7,8
Lake Ct. NE&SW ... 23W—43N 7,8
Lake St. E&W ... 24W—42N 7,8
Lakewood Dr. N&S 23W—43N 7,8
Larkman Terr. N&S 23W—42N 7,8
Liberty St. E&W ... 23W—42N 7,8
Linden Ln. E&W ... 23W—43N 7,8
Longview Dr. N&S ... 23W—42N 7,8
Loursen Ct. NW-SE ... 23W—42N 7,8
Maplewood Dr. E&W ... 23W—43N 7,8
McMiller St. E&W ... 23W—42N 7,8
Meadow Ct. NW-SE ... 22W—43N 8
Naber Av. E&W ... 23W—42N 7,8
Nelson Rd. N&S ... 22W—43N 8
Oakwood Dr. N&S ... 23W—43N 7,8
Orchard St. E&W ... 23W—42N 7,8
Osmond St. N&S ... 23W—42N 7,8
Park Av. E&W ... 23W—42N 7,8
Park Av. N&S ... 23W—43N 7,8
Parkway Av. N&S ... 23W—42N 7,8
Phillips Cir. E&W ... 23W—42N 7,8
Poplar Av. E&W ... 23W—42N 7,8
Ram Rd., S. E&W ... 23W—41N 7,8
Sequist Av. E&W ... 23W—42N 7,8
Spafford St. N&S ... 23W—42N 7,8
Turner Rd. N&S ... 23W—42N 7,8
Victoria St. N&S ... 23W—42N 7,8
Winsor Dr. N&S ... 23W—42N 7,8
Zilinger Ln. E&W ... 23W—43N 7,8
1st St. E&W ... 23W—42N 7,8

Bannockburn Streets

Atkin Dr. E&W ... 11W—22N 52
Audubon Ln. E&W 12W—22N 51,52
Bannockburn Ct. NE&SW ... 11W—22N 52
Bridle Ln. NW&SE ... 12W—23N 51,52
Cedar Crest Ln. E&W ... 11W—22N 52
Duffy Ln. E&W ... 12W—22N 51,52
Dunsiname East NW&SE ... 11W—23N 52
Dunsiname Ln. N&S ... 11W—23N 52
Hill Av. E&W ... 11W—22N 52
Hilltop Ln. E&W ... 12W—23N 51,52
Lakeside Dr. N&S ... 12W—23N 51,52
Lakewood Dr. E&W ... 12W—33N 51,52
Meadow Ln. N&S ... 11W—22N 52
Orchard Ln. N&S ... 11W—22N 52
Sterling Rd. SW&NE ... 11W—22N 52
Sunset Ln. E&W ... 12W—22N 51,52
Telegraph Rd. NW&SE ... 11W—22N 52
Thornapple Rd. N&S ... 12W—22N 51,52

Page
Valley Rd. E&W ... 11W—22N 52
Wilmont Rd. N&S ... 12W—22N 51,52

Barrington Streets

Applebee St. NW&SE ... 25W—20N 47
Berry Rd. E&W ... 25W—20N 47
Beverly Rd. N&S ... 24W—20N 47,48
Bosloorth Field N&S ... 25W—20N 47
Braeside Pl. E&W ... 26W—21N 47
Brandt Rd. E&W ... 26W—21N 47
Bryant Av. N&S ... 26W—20N 47
Burr Oak Ln. NW&SE ... 24W—20N 47,48
Carl Av. N&S ... 26W—20N 47
Castle Ct. N&S ... 24W—20N 47,48
Cemter Ct. E&W ... 24W—20N 47,48
Chestnut St. E&W ... 25W—20N 47
Cold Spring Rd. N&S ... 24W—20N 47,48
Commonwealth Ct. N&S ... 25W—20N 47
Cook St. N&S ... 25,26W—18,20N 47
Cumnor Av. N&S ... 26W—20N 47
Drury Ln. E&W ... 25W—20N 47
Ela St. N&S ... 25W—20N 47
Elm Av. E&W ... 25W—20N 47
Exmoor Av. N&S ... 26W—20N 47
Foxglove Ln. N&S,E&W ... 24W—20N 47,48
Fox Hunt Rd. N&S, E&W ... 24W—20N 47,48
Franklin St. E&W ... 25W—20N 47
Garfield St. N&S ... 25W—20N 47
Georgetowne Ln. N&S ... 25W—20N 47
Georgetowne Rd. N&S ... 25W—20N 47
Glendale Av. N. N&S ... 25W—20N 47
Grant St. N&S ... 26W—20N 47
Hager Av. N&S ... 26W—18,20N 47
Hampton Pk. E&W 25W—20N 47
Harrison St. N&S ... 25W—20N 47
Highland Rd. E&W 27W—21N 46
Hilltop Av. N&S ... 24W—20N 47,48
Home Av. N&S ... 26W—20N 47
Hough St. N&S ... 25W—18,20N 47
Indian Way N&S ... 24W—20N 47,48
James St. E&W ... 25W—20N 47
June Terr. E&W ... 25W—20N 47
Lake Shore Ct. NW&SE ... 24W—20N 47,48
Lake Shore Dr. N. E&W ... 24W—20N 47,48
Lake Shore Dr. S. E&W ... 24W—20N 47,48
Lake Zurich Rd. NE&SW ... 25W—20N 47
Laverne St. E&W ... 26W—20N 47
Liberty St. E&W ... 25W—20N 47
Linden Av. E&W ... 25W—20N 47
Lions Dr.E&W ... 25W—20N 47
Magnolia Av. N&S ... 25W—20N 47
Main St. E&W ... 25W—20N 47
Maple Av. E&W ... 25W—20N 47
Marlborough Rd. N&S ... 25W—20N 47
Meadow Way E&W 24W—20N 47,48
North Av. N&S ... 25W—20N 47
North St. E&W ... 26,27W—20N 46,47
North Shore Ct. NW&SE ... 24W—20N 47,48
Northwest Hwy. N&S,E&W ... 25,26W—20N 47
Oak Rd. NE&SW ... 25W—20N 47
Oxbow Ln. E&W ... 24W—20N 47,48
Park Ln. NW&SE ... 25W—20N 47
Pine St. E&W ... 25W—20N 47
Private Rd. N&S ... 26W—21N 47
Prospect Av. N&S ... 25W—20N 47
Providence Rd. E&W ... 25W—20N 47
Providence Rd. E&W ... 25W—20N 47
Raymond Av. N&S ... 26,27W—20N 46,47
Roslyn Rd. E&W ... 25W—20N 47
Scott Av. N&S ... 26W—20N 47
Sharon Dr. N&S ... 24W—20N 47,48
Shorely Dr. NE&SW ... 25W—20N 47
South Shore Ct. NE&SW ... 24W—20N 47,48
Spring Rd. E&W ... 26W—21N 47
Spruce St. N&S ... 25W—20N 47
Sunny Ln. N&S ... 25W—20N 47
Surrey Ln. E&W ... 24W—20N 47,48
Sycamore Av. N&S 25W—20N 47
The Point E&W ... 24W—20N 47,48
Towne Ln. N&S ... 25W—20N 47
Valencia Av. E&W ... 25W—20N 47
Valley Ct. N. NE&SW ... 24W—20N 47,48
Victoria St. E&W ... 25W—20N 47
Walnut Rd. NW&SE ... 25W—20N 47

Page
Washington St. E&W ... 25W—20N 47
Waverly Rd. E&W ... 26W—20N 47
Western Av. N&S ... 26W—20N 47
Williamsburg Pk. E&W ... 25W—20N 47
Willow Av. N&S ... 25W—20N 47
16th St. N&S ... 26W—20N 47

Barrington Hills Streets

Bisque Dr. NE&SW 27W—20N 46
Buckley Rd. N&S ... 28W—21N 46
County Line Rd. E&W ... 29,31W—20N 46
Cuba Rd. E& ... 28W—21,22N 46
Fox Hunt Rd. E&W 29W—20N 46
Hickory Ln. N&S ... 28W—21N 46
Jane Ct. E&W ... 29W—22N 46
Jane Ln. NE&SW ... 29W—22N 46
Lake Cook Rd. E&W ... 28,30W—20W 46
Meadow Rd. N&S ... 27W—20N 46
Merri Oaks Rd. E&W ... 28,30W—21N 46
Merryoaks Rd. E&W ... 28W—21N 46
Mid Oaks Ln. N&S 27W—20N 46
New Hart Rd. N&S 26W—20N 47
Oak Knoll Rd. E&W ... 26,28W—20N 46,47
Oakwood Dr. E&W 26W—20N 47
Old Hart Rd. N&S ... 26W—20N 47
Pagancia Dr. N&S ... 27W—20N 46
Park Av. N&S ... 29W—22N 46
Pheasant Dr. E&W 28W—21N 46
Plum Tree Rd. E&W ... 28,30W—21,22N 46
Pvt. NW&SE ... 27W—20N 46
Rein Dr. NE&SW ... 27W—20N 46
Ridgecroft Ln. N&S, E&W ... 29W—20N 46
Ridge Rd. N&S ... 29W—21N 46
Rock Ridge Rd. N&S ... 29W—21N 46
Sieberts Ridge Rd. NE&SW ... 28W—21N 46
Steeplechase E&W ... 28W—20N 46
Surrey Ct. E&W ... 29W—22N 46
Surrey Ln. E&W, N&S ... 29W—22N 46
Wagon E&W ... 29W—22N 46
Wagon Wheel Ln. E&W ... 29W—22N 46
Wooddale Dr. NW&SE ... 28W—20N 46

Buffalo Grove

Aberdeen Ct. E&W 16W—20N 50
Aberdeen Ln. N&S 16W—20N 50
Acorn Ct. E&W ... 16W—20N 50
Alden Ln. NW&SE ... 17W—21N 50
Amherst Ct. E&W ... 17W—21N 50
Anderson Ln. N&S 18W—21N 50
Apollo Dr. NW&SE 16W—20N 50
Appletree Ct. N&S ... 17W—20N 50
Arbor Gate Ln. NW&SE ... 17W—20N 50
Armstrong Ct. N. N&S ... 15W—20N 50,51
Armstrong Dr. E&W ... 16W—20N 50
Ashland Ct. NE&SW ... 17W—20N 50
Aspen Ct. N&S ... 17W—20N 50
Aspen Dr. N&S ... 17W—20N 50
Auburn Ln. E&W ... 17W—20N 50
Autumn Ct. E&W ... 16W—21N 50
Banbury Ln. E&W ... 17W—21N 50
Barclay Blvd. N&S 15W—21N 50,51
Bedford Ct. N&S ... 18W—21N 50
Bellmont Ct. NW&SE ... 16W—21N 50
Belmar Ct. NE&SW ... 17W—21N 50
Belmar Ln. NW&SE ... 17W—21N 50
Berkley Ct. N&S ... 16W—21N 50
Blossom Ct. N&S ... 17W—20N 50
Bordeaux Ct. E&W 17W—21N 50
Brandywyn Ct. E&W ... 17W—21N 50
Brandywyn Ln. N&S ... 17W—21N 50
Bristol Ln. NW&SE 18W—21N 50
Buckingham Ln. E&W ... 16W—20N 50
Buckthorn Terr. N&S ... 15W—20N 50,51
Buffalo Grove Rd. N&S ... 16W—17,20N 50
Bunescu Ct. N&S ... 18W—21N 50
Bunescu Ln. E&W ... 18W—21N 50
Burgess Cir. E&W ... 18W—21N 50
Burnt Ember Ln. NW&SE ... 17W—20N 50
Busch Pkwy. E&W 15W—21N 50,51
Camden Ct. E&W ... 18W—21N 50
Canterbury Ln. E&W ... 16W—21N 50

Page
Caren Ct. N&S ... 17W—21N 50
Caren Dr. E&W ... 17W—21N 50
Carlton Pl. E&W ... 17W—21N 50
Carman Av. N&S ... 15W—20N 50,51
Cary Ln. NW&SE ... 17W—20N 50
Castlewood Ln. NW&SE ... 17W—20N 50
Chase Ct. E&W ... 18W—21N 50
Chaucer Way E&W 17W—21N 50
Checker Dr. N&S ... 17W—21N 50
Checker Dr. NE&SW ... 17W—20N 50
Checker Rd. E&W ... 17,18,19W—20N 49,50
Chicory Ln. E&W ... 16W—20N 50
Churchill Ct. N&S ... 16W—21N 50
Circle Dr. NW&SE ... 16W—20N 50
Clearview Ct. N&S 16W—21N 50
Clohessey Dr. N&S 17W—20N 50
Cloverdale Ct. E&W ... 17W—21N 50
Cobbler Ln. E&W ... 16W—21N 50
Cobblestone Ct. N&S ... 16W—20N 50
Cobblestone Ln. N&S ... 16W—20N 50
Common Way E&W ... 16,17W—20,21N 50
Cooper Ct. E&W ... 18W—21N 50
Copperwood Dr. N&S, E&W ... 16W—21N 50
Corporate Grove Dr. E&W ... 15W—21N 50,51
County Line Rd. E&W ... 16W—20N 50
Courtland Dr. E&W 17W—21N 50
Crossfield Ct. N&S 16W—21N 50
Crown Point Ct. N&S ... 17W—20N 50
Crown Pt. Dr. N&S 17W—20N 50
Cumberland Ln. NW&SE ... 16W—21N 50
Dannet Ct. N&S ... 17W—21N 50
Dannet Rd. E&W ... 17W—21N 50
Dartmouth Ln. E&W ... 15W—20N 50,51
Dayton Ct. E&W ... 17W—21N 50
Dayton Rd. N&S ... 17W—21N 50
Devlin Rd. N&S ... 17W—21N 50
Devonshire Rd. N&S,E&W ... 17W—21N 50
Devonwood Ct. N&S ... 16W—21N 50
Dogwood Terr. N&S ... 16W—20N 50
Dorncliff Ln. NE&SW ... 17W—20N 50
Dover Drl E&W ... 17W—20N 50
Dundee Pkwy. E&W ... 16W—18N 50
Dunham Ln. NE&SW ... 17W—21N 50
Dunhill Dr. N&S,E&W ... 16W—20N 50
Eastwood Ln. E&W ... 15W—20N 50,51
Essington Ln. N&S 17W—20N 50
Euclid Ct. N&S ... 16W—21N 50
Fabish Ct. N&S ... 16W—21N 50
Fabish Dr. E&W ... 16W—21N 50
Fairfax Ln. E&W ... 18W—21N 50
Farnsworth Ct. N&S ... 18W—21N 50
Farnsworth Ln. NE&SW ... 18W—21N 50
Farrington Dr. E&W ... 17W—20N 50
Ferndale Ct. N&S ... 16W—20N 50
Fox Ct. F NW&SE 16W—20N 50
Fox Hill Ct. E. NW&SE ... 16W—20N 50
Fox Hill Ct. W. N&S ... 16W—20N 50
Franklin Ln. N&S ... 18W—20N 50
Fremont Way N&S 18W—21N 50
Gail Ct. NE&SW ... 17W—21N 50
Gail Dr. NE&SW ... 17W—21N 50
Gardenia Ln. E&W 17W—20N 50
Green Knolls Dr. N&S ... 17W—21N 50
Greenwich Ln. E&W ... 18W—21N 50
Hampshire Ct. E&W ... 16W—20N 50
Harris Dr. N&S ... 17W—20N 50
Harvest Ct. NW&SE ... 16W—21N 50
Hastings Ln. E&W ... 15W—20N 50,51
Hazelwood Terr. N&S ... 16W—20N 50
Heatherdown Way E&W ... 17W—20N 50
Heritage Pl. E&W ... 18W—21N 50
Hidden Lake Dr. E&W ... 16W—21N 50
Highland Grove Ct. N. NE&SE ... 16W—21N 50
Highland Grove Dr. N&S ... 16W—20,21N 50
Hill Ct. E. E&W ... 16W—20N 50

Page
Hill Ct. W. E&W ... 16W—20N 50
Hilldale Ln. N&S ... 16W—21N 50
Hobson Ct. NE&SW ... 16W—20N 50
Hobson Dr. N&S ... 16W—21N 50
Hollystone Ln. NE&SW ... 17W—20N 50
Horatio Blvd. N&S ... 16W—20N 50
Indian Spring Ln. N&S ... 17W—20N 50
Ivy Hall Ln. E&W ... 17W—21N 50
Kent. Ln. N&S ... 17W—21N 50
Kingsbridge Way E&W ... 17W—21N 50
Knight Hill Ct. NW&SE ... 17W—20N 50
Knollwood Ct. W.&E. N&S ... 17W—21N 50
Knollwood Dr. E&W ... 17W—21N 50
Lamont Terr. E&W ... 17W—21N 50
Landcaster Ct. NW&SE ... 16W—20N 50
Laraway Dr. N&S ... 17W—21N 50
Larchmont Dr. N&S ... 17W—21N 50
LaSalle Ct. N. E&W ... 17W—21N 50
LaSalle Ln. E&W ... 17W—21N 50
Lawn Ct. NE&SW ... 16W—21N 50
Lee Ct. N&S ... 18W—21N 50
Le Park Cir. N&S, E&W ... 15W—20N 50,51
Lexington Dr. N&S 15W—20N 50,51
Lilac Ln. N&S,E&W ... 15W—20N 50,51
Lockwood Ct. E. N&S ... 17W—21N 50
Lockwood Ct. W. N&S ... 17W—21N 50
Lockwood Dr. N&S 17W—21N 50
Logsdon Ln. N&S ... 17W—21N 50
Lyon Ct. E&W ... 17W—21N 50
Lyon Dr. E&W ... 17W—21N 50
Mahogany Dr. E&W ... 16W—20N 50
Morningside Ln. E. E&W ... 16W—21N 50
Morningside Ln. W. E&W ... 16W—21N 50
Mundelein Rd. NW&SE ... 17W—21N 50
Newfield Dr. E&W ... 16W—21N 50
Newport Ct. N&S ... 18W—21N 50
Newton Ct. N&S ... 16W—20N 50
Newton Dr. NW&SE ... 16W—20N 50
Osage Terr. N&S ... 16W—20N 50
Oxford Dr. E&W ... 17W—21N 50
Pauline Av. E&W ... 16W—20N 50
Pecan Cir. N&S ... 16W—20N 50
Penny Ln. N&S ... 17W—20N 50
Pin Oak Terr. E&W 16W—20N 50
Pinehurst Ln. N&S 16W—20N 50
Prairie Ln. N&S ... 16W—20N 50
Providence Ct. N&S ... 18W—21N 50
Providence Ln. E&W ... 18W—21N 50
Ranchview Ct. N&S ... 17W—21N 50
Raphael Av. N&S ... 15W—20N 50,51
Raupp Blvd. NW&SE ... 17W—20N 50
Redbud Pl. E&W ... 16W—20N 50
Ridgefield Ln. NW&SE ... 17W—21N 50
Ronnie Dr. N&S,E&W ... 17W—21N 50
Russelwood Cr. N&S ... 16W—21N 50
Sandhurst Dr. N&S, E&W ... 16W—21N 50
Say Brook Ln. N&S ... 18W—21N 50
Shady Grove Ln. N&S ... 17W—20N 50
Shambliss Ct. N&S 18W—21N 50
Shambliss Ln. N&S ... 18W—21N 50
Silver Rock Ln. N&S ... 17W—20N 50
Somerset Ln. NW&SE ... 16W—20N 50
Springside Ct. NW&SE ... 17W—20N 50
Springside Ln. NE&SW ... 17W—20N 50
Steeple Dr. E&W ... 15W—20N 50,51
Sunridge Ln. NW&SE ... 16W—20N 50
Teawood Cir. N&S ... 16W—20N 50
Thompson Blvd. E&W ... 16,17W—20,21N 50
Thompson Ct. N&S ... 16W—21N 50
Thornapple Ct. NE&SW ... 17W—20N 50
Thorndale Ct. N&S 16W—20N 50
Trotwood Ct. N&S ... 16W—21N 50

Page

Twilight Pass NE&SW
............17W—20N 50
Twisted Oak Ln. N&S
............17W—20N 50
Wakefield Dr. NW&SE
............16W—20N 50
Wakefield Ln. NW&SE
............16W—20N 50
Wellington Ct. N&S 16W—21N 50
West Bourne Ln. NE&SW
............17W—20N 50
Wheeling Av. N&S .15W—20N 50,51
Whitebranch Ct. N&S
............16W—21N 50
Wildflower Ct. N&S 16W—21N 50
Winding Oak Ln. E&W
............16W—20N 50
Windover Cir. N&S 17W—20N 50
Windwood Ct. N&S 16W—21N 50
Wood Hollow Ln. N&S
............17W—20N 50
Woodbury Rd. N&S
............16W—20N 50
Woodridge Ln. N&S
............16W—20N 50
Wyngate Ln. N&S .17W—20N 50

Deerfield Streets

Alden Ct. N&S ......11W—21N 52
Ambleside Dr. E&W
............11W—20N 52
Anthony Ln. E&W ..11W—20N 52
Appletree Ct. NW&SE
............11W—20N 52
Appletree Ln. N&S
............11W—20,21N 52
Arbor Vitae Rd. E&W
............11W—21N 52
Arthur Ct. N&S ....11W—20N 52
Augusta Dr. E&W ..10W—20N 52
Barclay Ln. NW&SE
............11W—21N 52
Bayberry Ln. E&W 11W—20N 52
Bent Creek Ridge N&S
............9W—20N 53
Berkley Ct. E&W
............11,12W—21N 51,52
Beverly Pl. N&S ....10W—21N 52
Birch Rd. E&W ....11W—21N 52
Birchwood Av. N&S
............11W—20N 52
Blackthorn Ln. N&S
............10W—21N 52
Brand Ln. N&S ....10W—21N 52
Brierhill Rd. N&S ..10W—20N 52
Broadmoor Pl. N&S
............11W—21N 52
Brookside Ln. E&W
............11W—20N 52
Burning Tree Ln. N&S
............11W—20N 52
Burr Oak Ln. N&S ..11W—20N 52
Burr Oak Ct. N&S .11W—20N 52
Byron Ct. N&S ....10W—20N 52
Cambridge Cir. NE&SW
............11W—20N 52
Camille Av. E&W ...11W—21N 52
Carlisle Av. N&S
............9W,10W—20N 52,53
Carlisle Pl. N&S ...10W—21N 52
Caroline Ct. E&W ..11W—20N 52
Carol Ct. E&W ....12W—21N 51,52
Carol Ln. E&W ......12W—21N 51,52
Carriage Way N&S ..9W—20N 53
Castlewood Ln. N&S
............12W—21N 51,52
Cedar St. N&S ....11W—20N 52
Cedar Terr. N&S ....11W—21N 52
Cedar Crest Dr. NW&SE
............10W—21N 52
Central Av. E&W
............11W,12W—20N 51,52
Chapel Ct. E&W ....11W—21N 52
Charing Cross Rd. E&W
............11W—21N 52
Chatham Cir. NE&SE
............11W—20N 52
Cherry St. N&S ....11W—21N 52
Chestnut St. N&S .11W—21N 52
Christopher Dr. E&W
............12W—20N 51,52
Circle Dr. E&W ....11W—20N 52
Clavina Av. NE&SW
............12W—20N 51,52
Clay Av. N&S ......11W—20N 52
Cody Ct. NE&SW ...10W—20N 52
Cody Ln. NE&SW ...10W—20N 52
Colony Ln. E&W ....9W—20N 53
Colwyn Terr. E&W ..10W—21N 52
Constance Ln. N&S
............12W—20N 51,52
Country Ct. N&S ...11W—20N 52
Country Ln. E&W ..11W—20N 52
County Line Rd. N&S
............10W—20N 52
Crabtree Ln. E&W ..11W—20N 52
Craig Ct. E&W ....12W—21N 51,52
Cranshire Ct. N&S .12W—21N 51,52
Crestview Dr. E&W .9W—20N 53
Cumnor Ct. E&W ..10W—21N 52

Page

Dartmouth Ln. E&W
............11W,12W—20N 51,52
Davis Av. E&W ....11W—21N 52
Deere Park Ct. E&W
............11W—21N 52
Deere Park Ln. N&S
............11W—21N 52
Deerfield Av. N&S .10W—20N 52
Deerfield Dr. N&S .11W—20N 52
Deerfield Rd. E&W 11W—20N 52
Deer Lake Rd. N&S
............10W—20N 52
Deerpath Ct. N&S .11W—20N 52
Deerpath Dr. N&S .11W—20N 52
Dimmeydale Dr. E&W
............10W—21N 52
Doral Ct. E&W .....10W—20N 52
Earls Ct. N&S ......11W—20N 52
East Canton Ct. E&W
............10W—21N 52
E. St. Andrews Ln. E&W
............10W—20N 52
Eastwood Dr. N&S 10W—20N 52
East Summit Ct. N&S
............11W—22N 52
Elder Ln. E&W ......10W—21N 52
Elizabeth Ct. NW&SE
............12W—21N 51,52
Ellendale Dr. E&W 10W—20N 52
Elm St. N&S ......11W—20N 52
Elmwood Av. E&W 11W—21N 52
Essex Ct. E&W ....10W—21N 52
Evergreen Ct. NW&SE
............11W—20N 52
Exmoor Ct. E&W ..10W—20N 52
Fairoaks Av. E&W .11W—21N 52
Fairview Av. N&S ..11W—20N 52
Ferndale Rd. N&S ..9W—20N 53
Forest Av. N&S ....11W—21N 52
Forest Way Dr. N&S
............11W—20N 52
Forsythia Dr. N&S .12W—20N 51,52
Foxhunt Tr. N&S .....9W—20N 53
Franklin Av. E&W ..11W—20N 52
Gahol Ct. E&W ....12W—21N 51,52
Garand Dr. E&W ..12W—21N 51,52
Green Ct. NW&SE 11W—20N 52
Greenbriar Dr. E&W
............10W—20N 52
Green Park Ct. NW&SE
............10W—20N 52
Greentree Av. E&W
............11W—21N 52
Greenwood Av. E&W
............11W—21N 52
Greenwood Ct. N&S
............11W—21N 52
Grove Av. N&S ......11W—20N 52
Gordon Av. E&W ...11W—20N 52
Gordon Terr. E& ...11W—20N 52
Hackberry Rd. E&W
............11W—20N 52
Hamilton Ln. N&S .10W—21N 52
Hampton Ct. N&S .12W—21N 51,52
Hawthorne Pl. N&S
............11W—21N 52
Hazel Av. E&W ....11W—21N 52
Heather Rd. NW&SE
............10W—21N 52
Hemlock St. N&S ..11W—21N 52
Hermitage Dr. E&W
............10W—20N 52
Hertzel Ln. E&W ..12W—21N 51,52
High School Dr. N&S
............11W—22N 52
Hillside Av. N&S ...11W—21N 52
Hoffman Ln. N&S ..11W—20N 52
Holly Ct. N&S ....11W—21N 52
Holly Ln. E&W ....11W—21N 52
Holmes Av. N&S ..11W—20N 52
Huehl Rd. N&S ....11W—20N 52
Hunter Ct. N&S ....11W—21N 52
Hyacinth Ln. E&W .11W—20N 52
Indian Hill Ct. NW&SE
............11W—22N 52
Indian Hill Rd. N&S 11W—20N 52
Jewett Park Dr. E&W
............11W—21N 52
Jonquil Terr. N&S ..11W—21N 52
Journal Pl. N&S ...10W—21N 52
Juniper Ct. N&S ...11W—21N 52
Kates Rd. E&W ....10W—21N 52
Kenmore Av. N&S .11W—20N 52
Kenton Rd. N&S ...11W—20N 52
Kerry Ln. N&S ....10W—20N 52
Kildare Ct. N&S ...10W—20N 52
Kildare Ln. E&W ..10W—20N 52
Kimberly Ct. E&W .11W—20N 52
King Richards Ct. N&S
............12W—21N 51,52
Kingston Terr. E&W
............10W—21N 52
Kipling Pl. N&S ....10W—20N 52
Knollwood Dr. E&W
............11W—20N 52
Lake Cook Rd. E&W
............11W—20N 52
Lake Eleanor Ct. E&W
............12W—21N 51,52
Lake Eleanor Dr. E&W
............12W—21N 51,52

Page

Lampton Ln. N&S .10W—21N 52
Landis Ln. E&W ....10W—21N 52
Larkdale Rd. E&W 10W—20N 52
Laurel Av. E&W ....11W—20N 52
Linden Av. E&W ...11W—20N 52
Lisa Marie E&W
............12W—20N 51,52
Locus Pl. N&S .....11W—20N 52
Lombardy Ct. N&S 11W—20N 52
Lombardy Ln. N&S 11W—21N 52
Longfellow Av. E&W
............10W—20N 52
Mallard Ln. E&W
............11W—20N 52
Manor Dr. NE&SW 10W—21N 52
Maple Ct. NW&SE 11W—20N 52
Marcie Ct. E&W ...10W—20N 51,52
Margate Terr. E&W 10W—20N 52
Meadow Ln. E&W .11W—20N 52
Meadowbrook Ln. N&S
............10W—21N 52
Merlin Ct. N&S ....11W—20N 52
Millstone Rd. E&W ..9W—21N 53
Montgomery Ct. NE&SW
............12W—20N 51,52
Montgomery Dr. N&S
............12W—20N 51,52
Montgomery Rd. E&W
............12W—20N 51,52
Mountain Ct. N&S .11W—22N 52
Mountain Dr. E&W 11W—22N 52
Mulberry Rd. E&W 10W—20N 52
Myrtle Ct. E&W ...11W—20N 52
Norman Ln. N&S ...10W—21N 52
North Av. E&W ....11W—22N 52
Northwoods Cir. N&S
............11W—21N 52
Northwoods Ct. NE&SW
............11W—20N 52
Northwoods Rd. N&S
............11W—20N 52
Oakley Av. N&S ...11W—21N 52
Oakmont Dr. E&W .10W—20N 52
Oakwood Pl. N&S .11W—21N 52
Orchard Ln. E&W ..10W—20N 52
Osterman Av. E&W
............11W—20N 52
Overland Ct. NW&SE
............11W—22N 52
Overland Tr. N&S ..11W—22N 52
Oxford Rd. N&S ...10W—21N 52
Park Av. N&S .....11W—21N 52
Park Ln. N&S .....11W—21N 52
Parkside Ln. N&S .11W—21N 52
Paula Ct. E&W ....12W—20N 51,52
Peachtree Ln. NE&SW
............11W—20N 52
Pear Tree Rd. E&W
............12W—20N 51,52
Pembroke Ct. N&S 11W—21N 52
Peterson Ln. N&S .11W—21N 52
Pine St. N&S ....11W—20,21N 52
Plum Tree Rd. N&S
............11W—20N 52
Portage Pass N&S 11W—22N 52
Potomac Av. N&S ..11W—20N 52
Prairie Av. N&S ...11W—20N 52
Price Ln. N&S .....11W—20N 52
Princeton Ln. NW&SE
............11W—20N 52
Radcliff Cir. NW&SE
............11W—20N 52
Rago Av E&W .....11W—20N 52
Ramsay Rd. E&W .10W—20N 52
Revere Ct. NE&SW
............10W—20N 52
River Rd. N&S .....9W—20N 53
Rosemary Terr. N&S
............10W—21N 52
Rosewood Ln. E&W
............11W—20N 52
Sapling Ln. N&S ...12W—20N 51,52
School St. E&W ...11W—21N 52
Sequoia Ln. E&W .10W—20N 52
Shagbark Ln. N&S ..9W—20N 53
Shannon Rd. NE&SW
............9W—20N 53
Shenandoah Ct. N&S
............10W—20N 52
Shenandoah Rd. E&W
............9W—20N 53
Sheridan Av. N&S .11W—20N 52
Smoke Tree Rd. N&S
............9W—20N 53
Somerset Av. E&W 11W—21N 53
Springfield Rd. NW&SE
............11W—21N 52
Spruce St. N&S ...11W—21N 52
Sprucewood Ln. E&W
............10W—20N 52
St. Andrews Ln. E&W
............10W—20N 52
Standish Dr. N&S ..10W—20N 52
Stratford Rd. N&S .11W—21N 52
Summit Ln. E&W ..11W—20N 52
Sunset Ct. E&W ...12W—20N 51,52
Susan Ln. E&W ...12W—20N 51,52
Tall Treet Ln. E&W 12W—21N 51,52
Tamarisk Ln. E&W 10W—20N 52

Page

Tanglewood Ct. N&S
............9W—20N 53
Terrace Ct. E&W ...11W—20N 52
Timberhill Rd. N&S 11W—20N 52
Todd Ct. N&S .....10W—21N 52
Vale Ct. E&W ......11W—20N 52
Village Green Ct. E&W
............12W—21N 51,52
Walden Ln. N&S ...10W—21N 52
Walnut St. E&W ...11W—20N 52
Warrington Rd. N&S
............11W—20N 52
Warwick Ct. NW&SE
............11W—20N 52
Warwick Rd. E&W .10W—20N 52
Waukegan Rd. NW&SE
............10,11W—20,22N 52
Waverly St. NW&SE
............11W—20N 52
Wayne Av. N&S ...11W—20N 52
WE-Go Ct. NW&SE
............12W—20N 51,52
WE-Go Trail E&W .12W—20N 51,52
Westcliff Ln. N&S ..11W—21N 52
Westgate Rd. E&W 10W—21N 52
West Summit Ct. N&S
............11W—22N 52
W. St. Andrews Ln. E&W
............10W—20N 52
W. Canton Ct. E&W
............11W—20N 52
Whittier Av. E&W ..10W—20N 52
Wicklow Ct. N&S ....9W—20N 53
Wicklow Rd. NW&SE
............9W—20N 53
Williams Av. N&S .11W—20N 52
Willow Av. N&S ...11W—20N 52
Wilmot Ln. E&W ..12W—21N 51,52
Wilmot Rd. N&S
............12W—20N,22N 51,52
Wincanton Dr. N&S
............11W—21N 52
Wincrest Rd. N&S .11W—20N 52
Wood Av. N&S ....11W—20N 52
Woodbine Ct. N&S 11W—20N 52
Woodland Dr. E&W 11W—20N 52
Woodridge Ct. N&S
............10W—21N 52
Woodruff Av. N&S .11W—21N 52
Woodward Av. N&S
............11W—20N 52
Woodvale Av. NW&SE
............10W—21N 52

Deer Park Streets

Bobwhite Ln. N&S .23W—21N 48
Bramble Ln. E&W .22W—20N 48
Briargate Ln. N&S .22W—20N 48
Buckeye Rd. E&W .23W—20N 48
Cardinal Ln. E&W .23W—21N 48
Circle Dr. N&S,E&W
............23W—20N 48
Clearwater Ct. E&W
............22W—21N 48
Clover Ln. N&S ....23W—20N 48
Corners Dr. E&W ..22W—20N 48
Country Ln. N&S ...22W—20N 48
County Line Rd. E&W
............23W—20N 48
Covington Dr. E&W
............22W—20N 48
Cuba Rd. E&W 24,26W—21N 47,48
Deer Lake Rd. 23W—20N 48
Deerpath Rd. N&S
............22,23W—21N 48
Deer Valley Dr. N&S
............22W—20N 48
Dogwood Ct. E&W 22W—20N 48
Dorthea Rd. N&S ..22W—20N 48
Edgeview Ct. NW&SE
............23W—20N 48
Ela Rd. N&S ....23W—21N 48
Elm Grove Dr. E&W
............25W—21N 47
Farthingdale N&S
............23W—21N 48
Ferndale Rd. N&S
............23,24W—20N 47,48
Green Forest Rd. NE&SW
............24,25W—21N 47,48
Grover Dr. E&W ...25W—21N 47
Harbor Dr. E. NW&SE
............22W—20N 48
Hearthside Dr. E&W
............23W—20N 48
Heather Ln. E&W ..22W—20N 48
Hedgeworth Dr. E&W
............23W—20N 48
Hidden Pines Dr. E&W
............22W—20N 48
Hollington Ln. E&W
............22W—20N 48
Hummingbird Ct. NW&SE
............24W—21N 47,48
Hunters Ln. NE&SW
............24W—21N 47,48
Hypoint Dr. N&S
............23,24W—21N 47,48
Inglenook Ct. 23W—21N 48
Inglenook Ln. N&S 23W—21N 48

Page

Jordon N&S ......22W—20N 48
Juniper Ct. E&W ..23W—20N 48
Juniper Ln. N&S ...23W—20N 48
Lagrou Ct. N&S ...22W—20N 48
Lakeview Ct. NE&SW
............23W—20N 48
Landmark Ln. N&S 22W—20N 48
Laurel Dr. N&S ....23W—20N 48
Lea Rd. N&S ......23W—20N 48
Lee St. E&W ......23W—20N 48
Lois Ln. E&W ......23W—20N 48
Long Grove Rd. E&W
............23W—20N 48
Madoch Dr. N&S ..22W—20N 48
Mallard Ct. NE&SW
............23W—21N 48
Meadow Ct. N&S ..23W—20N 48
Meadow Ln. N&S ..23W—20N 48
Oak Ridge Ln. N&S
............23W—20N 48
Old Farm Rd. N&S,E&W
............24W—21N 47,48
Park Hill Dr. N&S .23W—20N 48
Pheasant Hill Rd. NE&SW
............23W—20N 48
Pheasant Trail N&S
............23W—21N 48
Primrose Ln. E&W .23W—20N 48
Quail Ct. NE&SW .23W—20N 48
Rainbow Rd. N&S .24W—21N 47,48
Royale E&W ....23W—20N 48
Rue Cramonly E&W
............22W—20N 48
Rue Orleanais E&W
............23W—20N 48
Rue Tourain N&S ..22W—20N 48
Shady Ln. N&S ....23W—20N 48
Sumac Ct. NW&SE
............23W—21N 48
Sunset Ln. E&W ...25W—21N 47
Sunsetview Rd. N&S
............23,24W—20N 47,48
Sunset View Rd. N&S
............23W—20N 48
Surrey Ct. N&S 22,23W—20N 48
Swallow Ct. E&W ..23W—20N 48
Swansway N&S ...22W—20N 48
Sylvander Dr. N&S
............24,25W—21N 47,48
Tanager Ct. NW&SE
............24W—21N 47,48
Teal Ct. E&W ......23W—21N 47
Terrace Dr. N&S
............25,26W—21N 47
Thornhill Ct. E&W .23W—20N 48
Thrush Ct. NE&SW
............23W—21N 48
Touraine Ct. E&W .22W—20N 48
Wagon Ct. E&W ...23W—20N 48
Wehrhem Rd. N&S 22W—20N 48
Wheel Ct. E&W ....22W—20N 48
Wicker Dr. N&S ...22W—20N 48
Willow Ct. E&W ...22W—20N 48
Woodberry Rd. NE&SW
............23W—20N 48

Fox Lake Streets

Abbott Dr. N&S ...28W—39N 14
Adam St. N&S .....26W—35N 22,23
Amundsen St. E&W
............28W—36N 14
Arlington Rd. E&W 28W—39N 14
Arthur Av. N&S ....27W—37N 14
Ash St. N&S ......28W—39N 14
Atwater Pkwy. N&S 27W—36N 14
Bay Ln. E&W ......28W—36N 14
Bay Rd. N&S ......28W—36N 14
Benjamin Av. E&W 28W—36N 14
Boulder Pl. N&S ...27W—36N 14
Brewer Cypress Av E&W
............27W—36N 14
Castle Rd. N&S ...28W—37N 14
Cathryn St. E&W ..27W—37N 14
Channahon Ct. N&S
............28W—39N 14
Channel Dr. E&W .27W—35N 22
Channel Dr. NW-SE
............28W—38N 14
Chevy Chase Ct. NW-SE
............28W—39N 14
Christopher Way NE-SW
............28W—36N 14
Cedar Av. E&W ...27W—36N 14
Center St. N&S ...27W—36N 14
Clarendon Ct. NW-SE
............28W—39N 14
Commercial Av. NW-SE
............27W—36N 14
Concord Cir. NE-SW
............28W—39N 14
Cora Av. N&S .....27W—37N 14
Cottage Pl. NE&SW
............27W—36N 14
Covington Rd. E&W
............28W—36N 14
Crest Hill Ct. NE&SW
............28W—39N 14
Cross St. N&S .....28W—36N 14
Custor Ct. N&S ...28W—39N 14
Devlin Rd. N&S ....27W—36N 14

	Page
Dunns Pl. E&W .....28W—38N	14
Dunwood Ct. E&W 28W—39N	14
Eagle Point Rd. E&W	
.................28W—36N	14
East Leisure Av. N&S .28W—36N	14
Edison Ct. E&W .....27W—37N	14
Elm Av. N&S ....27W—36N	14
Elm St. E&W ....28W—39N	14
Ernie St. E&W ....28W—36N	14
Firpax Rd. E&W .....28W—36N	14
Fern Pl. E&W ....27W—36N	14
Forest Av. N&S .....27W—37N	14
Fortress Dr. NE-SW	
.................28W—37N	14
Fossil Dr. E&W .....26W—36N	14,15
Frazier Ct. E&W .....27W—35N	22
Fremont Rd. E&W .28W—36N	14
Garfield Av. E&W .26W—35N	22,23
Glenview Av. E&W 27W—36N	14
Glenview Pl. NE-SW	
.................27W—36N	14
Grand Av. E&W 27,28W—36N	14
Grass Lake Rd. E&W	
.................28W—39N	14
Greenwood Av. E&W	
.................28W—38N	14
Harding Av. N&S ...28W—35N	22
Hawthorne Ln. N&S	
.................27W—36N	14
Hazel Av. E&W ......27W—36N	14
Hickory Av. N&S ....27W—36N	14
Highland Av. .27W—36N	14
Highview Av. N&S .27W—36N	14
Hillcrest Dr. ...27W—36N	14
Hill Rd. NE&SW ...28W—36N	14
Hillside Av. NE&SW	
.................27W—36N	14
Hillside Dr. E&W ...27W—37N	14
Hilltop Av. E&W ....28W—36N	14
Hilltop Rd. N&S ....28W—36N	14
Holly Av. N&S ....27W—36N	14
Hook Ln. N&S ....28W—37N	14
Howard Av. E&W ...27W—37N	14
Howard Ct. NE&SW	
.................27W—37N	14
Industrial Av. NW&SE	
.................27W—36N	14
Jack Frost Ln. NE&SW	
.................28W—36N	14
Jackson Dr. N&S ...28W—39N	14
Jefferson St. N&S .26W—35N	22,23
Keystone Av. NE&SW	
.................27W—36N	14
Kings Rd. NE&SW 28W—35N	22
Kingston Blvd. N&S	
.................28W—37N	14
Knollwood Dr. NW&SE	
.................27W—35N	22
Lagoon Arlington Rd. N&S	
.................28W—36N	14
Lakeland Av. E&W 28W—35N	22
Lakelane Rd. NE&SW	
.................28W—36N	14
Lakeshore Dr. N&S 28W—38N	14
Lakeside Av. .27W—36N	14
Lakeside Rd. E&W 27W—37N	14
Lakeview Av. N&S 27W—36N	14
Lakewood Av. N&S 27W—36N	14
Lexington Ln. E&W 28W—39N	14
Linden N&S ....27W—36N	14
Lindy St. E&W ....27W—36N	14
Lippencott Rd. N&S	
.................27W—36N	14
Lippencott Ln. NW&SE	
.................27W—36N	14
Livingston St. N&S 28W—37N	14
Longwood Dr. E&W	
.................27W—35N	22
Lotus Av. E&W .....27W—38N	14
Madison Av. N&S .26W—35N	22,23
Manor Av. NE&SW 28W—36N	14
Maple Av. N&S .....27W—36N	14
Maruin St. N&S .....28W—36N	14
Mastodon Dr. N&S 26W—36N	14
Matts Rd. E&W .....28W—36N	14
Maude Av. E&W ....27W—36N	14
McHenry Rd. E&W 28W—36N	14
McKinley St. N&S	
..........26,28W—36N	14,15
Mead Ct.E&W ......28W—36N	14
Medinah N&S ....27W—36N	14
Mineola Rd. NE&SW	
.................27W—36N	14
Monterrey Terr .....28W—37N	14
Nippersink Blvd. NE&SW	
.................27W—37N	14
North End Av. E&W	
.................27W—37N	14
N. Lake Av. N&S ...27W—36N	14
N. Rushmore Rd. N&S	
.................26W—36N	14
Northway N&S .....27W—38N	14
Oak Av. N&S ....27W—36N	22
Oak Ct. N&S ....28W—36N	14
Oak St. E&W ....27W—36N	14
Orchard Pl. E&W ...27W—36N	14
Park Av. N&S ....28W—35N	22
Park Ln. NE&SW ...27W—35N	22
Park Rd. E&W ....28W—39N	14
Pine Av. E&W ....27W—36N	14

	Page
Pistakee Lake Rd. N&S	
.................28W—36N	14
Pistakee Pkwy E&W	
.................28W—35N	22
Poplar Av. N&S .....28W—36N	14
Rand York St. N&S 27W—36N	14
Ridgewood Av. N&S	
.................27W—36N	14
Riverside Dr. NE&SW	
.................28W—37N	14
Riverside Island Av. NW&SE	
.................28W—37N	14
Riverview Av. E&W 27W—37N	14
Rolland Pl. E&W ...28W—36N	14
Rollins Rd. NW&SE	
.................27W—36N	14
Rose Av. N&S ....27W—36N	14
Rushmore Rd. N&S	
.................27W—36N	14
Saxton Rd. N&S ...27W—36N	14
Scenic Ln. N&S ...28W—36N	14
Shady Ln. E&W ....27W—36N	14
Shillen St. E&W ...28W—36N	14
Shore Dr. N&S .....27W—39N	14
Silaom Av. NW&SE	
.................27W—36N	14
S. Lake Av. N&S ...27W—36N	14
South St. E&W .....28W—36N	14
Spring Dr. N&S .....27W—36N	14
Spruce Av. E&W ...27W—36N	14
Trout Av. NW&SE ..28W—38N	14
Troy St. NW&SE ...27W—36N	14
Tweed Rd. N&S ...28W—36N	14
Venice Av. NW&SE 27W—36N	14
Washington Av. N&S	
.......26,27W—36,38N	14,15
W. Grass Lake Dr. E&W	
.................27,28W—39N	14
Wildwood Dr. E&W 27W—35N	22
Woodland Av. N&S 27W—36N	14
Woodstock St. N&S	
.................27W—36N	14

Gages Lake Streets

	Page
Algonquin Dr. N&S 18W—33N	26
Avon Ct. NW&SE ..18W—33N	26
Battersol Dr. N&S ..18W—33N	26
Belvedere Rd. E&W	
.................18W—33N	26
Big Oaks Rd. E&W 18W—33N	26
Blackhawk Dr. E&W	
.................17W—33N	26
Cherokee Ct. 17W—33N	26
Cheyenne Ct. E&W	
.................17W—33N	26
Chippewa Rd. E&W	
.................17W—33N	26
Circle Ct. E&W .....18W—33N	26
Country Ln. E&W ..18W—33N	26
Cove Rd. NW&SE .18W—33N	26
Dady Ct. E&W ......18W—33N	26
Deer Path Rd. E&W	
.................18W—33N	26
Eastview Av. N&S .17W—33N	26
Eastwood Rd. N&S 17W—33N	26
Elm St. E&W ....18W—33N	26
Evergreen Dr. N&S 18W—33N	26
Fairfield Ln. E&W ..17W—32N	26
Forest Dr. N&S ....18W—33N	26
Gagemere Dr. N&S	
.................18W—33N	26
Gages Lake Dr. N&S	
.................18W—33N	26
Glen Rd. N&S .....18W—33N	26
Grand Dr. E&W ...18W—33N	26
Greentree Pl. N&S 18W—33N	26
Greentree Rd. E&W	
.................17W—33N	26
Hickory Pl. E&W ...18W—33N	26
Idlewild Dr. N&S ...18W—33N	26
Indian Ln. E&W ...18W—33N	26
Iroquois Dr. N&S ..17W—33N	26
Iroquois Dr. E&W ..17W—33N	26
Island Av. N&S ....18W—33N	26
Island Ct. N&S ....18W—33N	26
Ivy Ln. N&S ....17W—33N	26
John Magg Rd. N&S	
.................18W—33N	26
Kewaunee Dr. E&W	
.................17W—33N	26
Lake Rd. N&S, E&W	
.............17,18W—33N	26
Lake Shore Dr. NW&SE	
.................18W—33N	26
Lakeview Ct. NW&SE	
.................18W—33N	26
Lindenwood Dr. E&W	
.................18W—33N	26
Lone Rock Rd. N&S	
.................18W—33N	26
Lovers Ln. NE&SW	
.................18W—33N	26
Main St. E&W ......18W—33N	26
Manitowoc Dr. E&W	
.................18W—33N	26
Meadow Rd. N&S .18W—33N	26
Mill Rd. N&S ....18W—33N	26
Oakland Av. N&S ..18W—33N	26
Oak St. N&S ....18W—33N	26

	Page
Old Plank Rd. E&W	
.................18W—33N	26
Orchard Ln. E&W ..18W—33N	26
Park St. N&S ....18W—33N	26
Prospect Dr. N&S .18W—33N	26
Public Rd. NW&SE 18W—33N	26
Ridge Rd. NW&SE 18W—33N	26
Rolling Hills Rd. NW&SE	
.................18W—33N	26
Rule Ct. NW&SE ...18W—33N	26
Sears Blvd. N&S, E&W	
.................18W—33N	26
Sunset Av. N&S ...18W—33N	26
Thornapple Ln. N&S	
.................18W—33N	26
Timber Ln. E&W ...18W—33N	26
Tomahawk Pl. NW&SE	
.................18W—33N	26
Twin Lakes Blvd. N&S	
.................18W—33N	26
Valley Dr. E&W ....18W—33N	26
Valley View Dr. NW&SE	
.................18W—33N	26
Warren Av. E&W ...17W—33N	26
Wayside Pl. N&S ..18W—33N	26
Willow Point Dr. E&W	
.................18W—33N	26
Winnebago Ct. NW&SE	
.................17W—33N	26
Winnebago Dr. N&S, E&W	
.................17W—33N	26
Woodland Terr. N&S	
.................18W—33N	26
Wright Av. N&S ....18W—33N	26
1st St. N&S ....18W—33N	26
2nd St. N&S ....18W—33N	26

Grayslake Streets

	Page
Allen Av. E&W ......20W—33N	25
Allison Ct. E&W ....21W—32N	25
Alta Dr. N&S ....21W—32N	25
Augusta St. N&S ..21W—32N	25
Barron N&S ....20W—33N	25
Behm Dr. NW&SE .21W—33N	25
Berry Av. E&W .....20W—33N	25
Bluff Av. NE&SW ..21W—32N	25
Bonnie Brae Av. E&W	
.................20W—33N.	25
Briar Gate Dr. E&W	
.................20W—33N	25
Bristol Ln. N&S ....20W—33N	25
Brittan Av. N&S ....21W—32N	25
Brittany Sq.,E. NW&SE	
.................20W—33N	25
Burton St. N&S ....21W—33N	25
Cardinal Ct. N&S ..20W—33N	25
Carol Ln. E&W .....20W—33N	25
Ceceila St. N&S ...21W—33N	25
Center St. E&W ...20W—33N	25
Chard St. E&W ....20W—33N	25
Cove Ct. N&S ......20W—33N	25
Dawn Cir. N&S .....20W—33N	25
Durham Ln. E&W ..20W—33N	25
East St. N&S ....20W—33N	25
Flanders Ln. E&W .20W—33N	25
George St. E&W ...21W—33N	25
Getchell Av. E&W ..21W—32N	25
Glen St. E&W ......21W—33N	25
Gray Ct. NW&SE ..20W—33N	25
Greenwood Av. E&W	
.................21W—33N	25
Hamlitz E&W ....21W—33N	25
Harding St. N&S ...20W—33N	25
Harvey Av. E&W ...21W—33N	25
Hawley Ct. N&S ...21W—33N	25
Hawley St. E&W ...21W—33N	25
Heather Av. E&W ..20W—33N	25
Hickory St. E&W ...20W—33N	25
Highland Rd. E&W 20W—33N	25
Hillside Av. E&W ...21W—33N	25
Hojem Ln. E&W ....21W—32N	25
Jackson Blvd. E&W	
.................20W—32N	25
Junior Av. E&W ....20W—33N	25
Lake St. N&S ....21W—32N	25
Laurence St. N&S .20W—33N	25
Laurel Terr. N&S ...20W—33N	25
Lincoln Av. N&S ...20W—33N	25
Manor Av. N&S .....20W—33N	25
May St. N&S ....21W—33N	25
McMillan St. N&S ..20W—33N	25
Merrill Ln. E&W ....20W—33N	25
Mitchell Dr. E&W ..21W—33N	25
Neville Dr. N&S ....21W—32N	25
Normandy Ln. E&W	
.................20W—33N	25
Oak Av. E&W ....20W—33N	25
Oakwood Dr. N&S .20W—33N	25
Old Center St. E&W	
.................20W—33N	25
Oriole Ct. E&W .....20W—33N	25
Park Pl. E&W ....20W—33N	25
Paul St. NW&SE ...20W—33N	25
Pheasant Ct. N&S .20W—33N	25
Pierce St. N&S .....20W—33N	25
Pine St. E&W ....20W—33N	25
Prairieview Av. E&W	
.................21W—33N	25
Proctor St. E&W ...21W—33N	25

	Page
.................20W—33N	25
Quist St. N&S ....21W—33N	25
Railroad Av. NW&SE	
.................20W—33N	25
Robin Ct. N&S ......20W—33N	25
School St. N&S .....21W—33N	25
Seymour Av. N&S	
.................20W—32,33N	25
Shakespeare Dr. E&W	
.................20W—34N	25
Sheffield Ln. E&W .20W—33N	25
Siwiha Dr. E&W ....21W—33N	25
Slusser St. N&S ...21W—33N	25
S. Stewart St. N&S 20W—33N	25
Stratford Ct. N&S ..20W—34N	25
Stuart St. N&S ......20W—33N	25
Swan Dr. N&S ......20W—33N	25
Warren Ln. E&W ...21W—32N	25
Washington Blvd. E&W	
.................20W—32N	25
Webb St. N&S ......20W—33N	25
Westerfield Pl. N&S	
.................20W—32N	25
West Shore Dr. NW&SE	
.................21W—33N	25
White St. E&W .....20W—32N	25
Whitney St. N&S ...20W—33N	25
Wick St. E&W ....20W—32N	25
Woodland Dr. E&W 21W—33N	25
Ziegler Dr. N&S ....20W—33N	25
1st St. N&S ....21W—33N	25
2nd St. N&S ....21W—33N	25

Great Lakes Naval Training Center Streets

	Page
A St. E&W ....10W—30N	37
Alaska Av. E&W ...12W—30N	37
Allan Ln. E&W ......11W—31N	37
Argonaut Pl. N&S .11W—30N	37
Arizonia Av. N&S ..11W—30N	37
Arkansas Rd. N&S 12W—29N	37
Atlantic Rd. N&S ..11W—29N	37
Av. Pacific N&S .....11W—30N	37
B St. E&W ....10W—30N	37
Barry Av. E&W .....12W—30N	37
Barry Pl. N&S ....10W—30N	37
Barry Rd. E&W .....10W—30N	37
Bassett Av. N&S ...11W—30N	37
Beacon Av. E&W ..12W—30N	37
Berwyn Av. E&W ..12W—30N	37
Broadway Av. E&W	
.................11W—30N	37
Bronson Av. .10W—31N	37
Buckley Rd. E&W ..12W—30N	37
Burnham Av. E&W 10W—31N	37
C St. E&W ....10W—30N	37
California Av. E&W 11W—29N	37
Cavin Dr. E&W .....11W—30N	37
Clark Av. E&W .....10W—31N	37
Cluerius Av. E&W ..11W—30N	37
Connecticut Av. E&W	
.................12W—30N	37
Connecticut Ct. N&S	
.................11W—30N	37
Crosley Dr. E&W ...10W—30N	37
Crosley Dr. N&S ...10W—31N	37
D St. E&W ....10W—30N	37
Dahlgren St. N&S .10W—31N	37
Decatur Av. E&W ..10W—30N	37
Delaware Av. E&W 11W—29N	37
Depot Dr. E&W ....12W—30N	37
Dewey Av. E&W ...10W—31N	37
Downes Dr. N&S ..10W—30N	37
E St. E&W ....10W—30N	37
E. Alabama Av. E&W	
.................11W—30N	37
E.C.I. Ln. E&W ......11W—31N	37
Ellis St. N&S ....10W—31N	37
Enterprise Av. NE&SW	
.................11W—30N	37
Erie Ct. E&W ....12W—30N	37
Essex Av. N&S .....11W—31N	37
Evans Av. E&W ....10W—30N	37
E. Wyoming Av. E&W	
.................12W—30N	37
F St. E&W ....10W—30N	37
Farragut Av. E&W .10W—31N	37
Fisher Rd. NE&SW 10W—30N	37
Florida Av. E&W ...12W—30N	37
Forrestal Dr. N&S .11W—29N	37
Frontenac Av. N&S 12W—30N	37
Fullam Av. E&W ...10W—31N	37
G St. E&W ....10W—30N	37
Georgia Rd. N&S ..12W—29N	37
Grassie Lake Dr. N&S	
.................10W—31N	37
Great Lakes Dr. N&S	
.................12W—30N	37
Greenfield St. E&W 11W—30N	37
Hawaii Av. N&S ....11W—29N	37
Hennepin St. N&S .10W—31N	37
Hennepin St. N&S 10W—31N	37
Hines St. N&S ......10W—30N	37
Hopkins St. N&S ...10W—30N	37
Huron St. N&S .....12W—30N	37
Idaho Ct. N&S ......12W—30N	37
Idaho St. N&S ......12W—30N	37
Illinois St. N&S .....11W—29N	37
Indiana St. N&S ...11W—30N	37

	Page
Interepid St. N&S ..11W—30N	37
Iowa St. N&S ....11W—31N	37
Isherwood Av. N&S 10W—31N	37
Kentucky Ct. N&S .11W—29N	37
Kentucky St. N&S ..11W—30N	37
Langley St. NW&SE	
.................11W—31N	37
Lawrence St. N&S 10W—31N	37
Loth St. N&S ....11W—31N	37
Luce Blvd. N&S ...10W—31N	37
Lucee Blvd. N&S ...10W—31N	37
Mac Douvough N&S	
.................10W—31N	37
Mahan Rd. NW&SE	
.................10W—30N	37
Main St. N&S ....11W—30N	37
Maine Av. N&S .....11W—30N	37
Meridan Dr. N&S	
.................11W—29,30N	37
Meyer Cir. NW&SE 10W—31N	37
Michigan Ct. N&S .12W—30N	37
Minnesota Av. N&S 12W—30N	37
Mississippi St. N&S	
.................12W—30N	37
Missouri St. N&S	
.................11W—30,31N	37
Moffet Dr. E&W ....10W—31N	37
Moffet St. N&S .....10W—31N	37
Montana Av. N&S ..11W—30N	37
N. Admiral Rd. N&S	
.................11W—30N	37
Nebraska Ct. N&S .11W—30N	37
Nevada Ct. N&S ...12W—30N	37
New York Av. E&W 11W—29N	37
Neyer Cir. NW&SE 10W—31N	37
Nimitz Av. E&W ....10W—31N	37
Oklahoma Av. N&S 12W—30N	37
Oklahoma St. N&S 12W—30N	37
Ohio Av. E&W ....11W—29N	37
Ohio St. N&S ....11W—29N	37
Ontario Ct. E&W ...12W—30N	37
Oregon Ct. E&W ...12W—30N	37
Paul Jones Ct. N&S	
.................10W—31N	37
Paul Jones St. N&S	
.................10W—31N	37
Pennsylvania Av. E&W	
.................11W—30N	37
Perry St. N&S ....11W—30N	37
Porter Av. N&S .....10W—31N	37
Prebel Pl. N&S .....10W—30N	37
Preble Av. E&W ....10W—30N	37
Ranger Ct. N&S ....11W—30N	37
Ray St. N&S ....10W—31N	37
Remora Ct. E&W ..11W—30N	37
Rhode Island Av. N&S	
.................12W—29N	37
Rhode Island Ct. N&S	
.................12W—30N	37
Rogers St. N&S ....10W—31N	37
S. Admiral Rd. N&S	
.................11W—29N	37
Sampson Rd. N&S 10W—30N	37
Sampson St. N&S .10W—31N	37
Saratoga St. NW&SE	
.................11W—30N	37
Spaulding St. N&S 11W—30N	37
Sutton Ct. N&S .....12W—29N	37
Superior St. N&S ..12W—30N	37
Tennessee Ct. E&W	
.................12W—30N	37
Texas Ct. E&W .....11W—30N	37
Thresher St. N&S ..11W—30N	37
Utah Ct. E&W ....12W—30N	37
Vermont Ct. No.	
.................12W—30N	37
Vermont Ct. So. E&W	
.................12W—30N	37
Virginia Ct. NW&SE	
.................12W—30N	37
Virginia Rd. E&W ..11W—30N	37
W. Alabama Av. E&W	
.................12W—29N	37
Washington Av. E&W	
.................11,12W—30N	37
W. Colorado .12W—30N	37
W. Florida Ct. E&W	
.................12W—30N	37
Wisconsin Dr. E. NE&SW	
.................12W—30N	37
Wurtsbaugh N&S	
.................10W—30N	37
W. Wyoming Av. E&W	
.................12W—30N	37
Wyoming Ct. E&W 12W—30N	37
Yeager N&S ....11W—30N	37
Zegemeier St. N&S	
.................10W—31N	37
1st Av. E&W ....11W—29N	37
2nd Av. E&W ....11W—29N	37
3rd Av. E&W ....11W—30N	37
4th Av. E&W ....11W—30N	37
5th Av. E&W ....11W—30N	37
6th Av. E&W ....11W—30N	37
7th Av. E&W ....11W—30N	37
8th Av. E&W ....11W—30N	37
9th Av. E&W ....11W—30N	37
10th Av. E&W ......11W—30N	37
11th Av. E&W ......11W—30N	37
12th Av. E&W ......11W—30N	37

Page

1st St. N&S ....10W—30N 37
2nd St. N&S ....10W—30N 37
3rd St. N&S ....10W—30N 37
4th St. N&S ....10W—30N 37
5th St. N&S ....10W—30N 37
6th St. N&S ....10W—30N 37
7th St. N&S ....10W—30N 37
8th St. N&S ....10W—30N 37
9th St. N&S ....10W—30N 37
11th St. N&S ....10W—30N 37

Green Oaks Streets
Belmont Dr. E&W ..14W—30N 35 36
Benson Ln. N&S ....14W—29N 35 36
Benson Rd. N&S ....14W—29N 35,36
Berwick Way E&W 14W—30N 35,36
Brentwood Dr. E&W
..............14W—30N 35,36
Carriage Ct. N&S ..14W—30N 35,36
Cranbrook Rd. E&W
..............14W—30N 35,36
Crescent Knoll Dr. NE&SW
..............14W—28N 35,36
Crest Rd. N&S ......14W—29N 35,36
Dan Patch Cir. N.
..............14W—31N 35,36
Dan Patch Cir. S.
..............14W—31N 35,36
Fox Run N&S ....14W—29N 35,36
Glenmore Rd. N&S 14W—30N 35,36
Greenbriar Dr. E&W
..............14W—29N 35,36
Greenbriar Ln. E&W
..............14W—29N 35,36
Hamilton Rd. N&S .15W—31N 35,36
Harwood Dr. N&S .15W—31N 35,36
Haven Ln. E&W ....15W—31N 35,36
Heatcliff Dr. N&S ..14W—31N 35,36
Horace Ct. NW&SE
..............14W—30N 35,36
Irondale Rd. N&S ..15W—31N 35,36
Kathryn Ct. N&S ..14W—29N 35,36
Kenton Ln. E&W ..14W—30N 35,36
King Ct. E&W ......14W—30N 35,36
King Dr. N&S, E&W
..............14W—30N 35,36
Lexington Rd. NE&SW
..............14W—30N 35,36
Lockwood Dr. N&S 14W—30N 35,36
Margate Ln. E&W .14W—28N 35,36
Minard Ln. E&W ...14W—29N 35,36
Morgan Ct. E&W ..14W—31N 35,36
O'Plaine Rd. N&S
..............14W—30,31N 35,36
Pearson Rd. E&W .14W—29N 35,36
Placid Ln. E&W ....14W—30N 35,36
Rein Ct. NW&SE ...14W—31N 35,36
Saddle Hill Rd. N&S
..............14W—30N 35,36
Saratoga Ct. E&W 14W—30N 35,36
Scotland Ct. E&W .14W—31N 35,36
Shannondale Dr. E&W
..............14W—31N 35,36
Steeplechase Ct. E&W
..............14W—30N 35,36
Sunrise Rd. E&W ..14W—29N 35,36
Thornhill Rd. N&S 14W—30N 35,36
Tri-State Tollway N&S
..............14W—29N 35,36
White Fenos N&S
..............14W—30N 35,36
Wickham Dr. N&S .14W—30N 35,36
Wilton Ln. N&S ....14W—30N 35,36
Woodview Dr. E&W
..............15W—31N 35,36

Gurnee Streets
Abingdon Ct. N&S .16W—33N 26,27
Adaline Ct. E&W ...14W—35N 27,28
Adele Dr. E&W .....15W—35N 27
Alpine Ct. N&S .....15W—36N 19
Astor Pl. N&S ......14W—35N 27,28
Atlanta Av. E&W ...14W—35N 27,28
Avery NE&SW ......16W—33N 26,27
Beechwood Av. E&W
..............15W—36N 19
Belleplaine Av. N&S
..............13W—34,35N 27,28
Beth NW&SE ......16W—33N 26,27
Bennett Av. E&W ..14W—34N 27,28
Bicwell NW&SE ...16W—33N 26,27
Birch Rd. NW&SE .14W—34N 27,28
Birchwood NE&SW 15W—35N 27
Blackburn St. N&S 13W—35N 27,28
Blackstone Av. E&W
..............13W—35N 27,28
Boulevard View Av. N&S
..............13W—35N 27,28
Brierwood Ct. N&S 14W—33N 27,28
Brookhaven N&S ..14W—34N 27,28
Brown Cr. E&W ....14W—34N 27,28
Brown Pl. N&S .....14W—34N 27,28
Campbell N&S .....16W—33N 26,27
Carol E&W ....15W—35N 27
Carriage Rd. E&W 15W—35N 27
Cedar Av. E&W ....15W—35N 27
Centennial Ct. E&W
..............14W—35N 27,28
Chandler NE&SW .16W—33N 26,27
Charles Av. N&S ...14W—35N 27,28

Page

Charles Av. E&W ..14W—34N 27,28
Chase Ct. N&S .....16W—33N 26,27
Cheshire E&W ......15W—35N 27
Cheyenne Rd. E&W
..............13W—36N 19,20
Chip Ct. NE&SW ...16W—33N 26,27
Clearview Av. E&W
..............13W—36N 19,20
Clearview Ct. E&W 12W—36N 20
Colby Av. NW&SE .16W—33N 26,27
Colby Rd. N&S .....16W—33N 26,27
Cornell Av. E&W ...14W—33N 27,28
Country Club Av. E&W
..............13W—36N 19,20
Country Tr. E&W ..14W—33N 27,28
Coventry N&S ......15W—35N 27
Crescent Av. E&W 13W—35N 27,28
Darlene Ct. E&W ..15W—34N 27
Darlene Dr. E&W ..15W—34N 27
Deer Run NE&SW 15W—35N 27
Delany Rd. N&S
..............15W—33N 27
Dixon NW&SE .....16W—33N 26,27
Dorchester Av. E&W
..............13W—34N 27,28
Dordan N&S ....16W—33N 26,27
Drexel Av. E&W ...13W—34N 27,28
Drury NE&SW ......16W—33N 26,27
Dunham Rd. E&W 16W—33N 26,27
Eastwood Av. E&W 14W—33N 27,28
Eau Claire N&S ....15W—35N 27
Elm Rd. NE&SW ..14W—34N 27,28
Ellis Av. E&W ......14W—33N 27,28
Elsie Av. N&W .....15W—35N 27
Emerald Av. N&S .14W—35N 27,28
Estes St. N&S ...13W—34,35N 27,28
Evergreen Dr. E&W
..............15W—35N 27
Farmgate N&S .....14W—33N 27,28
Farwell N&S ....16W—33N 26,27
Ferndale St. N&S ..13W—35N 27,28
Fieldstone Ct. NE&SW
..............14W—34N 27,28
Finch Ct. E&W .....14W—34N 27,28
Florida Av. E&W ..13W—36N 19
Fox Ln. E&W ....15W—35N 27
Fuller Rd. N&S .....15W—35N 27
Gillings Dr. N&S ...14W—35N 27,28
Glendale Dr. NW&SE
..............15W—35N 27
Glen Flora Av. E&W
..............13W—35N 27,28
Glen Way E&W ...16W—33N 26,27
Grace St. N&S .....13W—34N 27,28
Grand Av. E&W ...14W—34N 27,28
Grand Av. NW&SE 15W—35N 27
Grandmore Av. E&W
..............13W—35N 27,28
Grandview Av. E&W
..............13W—35N 27,28
Grandville Av. E&W
..............13W—35N 27,28
Great America Parkway N&S
..............15W—35N 27
Green Brier Ct. E&W
..............14W—33N 27,28
Green Haven N&S,E&W
..............14W—34N 27,28
Greenleaf St. N&S
..............13W—34,35N 27,28
Greenwood Av. E&W
..............13W—36N 27,28
Grove Av. E&W ....13W—35N 27,28
Harper Av. N&S ...13W—34N 27,28
Hawthorne Av. N&S
..............13W—35N 27,28
Heatherridge Dr. E&W
..............13W—36N 19,20
Hickory Haven Dr. East N&S
..............15W—33N 27
Hickory Haven Dr. West N&S
..............15W—33N 27
Highland Av. E&W .13W—36N 19,20
Jeffery Av. E&W ...14W—34N 27,28
Johns Manville Av. N&S
..............13W—35N 27,28
Keith Av. E&W .....13W—35N 27,28
Kenwood Av. E&W 13W—34N 27,28
Kilbourne Rd. NE&SW
..............13W—35N 27,28
Lake Park Av. E&W
..............15W—33N 27
Lawrence Av. N&S 13W—34N 27,28
Lawson Blvd. NE&SW
..............15W—35N 27
Lee Av. E&W ....13W—35N 27,28
Lee Av. NW&SE ...13W—35N 27,28
Leonard Dr. NE&SW
..............16W—33N 26,27
Lind Ln. N&S ....15W—33N 27
Magnolia Av. .13W—34N 27,28
Manchester Dr. E&W
..............16W—33N 26,27
McClure Av. E&W .14W—34N 27,28
Milwaukee Av. NE&SW
..............15W—34N 27
Mint Haven N&S ...14W—34N 27,28

Page

Mitchell Ct. NW&SE
..............16W—33N 26,27
Morrison Dr. N&S ..13W—35N 27,28
Morman Av. E&W ..14W—34N 27,28
North Av. E&W .....14W—34N 27,28
Northwestern Av. N&S
..............13W—35N 27,28
Oak Ln. E&W ....13W—35N 27
Oakwood St. N&S .13W—35N 27,28
Oglesby Av. E&W ..14W—34N 27,28
Old Grand Av. NW&SE
..............14W—35N 27,28
Oriole Ct. E&W .....14W—34N 27,28
Pacific Av. E&W ...13W—35N 27,28
Pine Grove St. N&S
..............13W—34N 27,28
Pine St. N&S ....15W—35N 27
Porett Dr. E&W ....13W—35N 27,28
Portage NE&SW ...15W—35N 27
Prairie Oak Rd. E&W
..............15W—35N 27
Ralph Av. N&S .....14W—35N 27,28
Raven Ct. E&W ....14W—35N 27,28
Red Rine Av. E&W 15W—36N 27
Robin Cr. E&W .....14W—35N 27,28
Rockpoint Ct. E&W 15W—35N 27
Rogers Rd. N&S ...15W—35N 27
Russell Av. E&W ..14W—35N 27,28
St. Paul Av. NE&SW
..............14W—35N 27,28
Sanders N&S ....16W—33N 26,27
Scot Ct. N&S ....16W—33N 26,27
Shadow Rock Ct. E&W
..............14W—33N 27,28
Shagbark Ct. E&W 15W—35N 27
Shepard N&S ....16W—33N 26,27
Sherman Av. E&W 13W—35N 27,28
Sizer NE&SW ......16W—33N 26,27
South Rd. E&W ....15W—35N 27
Springhaven E&W .14W—34N 27,28
Stony Island Av. N&S
..............14W—34N 27,28
Stewart N&S ....15W—33N 27
Stout N&S ....15W—33N 27
Stratford N&S ......15W—35N 27
Sunnyside Av. N&S
..............14W—33N 27,28
Sunrise E&W ....15W—33N 27
Swanson Ct. N&S .13W—36N 27,28
Tanglewood SE NW
..............14W—33N 27,28
Taylor N&S ....16W—33N 26,27
University Av. E&W 13W—34N 27,28
Vose Dr. N&S ......16W—33N 26,27
Wakefield N&S .....16W—33N 26,27
Washington St. E&W
..............13W—34N 27,28
Wausau N&S ....15W—35N 27
Waveland Av. NW&SE
..............13W—34N 27,28
Waveland St. N&S 13W—34N 27,28
West St .... N&S 14W—34N 27,28
White E&W ....16W—33N 26,27
Whitney NW&SE ..16W—33N 26,27
White Oak Ct. NW&SE 14W—33N 27,28
Wilber NE&SW ....15W—33N 27
Williams N&S ....16W—33N 26,27
Willow NW&SE ....15W—35N 27
Windwood E&W ...15W—35N 27
Winona E&W ....15W—35N 27
Woodlawn Av. E&W
..............13W—34N 27,28

Hainesville Streets
Antioch St. N&S. 22W—33N 24
Belvedere Rd. E&W
..............22W—33N 24
Devoe N&S ....22W—33N 24
Gage St. N&S ......22W—33N 24
Hainesville Rd. N&S
..............22W—33N 24
North St. E&W .....22W—33N 24

Hawthorn Woods Streets
Aberdeen Rd. E&W
..............20W—24N 41
Acorn Dr. NE&SW .23W—24N 39,40
Albert Cir. NE&SW 19W—24N 41
Arthur Ct. N&S ....21W—24N 41
Bent Tree Ct. NW&SE
..............24W—25N 39,40
Birch Lake Dr. E&W
..............22W—24N 40
Bixtone Path NE&SW
..............24W—25N 39,40
Blackhawk Rd. N&S
..............20W—24N 41
Brierwoods Ln. N&S
..............24W—24N 39,40
Brighton Ct. E&W .20W—24N 41
Bruce Cir. N&S,E&W
..............23W—24N 39,40
Bruce Ct. NW&SE .23W—24N 39,40
Byron Cir. N&S ....22W—24N 40
Cambridge Dr. N&S
..............20W—25N 41
Canterbury Ln. E&W
..............20W—25N 41
Carlisle Rd. N&S,E&W
..............20W—25N 41

Page

Cayuga Ct. E&W ...19W—25N 41
Cherry Hill Cir.N&S 19W—24N 41
Conesug Ct. E&W .19W—25N 41
Cooper Ct. N&S ...20W—25N 41
Croydon Rd. N&S .20W—25N 41
Darlington Rd. N&S
..............20W—24N 41
Dartmouth Ln. E&W
..............21W—25N 41
David Ln. N&S .....22W—24N 40
Edward Ln. E&W ..20W—24N 41
Elm St. N&S ....20W—24N 41
Elmwood Dr. NW&SE
..............23W—24N 39,40
E. Lynn Dr. N&S ...21W—24N 41
Essex E&W ....21W—24N 41
Fairfield Rd. N&S .22W—24N 40
Falkirk Rd. E&W ..20W—24N 41
Fox Hunt Ct. E&W 24W—25N 39,40
Fox Hunt Trail NE&SW
..............24W—25N 39,40
Gino Ln. NW&SE ..19W—24N 41
Glen Ct. E&W ......21W—24N 41
Greenbriar Ln. N&S
..............19W—24N 41
Hampton Ln. E&W 20W—24N 41
Harvard Ln. N&S ..20W—25N 41
Hawthorne Dr. E&W
..............21W—24N 41
Heather E&W ......21W—24N 41
Heather Ln. E&W .21W—24N 41
Hickory Rd. E&W ..21W—24N 41
Highland Terr. N&S 21W—24N 41
Highpoint Cir. NW&SE
..............22W—25N 40
Highpoint Dr. NE&SW
..............22W—25N 40
Highview Cir. N&S .20W—24N 41
Hillcrest Dr. N&S ..20W—23N 49
Hilltop Ct. NE&SW 19W—23N 49
Holmes Av. NE&SW
..............22W—25N 40
Indian Dreek Rd. E&W
..............20W—25N 41
James Ct. NW&SE 20W—24N 41
James Dr. E&W ....20W—24N 41
Jamie Ln. E&W ....20W—24N 41
Jane Ct. N&S ......20W—24N 41
John Dr. N&S ......20W—24N 41
Juel Cir. E&W ......21W—24N 41
Juel Ct. E&W ....20W—24N 41
Juel Dr. E&W ....20W—24N 41
Karen Ct. NE&SW 19W—24N 41
Kathy Ln. E&W ....22W—25N 40
Keuka Ct. E&W ....19W—25N 41
Krueger Rd. E&W .22W—25N 40
Lagoon Dr. N&S ...20W—24N 41
Lake St. E&W ......21W—24N 41
Lakeview Rd. E&W 20W—23N 49
Lancelot Ln. NW&SE
..............21W—24N 41
Lisa Ln. N&S ....20W—24N 41
Lydia Ct. E&W .....23W—24N 39,40
Lynn Dr. N&S ......21W—24N 41
Magnolia Pkwy. E&W
..............19W—24N 41
Marilyn N&S ....20W—24N 41
Mark Dr. N&S ......20W—24N 41
Mary Ln. E&W .....19W—24N 41
McHenry Rd. NW&SE
..............24W—25N,20W—23N 47,48
Melody Ln. (Cherry Rd.) N&S
..............21W—24N 49
Midlothian Rd. NE&SE
..............22W—24N 40
Moorgate Trail E&W
..............24W—25N 39,40
Nancy Ct. E&W ...22W—25N 40
Newbury Ct. N&S .20W—24N 41
N. Bruce Cir. E&W 23W—24N 39,40
Norbert Dr. E&W ..20W—24N 41
Oak Ln. NW&SE ...21W—24N 41
Old Barn Rd. E&W 20W—23N 49
Oneida Ln. N&S ...20W—25N 41
Onondaga Dr. E&W
..............20W—25N 41
Orchard Ln. N&S ..21W—24N 41
Pheasant Run Rd. E&W
..............24W—25N 39,40
Piper Ln. N&S ......20W—24N 41
Princeton Ct. N&S .21W—25N 41
Princeton Ln. NE&SW
..............20W—25N 41
Public St. NW&SE .23W—24N 39,40
Quail Hollow Ct. N&S
..............20W—23N 49
Quail Hollow Rd. N&S
..............20W—23N 49
Ridge Dr. E&W ....23W—24N 39,40
Robert Ct. E&W ...20W—24N 41
Rutgers Ct. N&S ..20W—25N 41
S. Bruce Cir E&W .23W—24N 39,40
Seneca East Av. N&S
..............20W—25N 41
Seneca West Av. N&S
..............20W—25N 41
Sequoia Ln. N&S ..20W—25N 41
Squire Rd. N&S
..............21W—24N 41
St. John Dr. N&S ..19W—24N 41

Page

Stonehaven Dr. E&W
..............20W—24N 41
Sunset Ct. NE&SW
..............20W—23N 49
Sunset Rd. N&S ...23W—24N 39,40
Tanglewood Ct. N&S
..............24W—24N 39,40
Tanglewood Ln. E&W
..............24W—24N 39,40
Thornfield Ln. NW&SE
..............24W—24N 39,40
Trent Rd. N&S .....20W—24N 41
University Cir. NE&SW
..............20W—25N 41
Victoria Ln. N&S ..21W—24N 41
Wakla Ct. E&W ....20W—25N 41
Walnut Dr. N&S ...21W—24N 41
Washitay Av. NE&SW
..............20W—25N 41
Wayne Ln. N&S ...23W—24N 39,40
Whitman Terr. E&W
..............22W—25N 40
Wild Way E&W ....20W—24N 41
Winding Branch Rd. E&W
..............24W—25N 39,40
W. Lynn Dr. N&S ..21W—24N 41
Wooded Ln. N&S ..24W—26N 39,40
Yale Ct. E&W ......20W—25N 41

Highland Park Streets
Acorn Ln. N&S .....9W—20N 53
Alley Rd. N&S ......7W—20N 53
Alta Ln. E&W ....10W—22N 52
Alvin Pl. N&S ......7W—21N 53
Andean Pl. E&W ...9W—22N 53
Apple Tree Ln. E&W 9W—23N 53
Arbor Av. N&S .....9W—21N 53
Arlington Av. N&S .9W—23N 53
Ashland Pl. N&S ...7W—20N 53
Aspen Ln. E&W ....8W—20N 53
Auburn Av. E&W ..10W—23N 52
Auburn Av. E&W ..9W—23N 53
Auburn Pl. N&S ...9W—24N 45
Ava St. NE&SW ...7W—21N 53
Avignon Ct. E&W ..9W—20N 53
Baldwin Rd. NW&SE
..............7W—21N 53
Balsam Rd. E&W ..9W—21N 53
Barberry Rd. E&W .9W—21N 53
Barnard Ln. N&S ..7W—21N 53
Beaupre Ct. E&W ..9W—20N 53
Beech Ln. NW&SE .7W—21N 53
Beech St. NW&SE .9W—20N 53
Belle Av. NE&SW ..8W—22N 53
Belleview Pl. NE&SE
..............7W—21N 53
Berkeley E&W .....10W—22N 52
Beverly Pl. N&S .9W—21,22N 53
Birch Av. E&W .....9W—21N 53
Birchwood Av. E&W 9W—22N 53
Blackhawk Rd. NW&SE
..............7W—20N 53
Blackstone Pl. E&W 7W—20N 53
Bloom St. NE&SW .8W—23N 53
Blossom Ct. NE&SW
..............9W—20N 53
Bob-O-Link Rd. N&S
..............8,9W—21N 53
Boxer Ct. N&S .....10W—22N 52
Braeburn Ln. E&W .7W—20N 53
Braeside Rd. E&W .7W—20N 53
Briar Ln. N&S ......9W—20N 53
Briarcliff Ln. E&W .10W—23N 52
Briargate Dr. NW&SE
..............10W—21N 52
Briarwood Pl. E&W 7W—20N 53
Brittany Rd. E&W ..7W—20N 53
Broadview Av. NW&SE
..............7W—21N 53
Bronson Ln. NE&SW
..............7W—20N 53
Brooks Rd. N&S ...9W—24N 45
Brownville Rd. E&W 7W—20N 53
Burchell Av. E&W ..9W—23N 53
Burton Av. NW&SE .7W—21N 53
Burton Pl. NW&SE .7W—20N 53
Burr Oaks Ln. E&W 9W—20N 53
Byron Ln. N&S .....10W—22N 52
Cambridge Ct. E&W
..............10W—23N 52
Calais Pl. E&W .....8W—21N 53
Carlyle Terr. E&W ..8W—21N 53
Cardinal Ln. N&S ..10W—22N 52
Carol Ct. E&W .....7W—20N 53
Cary Av. E&W ......7W—21N 53
Castlewood Rd. E&W
..............10W—21N 52
Cavell Av. N&S .....9W—21N 53
Cedar Av. NE&SW .7W—21N 53
Centennial Ln. NW&SE 10W—23N 52
Centennial Pkwy. NE&SE
..............10W—23N 53
Centerfield Ct. E&W 9W—20N 53
Central Av. NE&SW 8W—21N 53
Central Ct. NE&SW 8W—21N 53
Chantilly Blvd. E&W 9W—20N 53
Charal N&S ....7W—20N 53
Chatham Cir. N&S .7W—20N 53
Chaucer Ln. N&S ..8W—21N 53
Cherokee Rd. E&W .7W—20N 53

Page
Cherry Ln. E&W ......9W—22N 53
Chicago Av. E&W ....8W—23N 53
Churchill Ct. N&S ..11W—22N 52
Churchill Ln. E&W .10W—22N 52
Clavey Ct. N&S ....8W—20N 53
Clavey Ln. NW&SE .8W—20N 53
Clavey Rd. E&W ..8,9W—20N 53
Clifton Av. N&S ....9W—22N 53
Cloverdale Av. N&S ....10W—22N 52
Cofton Av. N&S ....8W—21N 53
College Pl. E&W .....9W—24N 45
Compton Av. N&S ...9W—23N 53
Comstock Pl. E&W ..7W—20N 53
Concorde Cir. E&W .9W—20N 53
Concorde Dr. NW&SE ....9W—20N 53
Country Ln. NE&SW ....9W—20N 53
Court Av. E&W ....8W—21N 53
Crawford Pl. NE&SW ....7W—21N 53
Crescent Ct. NE&SW ....7W—22N 53
Crofton Ct. N&S ......8W—21N 53
Dale Av. NW&SE .....8W—22N 53
Dato Av. N&S ....8W—22N 53
Dean Av. NE&SW ...7W—21N 53
Deer Creek Pkwy. N&S ....8W—20N 53
Deerfield Ct. E&W ...9W—21N 53
Deerfield Pl. NW&SE ....9W—21N 53
Deerfield Rd. N&S,E&W ....9W—21N 53
Deere Pk. Ct. N&S ..6W—20N 53
Dell Ln. N&S ....7W—20N 53
Dell Pl. N&S ....7W—20N 53
Delta Rd. E&W ....7W—20N 53
Derrick St. N&S ....9W—23N 53
Detamble Av. NE&SW ....8W—21N 53
Devon Ct. NW&SE ..9W—21N 53
Division St. E&W .....9W—21N 53
Driscoll Ct. E&W .....8W—21N 53
Dryden Ln. E&W .....8W—21N 53
Eastwood Av. N&S 10W—21N 52
Eaton Ct. NE&SW .10W—23N 52
Edgecliff Dr. E&W ...8W—23N 53
Edgewood Ct. N&S .9W—21N 53
Edgewood Rd. E&W 9W—20N 53
Egandale Rd. NW&SE ....8W—22N 53
Elder Ln. NE&SW ...6W—20N 53
Elm Pl. E&W ....8W—22N 53
Elmwood Dr. N&S ...9W—22N 53
Ellridge Cir. N&S .....9W—20N 53
Euclid Av. E&W ....9W—23N 53
Euclid Ct N&S ....9W—23N 53
Exmoor Av. N&S .....9W—22N 53
Fairview Rd. E&W ...8W—21N 53
Ferndale Av. N&S ...9W—21N 53
First St. NW&SE .....8W—22N 53
Flora Pl. NW&SE ....7W—20N 53
Florence Pl. N&S ....8W—21N 53
Forest Av. N&S ....7W—21N 53
Fredrickson Pl. NE&SW ....9W—21N 53
Friar Tuck Av. E&W ....10W—22N 52
Ft. Sheridan Av. N&S ....8W—23N 53
Garland Av. E&W ..10W—21N 52
Glencoe Av. NW&SE ....8W—21N 53
Glenview Av. E&W ..8W—22N 53
Golf Av. E&W ....8,9W—21N 53
Grange Av. N&S ....10W—22N 52
Gray Av. E&W ....8W—21N 53
Green Bay Rd. NW&SE
...........7W—20N,8W—22,23N 53
Greenwood Av. N&S 9W—23N 53
Grove Av. E&W ....9W—21N 53
Groveland Av. N&S .7W—20N 53
Half Day Rd. E&W ..9W—23N 53
Halsted Ln. E&W ....8W—21N 53
Harvard Ct. E&W ....9W—22N 53
Hastings Av. N&S,E&W ....7W—20N 53
Havenwood Ct. NE&SW ....7W—20N 53
Hawthorne St. N&S .7W—21N 53
Hazel Av. E&W ....8W—22N 53
Heather Ln. E&W ....9W—21N 53
Hedge Run E&W .....7W—20N 53
Hemlock Ln. N&S ....9W—20N 53
Hiawatha Ct. E&W ..8W—20N 53
Hiawatha Tr. N&S ....8W—20N 53
Hickory St. NW&SE 8W—22N 53
Highland Pl. NE&SW ....7W—20N 53
Highmoor Rd. N&S 10W—22N 52
Hill N&S ....9W—20N 53
Hill St. E&W ....9W—24N 45
Hillcrest Av. NW&SE ....10W—21N 52
Hillside Dr. NW&SE .7W—20N 53
Holly Rd. E&W ......10W—22N 52
Homewood Av. E&W ....8W—22N 53
Huntington Ln. E&W ....9W—21N 53
Hyacinth Pl. E&W ....9W—24N 45
Idlewild Ln. N&S ......9W—23N 53
Indian Ln. NW&SE ..7W—20N 53
Iris Ln. E&W ....7W—20N 53
Ivy Ln. E&W ....6W—20N 53
Judson Av. NW&SE 7W—21N 53
Keats Ct. NW&SE .10W—22N 52
Keats Ln. N&S ......10W—22N 52
Kent Av. E&W ....9W—23N 53
Kimball Rd. E&W ....8W—21N 53
Kimballwood Ln. E&W ....8W—21N 53
Kincaid Av. N&S ......7W—20N 53
Kipling Ct. E&W ....10W—22N 52
Kipling Ln. N&S .....10W—22N 52
Knollwood Ln. NE&SW ....7W—21N 53
Krenn Av. NE&SW ..9W—24N 45
Lake Av. NW&SE ....7W—22N 53
Lakeside Pl. N&S .6,7W—20N 53
Lakeside Manor Pl. E&W ....6W—20N 53
Lakeview Terr. E&W 6W—20N 53
Lakewood Pl. E&W .7W—20N 53
Lament Thee Av. E&W ....7W—20N 53
Lancelot Av. E&W ...9W—22N 53
Larkspur Dr. N&S ...8W—20N 53
Laurel Av. NE&SW ..8W—22N 53
Laurietta Av. N&S ....8W—23N 53
Lawrence Ln. E&W .9W—20N 53
Leslee Rd. NE&SW .7W—20N 53
Lewis Ln. E&W ....9W—20N 53
Lexington Ln. NW&SE ....10W—23N 52
Lilac Ln. NW&SE ....9W—21N 53
Lincoln Av. E&W ...7,8W—21N 53
Lincoln Pl. NW&SE .8W—21N 53
Lincolnwood Rd. N&S ....7W—20N 53
Linden Av. N&S ......8W—22N 53
Linden Av. NW&SE .7W—21N 53
Linden Park Pl. NE&SW ....8W—22N 53
Little John Ct. E&W ....10W—22N 52
Livingston St. E&W .9W—23N 53
Llewellyn Av. E&W ..9W—23N 53
Logan St. NW&SE ..8W—23N 53
Lorraine Cir. E&W ...8W—20N 53
Lotus Pl. E&W ....9W—24N 45
Lyman Ct. N&S ....7W—20N 53
Lynn Terr. N&S,E&W ....10W—23N 52
Lyons Cir. E&W ......8W—20N 53
Magnolia Ln. NW&SE ....9W—20N 53
Manor Rd. N&W ....10W—22N 52
Maple Av. NE&SW ..8W—22N 53
Maple Ln. NW&SE ..8W—22N 53
Marion Av. EU&W ...8W—20N 53
Marl Oak Dr. N&S ...9W—23N 53
Marquette Rd. N&S .8W—20N 53
Marshman St. NE&SW ....7W—21N 53
Marvell Ln. E&W .....8W—21N 53
Mayor Ln. N&S ......10W—23N 52
McCarn Rd. NW&SE 9W—2N 53
McDaniels Av. N&S .8W—21N 53
McGovern St. NW&SE ....8W—22N 53
McKibben Rd ....8W—23N 53
Meadow Ln. E&W .10W—23N 52
Melba Ln. NW&SE ..8W—23N 53
Melody Ln. NE&SW 7W—20N 53
Midland Av. E&W ..10W—21N 52
Midlothian Av. N&S .8W—22N 53
Montgomery Av. N&S ....8W—23N 53
Moraine Rd. F&W ...8W—23N 53
Moseley Rd. E&W ...8W—21N 53
Mulberry Pl. E&W ...8W—21N 53
N. Deer Park Dr. NW&SE ....6W—20N 53
Naida Terr. E&W .....8W—22N 53
North Av. E&W ...9,10W—23N 52,53
Northland Av. E&W 10W—21N 52
Ny-O-Da Pl. E&W ...8W—20N 53
Oak St. N&S ....8W—22N 53
Oak Knoll Terr. N&S 6W—20N 53
Oakland Dr. NE&SW ....7W—20N 53
Oakmont Rd. E&W .7W—21N 53
Oakvale Rd. E&W ...7W—21N 53
Oakwood Av. N&S ...8W—21N 53
Oxford Ct. E&W ....10W—23N 52
Old Barn Ln. N&S ...8W—21N 53
Old Briar Rd. E&W ..9W—20N 53
Old Deerfield Rd. NE&SW ....9W—21N 53
Old Mill Rd. Pvt N&S ....10W—24N 45
Old Skokie Rd. NW&SE ....9W—21N 53
Old Trail E&W ....9W—23N 53
Orchard Ln. E&W ....8W—23N 53
Orchard St. E&W ....8W—23N 53
Orleans Cir. N&S .....9W—20N 53
Orleans Dr. N&S .....9W—20N 53
Park Av. NE&SW ....8W—22N 53
Park Ln. NW&SE ....8W—22N 53
Park Front Pl. NE&SW ....8W—22N 53
Parkside Dr. NW&SE ....10W—23N 52
Partridge Ln. E&W 10W—22N 52
Patten St. NW&SE ..8W—23N 53
Perennial Ln. N&S ..9W—22N 53
Picadilly Rd. NW&SE ....9W—21N 53
Pierce Rd. NE&SW .7W—20N 53
Pine Point Ct. E&W .6W—20N 53
Pleasant Av. NW&SE ....7W—20N 53
Poplar Rd. N&S ....9W—20N 53
Port Clinton Rd. N&S ....8W—23N 53
Princeton Av. E&W ..9W—22N 53
Pricilla Av. N&S ....9W—23N 53
Private Rd. N&S ....10W—24N 45
Prospect Av. E&W ...8W—22N 53
Rambler Ln. E&W ...7W—20N 53
Ravenswood Av. N&S ....9W—23N 53
Ravine Dr. E&W .....8W—21N 53
Ravine Ln. NW&SE 8W—22N 53
Ravine Terr. NE&SW ....8W—22N 53
Ravine Oaks Av. NE&SW ....7W—21N 53
Ravinia Park Rd. E&W ....7W—21N 53
Red Oaks Ln. N&S .9W—20N 53
Rice St. N&S ....7W—20N 53
Richfield Av. E&W .10W—21N 52
Ridge Rd. N&S ......10W—22N 52
Ridge Rd. NW&SE ....9,10W—20N 52,53
Ridgelee Rd. E&W ..9W—20N 53
Ridgewood Dr. NW&SE ....8W—21N 53
Ridgewood Pl. NW&SE ....8W—21N 53
Riparian Rd. E&W ...8W—23N 53
Robin Hood Pl. E&W ....9W—22N 53
Roger Williams Av. E&W ....7W—20N 53
Rolling Av. E&W ......8W—21N 53
Rosemary Rd. E&W 9W—20N 53
Rosewood Rd. Ln. E&W ....7W—21N 53
Roslyn Cir. N&S ......8W—23N 53
Roslyn Ln. N&S ....8W—23N 53
Russet Ln. N&S ......9W—20N 53
Ryders Ln. N&S ....10W—22N 52
Sandwick Ct. E&W ..9W—22N 53
Saxony Dr. NW&SE 8W—21N 53
Saxony Rd. NE&SW 8W—21N 53
Second St. NW&SSE ....8W—22N 53
Seven Pines Cir. NW&SE ....8W—20N 53
Shady Ln. N&S .....10W—22N 52
Sheahen Ct. N&S ....8W—22N 53
Sheldon Ln. N&S ....7W—20N 53
Sheridan Ct. N&S ....8W—22N 53
Sheridan Rd. N&S ....7,8W—20,21,22N 53
Sherwood Rd. N&S ....10W—21N 52
Shire Rd. E&W ....9W—21N 53
Shonee Rd. NW&SE ....8W—20N 53
Skokie Av. E&W ......8W—22N 53
Skokie Hwy. NW&SE ....8,10W—20,23N 52,53
South Deer Park Dr. NW&SE ....6W—20N 53
South Lane Av. E&W ....10W—21N 52
Spruce Av. N&S ....10W—22N 52
St. Charles Pl. N&S 7W—20N 53
St. Johns Av. N&S ....8W—21,23N 53
St. Trope Ct. E&W ..9W—20N 53
Stonegate Dr. E&W .7W—20N 53
Stratford Rd. E&W ..9W—20N 53
Strath Erin E&W ......9W—20N 53
Sumac Rd. NW&SE ....9W—20,21N 53
Summerdale Av. N&S ....10W—21N 52
Summit Av. N&S .....9W—23N 53
Sunnyside Av. N&S ....10W—22N 52
Sunset Av. N&S ....8W—22N 53
Sunset Rd. N&S .9W—21,22N 53
Sycamore Pl. E&W .7W—22N 53
Sylvester Pl. NE&SE ....7W—22N 53
Tanglewood Ct. E&W ....9W—20N 53
Taylor Av. E&W ....9W—22N 53
Tennyson Ln. N&S 11W—22N 52
Thackery Ln. N&S ...8W—21N 53
Thornapple Ln. E&W ....10W—23N 52
Thorntree Ln. E&W .8W—21N 53
Timber Hill Rd. E&W ....7W—20N 53
Toulon Ct. N&S ....8W—20N 53
Trailway N&S ....8W—20N 53
Trail Way N&S ....10W—23N 52
Tree Dr. E&W ....7W—20N 53
Turnbull Woods N&S ....7W—20N 53
Turnstile Ln. E&W ...9W—20N 53
Twin Oaks Dr. N&S 10W—23N 52
Underwood Av. E&W ....9W—23N 53
University Av. N&S ..9W—23N 53
Vine Av. E&W ....8W—22N 53
Virginia Rd. NW&SE 9W—21N 53
Wade St. NW&SE ...7W—21N 53
Wahwahtaysee Av. N&S ....8W—20N 53
Walker Av. E&W ......8W—23N 53
Walnut Av. NE&SW .8W—22N 53
Wake Robin Ln. N&S ....7W—20N 53
Warbler Ct. NE&SW 9W—23N 53
Warbler Pl. N&S ......9W—23N 53
Washington Pl. NE&SW ....7W—20N 53
Waverly Rd. NE&SW ....7W—21N 53
Western Av. N&S ....9W—23N 53
Westgate Terr. E&W ....10W—21N 52
White Oak Ln. Pvt NE&SW ....8W—21N 53
Willow Pl. E&W .....10W—23N 52
Willow Rd. N&S .....10W—22N 52
Wincanton Ln. N&S 7W—22N 53
Windsor Rd. N&S ....9W—21N 53
Windy Ln. E&W ....9W—20N 53
Winona Rd. N&S .....8W—20N 53
Winthrop Rd. N&S ...9W—21N 53
Woodbine Av. N&S ..9W—20N 53
Woodbine Rd. N&S .9W—21N 53
Woodbridge Ln. NE&SW ....8W—23N 53
Woodland Rd. NE&SW ....7W—20N 53
Wood Leigh Av. E&W ....9W—23N 53
Wood Path NE&SW 8W—22N 53
Wood Rd. N&S ....8W—21N 53
York Ln. E&W ....10W—21N 52
Yale Av. E&W ....9W—22N 53
Yager Av. E&W ....9W—21N 53
2nd St. NE&SW ......8W—23N 53
3rd St. NE&SW ......8W—23N 53
4th St. NE&SW ......8W—23N 53
5th St. NE&SW ......8W—23N 53
6th St. NE&SW ......8W—23N 53
7th St. NE&SW ......8W—23N 53
8th St. NE&SW ......8W—23N 53
9th St. NE&SW ......8W—23N 53
10th St. NE&SW .....8W—23N 53
11th St. NE&SW .....8W—23N 53
A St. NW&SE ....8W—23N 53
B St. NE&SW ....8W—23N 53
F St. NE&SW ....8W—23N 53
G St. N&S ....8W—23N 53
H St. N&S ....8W—23N 53

Highwood Streets

Ashland Av. E&W ....9W—23N 53
Central Av. N&S ......9W—23N 53
Clay Av. E&W ....9W—23N 53
Elm Av. N&S ....9W—23N 53
Euclid Av. E&W ....9W—23N 53
Euclid Ct. N&S ....9W—23N 53
Everts Pl. N&S ....9W—23N 53
Evolution Av. N&S ...9W—23N 53
Funston Av. N&S .....9W—23N 53
Greenbay Rd. NW&SE ....9W—23N 53
Grove St. N&S ....9W—23N 53
High St. N&S ....9W—23N 53
Highwood Av. E&W .9W—23N 53
Jeffery Pl. N&S ....9W—23N 53
Jocelyn Pl. E&W .....9W—23N 53
Llewellyn Av. E&W ..9W—23N 53
Maple St. N&S ....9W—23N 53
Mears Pl. E&W ....9W—23N 53
Michigan Av. E&W ...9W—23N 53
Morgan Pl. N&S ......9W—23N 53
North Av. N&S ....9W—23N 53
Oak Av. N&S ....9W—23N 53
Oak Terr. N&S ....9W—23N 53
Oakridge Av. E&W ..9W—23N 53
Palmer Av. N&S ......9W—23N 53
Pleasant Pl. N&S .....9W—23N 53
Prairie Av. E&W ....9W—23N 53
Sheridan Av. E&W ...9W—23N 53
Sheridan Rd. NW&SE ....9W—23N 53
Summit Av. E&W .....9W—23N 53
Washington Av. E&W ....9W—23N 53
Webster Av. E&W ....9W—23N 53
Western Av. N&S 9W—23,24N 45,53
Western Pl. E&W .....9W—24N 45
Wrendale Av. E&W .9W—23N 53

Indian Creek Streets

Circle Dr. NE&SW .17W—24N 42
Crestland Rd. E&W ....17W—24N 42
Mills Ct. E&W ....17W—24N 42
Shann Dr. N&S ....17W—24N 42
Valley Rd. E&W .....17W—24N 42

Island Lake Streets

Arbor Rd. E&W .....28W—28N 30
Beech St. N&S .....28W—28N 30
Briar Ct. E&W ....28W—28N 30
Briar Rd. E&W ....28W—28N 30
Briar Hill Dr. E&W .28W—28N 30
Carol Cir. NE&SW .28W—28N 30
Cedar Terr. N&S ....29W—28N 30
Channel Dr. E&W ..28W—28N 30
Charles Ct. E&W ...29W—28N 30
Clover Rd. E&W ....28W—28N 30
David Ct. E&W ......29W—28N 30
Eastway Dr. N&S ...28W—28N 30
Elder Dr. N&S ....28W—28N 30
Elm Av. N&S ....28W—28N 30
Ethel Terr. N&S .....29W—28N 30
Fairfield Dr. E&W ...28W—28N 30
Fern Dr. E&W ....28W—28N 30
Forest Dr. E&W .....28W—28N 30
Greenleaf Av. N&S 28W—28N 30
Hickory Terr. E&W .29W—28N 30
Highland Dr. N&S ..29W—28N 30
Hillside Dr. NE&SW ....29W—28N 30
Honeysuckle Dr. E&W ....29W—28N 30
Hyacinth Terr. N&D 29W—28N 30
Ivy Rd. E&W ....28W—28N 30
Judith Dr. NE&SW .28W—28N 30
Juniper Rd. E&W ..28W—28N 30
Kingston Dr. N&S ..28W—29N 30
Lakeside Ct. NE&SW ....28W—28N 30
Lakeview Dr. N&S .29W—28N 30
Les Circle Dr. E&W 28W—28N 30
Lillar Ct. NW&SE ...29W—28N 30
Locust Av. N&S .....28W—28N 30
Mallard Pt. N&S ....28W—29N 30
Midway Dr. N&S ....29W—28N 30
Northern Ct. E&W .28W—28N 30
Northern Terr. E&W ....28W—28N 30
Oak Terr. N&S ....29W—28N 30
Oakwood Av. N&S 28W—28N 30
Park Dr. N&S ....28W—28N 30
Pine Terr. N&S ......29W—28N 30
Poplar Dr. N&S ......28W—28N 30
Ralph Ct. E&W ......29W—28N 30
Richard Ct. E&W ...29W—28N 30
Ridge Av. N&S ....28W—28N 30
Rose Av. E&W ....28W—28N 30
Slocum Lake Rd. NW&SE ....28W—28N 30
Southern Terr. E&W ....28W—28N 30
South Shore Dr. E&W ....28W—28N 30
Spruce Terr. N&S ..29W—28N 30
Sumac Dr. N&S .....28W—28N 30
Timber Ln. E&W ....28W—27N 38
Willow Ln. N&S .....28W—28N 30
Woodbine Av. E&W ....28W—28N 30
Woodland Dr. N&S 28W—28N 30
Woodland Cir. N. N&S ....28W—28N 30
Woodland Cir. S. N&S ....28W—28N 30

Kildeer Streets

Acorn Ct. N&S ......21W—21N 49
Amberley Dr. NW&SE ....21W—20N 49
Andover Rd. N&S ..20W—21N 49
Barbara Ct. E&W ..21W—21N 49
Boschome Dr. E&W ....21W—21N 49
Brandon Rd. E&W 21W—21N 49
Buffalo Run N&S ...21W—20N 49
Chartwell Dr. NW&SE ....20W—20N 49
Chestnut Ridge Rd. E&W ....22W—21N 48
Circle Dr. E&W ......21W—21N 49
Cliffside Dr. E&W ..21W—21N 49
Cuba Rd. E&W 21,22W—21N 48,49
Dallas Ct. N&S .....20W—21N 49
Dorothea Ct. NW&SE ....20W—21N 49
Dr ....20W—20N 49
Elder Ct. NW&SE ..22W—21N 48
Ln. E&W ....21W—22N 49
Exeter Rd. E&W ....20W—21N 49
Grove Rd. N&S .....21W—21N 49
Hawthorne Ln. N&S ....22W—21N 48
Heather Ct. N&S ...21W—20N 49
Hickory Dr. E&W ...21W—21N 49
Hidden Valley Dr. E&W ....21W—21N 49
Highwood Rd. NE&SW ....22W—21N 48

Page

Hill Hampton Rd. NW&SE ...21W—21N 49
Kepwick Ln. NE&SW ...21W—20N 49
Kirkley Dr. E&W ...21W—20N 49
Lexington Ln. E&W 20W—21N 49
Linden Ln. E&W ...21W—21N 49
Little Pond Rd. NE&SW ...22W—21N 48
Long Meadows Dr. N&S ...20W—20N 49
Maple Ct. NW&SE 22W—21N 48
Marcy Ln. NW&SE 20W—21N 49
Meadow Ct. E&W .20W—20N 49
Middleton Dr. N&S 20W—21N 49
Oak Trail E&W ...21W—21N 49
Pine Lake Cir. E&W ...21W—21N 49
Pine Lake Ct. N&S 21W—21N 49
Tree Rd. N&S ...22W—21N 48
Valley View Rd. N&S ...21W—21N 49
Vermont Ct. N&S ..20W—21N 49
Weatherstone Ct. NE&SW ...20W—20N 49
Weatherstone Rd. E&W ...21W—20N 49
White Pine Rd. NW&SE ...22W—21N 48
Willow Dr. E&W ...21W—21N 49
York Ct. E&W ...21W—20N 49

Lake Barrington Streets

Alice Ln. N&S ...27W—23N 46
Apache Ln. E&W ...25W—24N 39
Apache Path NE&SW ...26W—24N 38,39
Bark Ct. N&S ...28W—24N 38
Barrington Rd. NW&SE ...27W—23N 46
Beacon Dr. N&S ...28W—23N 46
Buoy Ct. E&W ...28W—24N 38
Cayuga Tr. N&S,E&W ...27W—25N 38
Cedar Ridge NE&SW ...26W—24N 38,39
Cherokee Dr. N&S 25W—24N 39
Chippewa Ct. E&W 26W—24N 38,39
Club Cir. E&W ...26W—24N 38,39
Commercial Av. E&W ...28W—22N 46
Cove Ct. N&S ...28W—23N 46
Crestview Ln. N&S 27W—23N 46
Cutter Ln. E&W ...28W—24N 38
Deer Trail Ct. NE&SW ...26W—24N 38,39
Deer Trail Hill N&S 25W—24N 39
Dock Dr. N&S ...28W—23N 46
East Ln. NW&SE ...27W—23N 46
Farm View Cir. NW&SE ...27W—25N 38
Flint Dr. N&S ...27W—23N 46
Flint Creek Dr. N&S ...27W—21N 46
Foxwood Ln. NW&SE ...26W—24N 38,39
Golfview Ln. N&S ..27W—23N 46
Grayshire Ln. N&S 27W—23N 46
Harbor Rd. N&S,E&W ...28W—22N 46
Henry Ln. N&S ...27W—22N 46
Henry Rd. E&W ...27W—22N 46
Hickory Ln. N&S ...26W—24N 38,39
Hickory Ridge E&W ...27W—25N 38
Hillside Dr. E&W ...28W—22N 46
Hilltop Ct. NE&SW 25W—24N 39
Hillview Dr. N&S ...28W—22N 46
Hunt Trail E&W ...26W—24N 38,39
Industrial Av. E&W 28W—22N 46
Iroquois Ct. NW&SE ...27W—25N 38
Island View Ln. E&W ...26W—24N 38,39
Kazimour Dr. E&W 27W—25N 38
Kelsey Rd. N&S 28W—22,23N 46
Lake Shore Dr. W. E&W ...27W—25N 38
Lakeview Dr. NW&SE ...27W—23N 46
Lake Zurich-Highwood E&W ...26,28W—22N 46,47
Main Entrance E&W ...26W—24N 38,39
Mallard Pt. E&W ...25W—24N 39
Meadow Pl. E&W ..26W—24N 38,39
Meadow View Ct. N&S ...27W—25N 38
Miller Rd. E&W ...27W—24N 38
North Av. NE&SW .27W—23N 46
Oak Hill Rd. N&S,E&W ...26W—24N 38,39
Old Barn Rd. N&S,E&W ...26W—24N 38,39
Old Barrington Rd. NW&SE ...27W—23N 46
Old Roberts Rd. N&S ...27W—25N 38
Onandago Ct. NW&SE ...27W—25N 38

Page

Oneida Ln. N&S ...27,28W—25N 38
Oriole Rd. E&W ...27W—25N 38
Paddock Ln. N&S .26W—25N 38,39
Pawnee Rd. N&S ..25W—24N 39
Pepper Rd. N&S ...28W—22N 46
Pinecrest Cir. N&S 26W—24N 38,39
Riverbend Ct. E&W,N&S ...27W—25N 38
Riverbend Dr. E&W ...27W—25N 38
River Rd. N&S ..27W—24,25N 38
Roberts Rd. E&W .27W—25N 38
Rolling Wood E&W 26W—24N 38,39
Schooner Ln. E&W 28W—23N 46
Seneca Tr. N&S ...27W—25N 38
Shore Line Rd. N&S ...26W—24N 38,39
Thornhill Ct. E&W .26W—24N 38,39
Thornhill Ln. E&W .26W—24N 38,39
Timber Ridge N&S 26W—24N 38,39
Tioga Trail N&S ...26W—24N 38,39
Tuscarora Ct. N&S 27W—25N 38
Twin Pond Rd. NW&SE ...27W—25N 38
Valley View Rd. N&S ...26W—24N 38,39
Vance Ct. E&W ...28W—23N 46
Vista Ln. E&W ...27W—23N 46
Welch Cir. N&S ...28W—23N 46
West Ln. N&S ...27W—23N 46
White Pine Dr. N&S ...26W—24N 38,39
Woodland Dr. E&W 27W—23N 46
Woodview Rd. N&S ...25W—24N 39

Lake Bluff Streets

Arbor Ct. N&S ...10W—29N 37
Arbor Dr. E&W ...10W—29N 37
Arden Shore Rd. E&W ...10W—29N 37
Armour Dr. N&S,E&W ...11W—29N 37
Ascot Ct. NE&SW .11W—29N 37
Ashington Cir. E&W ...11W—29N 37
Bath And Tennis Club Rd. E&W ...11W—28N 37
Birch Rd. N&S ...10W—28N 37
Birkdale Rd. E&W .11W—28N 37
Blodgett Av. E&W ...10,11W—27N 45
Bluff Rd. N&S ...10W—28N 37
Bradford Ct. E&W .11W—29N 37
Briar Ln. N&S ...10W—28N 37
Brierfield Ct. E&W .11W—29N 37
Bristol Ct. E&W ...11W—29N 37
Buckminster Ct. E&W ...11W—29N 37
Cambridge Rd. E&W ...10W—28N 37
Carlyle Cir. N&S ...11W—29N 37
Carriage Park Av. E&W ...12W—28N 37
Center Av. E&W 10,11W—28N 37
Circle Dr. N&S ...10W—28N 37
Coventry Ct. E&W .11W—29N 37
Crescent Dr. E&W .10W—28N 37
Eva Terr. N&S ...11W—28N 37
Forest Cove Rd. E&W ...10W—28N 37
Forest Hills Rd. E&W ...11W—28N 37
Foss Ct. N&S ...10W—28N 37
Garfield Av. N&S ...11W—28N 37
Glen Av. N&S ...10W—28N 37
Grafton Ct. E&W ...11W—29N 37
Green Bay Rd. N&S ...11W—29N 37
Greenwich Ct. E&W ...11W—29N 37
Gurney Av. N&S ...10W—28N 37
Hamilton Ct. E&W .11W—29N 37
Hancock Av. NW&SE ...11W—28N 37
Hawthorne Ct. E&W ...10,11W—28N 37
Hearthrow Ct. E&W ...11W—29N 37
Hickory Ct. N&S ...11W—28N 37
Hirst Ct. N&S ...10W—28N 37
Indian Rd. E&W ...10W—28N 37
Inverness Ct. E&W 11W—29N 37
Kohl Dr. E&W ...11W—29N 37
Lake Av. N&S ...10W—28N 37
Lakeland Dr. E&W .10W—28N 37
Leeds Ct. NW&SE 11W—29N 37
Lincoln Av. N&S ...11W—28N 37
Main St. E&W ...11W—28N 37
Maple Av. N&S ...10W—28N 37
Market Sq. East N&S ...11W—28N 37
Market Sq. West N&S ...11W—28N 37
Marvin Rd. E&W ...11W—28N 37
Mawman Av. NE&SW ...11W—28N 37
MacLaren Ln. N&S 11W—28N 37
Moffet Rd. N&S ...10W—28N 37

Page

Mountain Av. N&S .10W—28N 37
Neuman Ct. N&S ..10W—28N 37
North Av. E&W ...10W—28N 37
N. Shore Dr. E&W .12W—28N 37
Oak Av. N&S ...10W—28N 37
Oak Terr. Ct. N&S .10W—28N 37
Oaks Dr. N&S ...11W—29N 37
Park Av. E&W ...10W—28N 37
Park Ln. E&W ...11W—28N 37
Park Pl. E&W ...10W—28N 37
Pine Av. N&S ...11W—28N 37
Pine Ct. N&S ...11W—28N 37
Prospect Av. E&W ...10,11W—28N 37
Ravine Av. E&W ...10W—28N 37
Ravine Forest Dr. E&W ...10W—28N 37
Rebecca Terr. N&S 11W—28N 37
Rockland Av. N&S .11W—28N 37
Roselle Terr. N&S .11W—28N 37
Scranton Av. E&W 10W—28N 37
Sheridan Pl. E&W .10W—28N 37
Sheridan Rd. E&W 10W—28N 37
Sheridan Rd. N&S 10W—29N 37
Sheridan Dr. E&W .12W—28N 37
Sherwood Terr. N&S ...12W—28N 37
Shore Acres Rd. E&W ...10W—29N 37
Signe Ct. E&W ...11W—29N 37
Simpson Av. N&S ..10W—28N 37
State St. N&S ...11W—28N 37
Sunrise Av. N&S ...10W—28N 37
Sunset Ln. N&S ...11W—28N 37
Sunset Pl. E&W ...10W—28N 37
Surrey Ln. N&S ...12W—28N 37
Sylvan Rd. E&W ...10W—28N 37
Thorn Valley Ln. E&W ...11W—29N 37
Thornwood Ln. NE&SW ...11W—28N 37
Vincent Ct. N&S ...10W—28N 37
Walnut Av. N&S ...10W—28N 37
Warrington Ct. E&W ...11W—29N 37
Warrington Dr. N&S, E&W ...11W—29N 37
Washington Av. E&W ...11W—28N 37
Washington St. E&W ...10W—28N 37
Waukegan Rd. NW&SE ...12W—28N 37
Weatherford Ct. E&W ...11W—29N 37
Wimbledon Ct. N&S ...11W—28N 37
Wimbleton Rd. N&S ...11W—28N 37
Witchwood Ln. E&W ...10,11W—28N 37
Woodland Rd. E&W ...10,11W—28N 37

Lake Forest Streets

Ahwahnee Ln. N&S ...11W—26N 45
Ahwanee Rd. N&S 11W—26N 45
Alden Ln. E&W ...11W—27N 45
Alison Ln. E&W ...12W—27N 44
Arbor Ln. E&W ...12W—23N 51,52
Arcady Dr. E&W ...12W—24N 44
Armour Cir. E&W ...12W—26N 44
Ashlawn Dr. E&W ..12W—26N 44
Ashley Rd. E&W ...9W—25N 45
Atteridge Rd. E&W 10W—27N 45
Bank Ln. N&S ...10W—26N 45
Barat Ct. N&S ...10W—25N 45
Barberry Ln. E&W .10W—27N 45
Barn Swallow Rd. NE&SW ...11W—25N 45
Basswood Rd. E&W ...11W—25N 45
Behr Ct. N&S ...12W—26N 44
Beverly Pl. NW&SE ...10W—25N 45
Big Oaks Ct. E&W 12W—23N 51,52
Birch Ct. E&W ...11W—25N 45
Blackthorne Ln. NE&SW ...11W—25N 45
Bluffs Edge Dr. NW&SE ...9W—25N 45
Bowling Green Dr. E&W ...13W—24N 43,44
Breckenridge Av. N&S ...11W—24N 45
Breckenridge Ct. N&S ...11W—24N 45
Brair Ln. E&W ...10W—25N 45
Buena Rd. N&S 10,11W—25N 45
Burr Oak Rd. N&S 11W—27N 45
Burton Dr. N&S ...12W—26N 44
Butler Rd. N&S ...10W—25N 45
Cardinal Ct. NE&SW ...11W—25N 45
Cascade Ct. N. E&W ...12W—24N 44
Cascade Ct. S. E&W ...12W—24N 44

Page

Castlegate Ct. E&W ...12W—26N 44
Cherokee Rd. E&W ...10W—25N 45
Cherry Av. E&W ...10W—26N 45
Chiltern Dr. N&S ...12W—26N 44
Christina Ln. NE&SW ...11W—24N 45
Church Rd. NW&SE ...10W—27N 45
Circle Ln. N&S ...9W—25N 45
Clover Av. N&S ...11W—26N 45
College Rd. E&W ..10W—26N 45
Concord Dr. E&W ..12W—26N 44
Coventry Ct. N&S .12W—25N 44
Coventry Dr. E&W .12W—25N 44
Crab Tree Ln. E&W ...10W—27N 45
Crest Ct. E&W ...10W—24N 45
Deerpath E&W .10,12W—26N 44,45
Deerpath Sq. N&S 11W—26N 45
De Fontaine Ln. N&S ...12W—24N 44
Devonshire Ct. NW&SE ...13W—23N 51
Devonshire Ln. NE&SW ...13W—23N 51
Douglas Dr. N&S ...9W—25N 45
Dover Rd. E&W ...11W—23N 52
Edgecotle Ln. NW&SE ...11W—26N 45
Edgewood Rd. N&S ...10W—27N 45
Effner Av. E&W ...10W—27N 45
Elder Path NE&SW ...10W—27N 45
Elm Tree Rd. N&S 10W—27N 45
Estate Ln. E. N&S ...12,13W—24N 43,44
Estes Av. N&S ...11W—24N 45
Everett Rd. E&W ...12W—24N 44
Exter Pl. N&S ...12W—26N 44
Fairview Av. N&S ..11W—24N 45
Fairway Dr. E&W ...12W—24N 44
Farm Rd. E&W ...13W—24N 43,44
Farnham Mill Trail E&W ...11W—23N 52
Fletcher Cir. N&S ..12W—26N 44
Forest Hill Rd. N&S ...10W—24,25N 45
Foster Pl. NE&SW 10W—25N 45
Franklin Pl. E&W ...10W—27N 45
Frnz Dr. N&S ...12W—24N 44
Frost Pl. NE&SW ..10W—26N 45
Glenwood Dr. E&W 10W—25N 45
Glenwood Rd. E&W ...10W—25N 45
Golf Ln. N&S ...11W—26N 45
Grace Ln. E&W ...12W—27N 44
Granby Rd. E&W ..10W—27N 45
Grandview Ln. N&S ...10W—24N 45
Griffith Rd. N&S ...10W—27N 45
Green Bay Rd. N&S ...10,11W—24,27N 45
Green Briar Ln. E&W ...10W—26N 45
Greenleaf Av. N&S 10W—27N 45
Greenvale Rd. N&S ...12W—26N 44
Greenview Pl. E&W ...10W—25N 45
Greenwood Av. E&W ...10W—24N 45
Grovect NW&SE ...12W—24N 44
Hackberry Ln. E&W ...13W—24N 43,44
Harlan Ct. N&S ...11W—24N 45
Harlan Ln. N&S ...11W—24N 45
Hastings Ct. N&S ..11W—26N 45
Hathaway Cir. N&S 12W—26N 44
Haven Wood Ln. E&W ...9W—25N 45
Hawkweed Ln. N&S ...11W—27N 45
Hawthorne Pl. N&S ...10W—27N 45
Heather Ln. E&W ..10W—26N 45
Heritage Ct. N&S ..12W—24N 44
Heron Rd. E&W ...11W—25N 45
Hickory Ct. E&W ...10W—24N 45
High Holborn E&W 12W—26N 44
Highland Av. N&S .11W—24N 45
Highview Terr. E&W ...10W—25N 45
Hilldale Pl. E&W ...10W—25N 45
Holland Ct. N&S ...11W—26N 45
Honeysuckle Rd. NE&SW ...11W—25N 45
Illinois Rd. E&W ...10W—26N 45
Inverlieth Rd. E&W 12W—26N 44
Inverlieth Terr. E&W ...12W—26N 44
Inverton Rd. E&W .12W—26N 44
Ivy Ct. E&W ...10W—25N 45
June Terr. N&S ...10W—25N 45
Keith Ln. NE&SW ...9W—25N 45
Kendler Ct. NE&SW 9W—25N 45
Kennett Ln. E&W ..12W—24N 44

Page

Kennington Terr. E&W ...11W—26N 45
Kimberly Ln. E&W .11W—24N 45
King Muir Rd. N&S 12W—26N 44
Knollwood E&W ...12W—27N 44
Knollwood Cir. NE&SW ...12W—28N 37
Knollwood Ln. N&S ...12W—28N 37
Knollwood Rd. NW&SE ...12W—28N 37
Lake Rd. NW&SE ...9,10W—27N 45
Larchmont Ln. E&W ...12W—26N 44
Laurel Av. E&W ...11W—27N 45
Lawrence Av. E&W 12W—24N 44
Lexington Dr. N&S 12W—26N 44
Linden Av. E&W ...10W—24N 45
Loch Ln. E&W ...9W—25N 45
Longwood Dr. E&W ...10W—24N 45
Lorraine Ln. E&W .12W—26N 44
Louis Av. E&W ...11W—24N 45
Lowell Ln. N&S ...12W—23N 51,52
Mallard Ln. E&W ...11W—25N 45
Marion Av. E&W ...10W—24N 45
Maple Ct. N&S ...9W—26N 45
Maplewood Rd. E&W ...9W—26N 45
Mayflower Rd. NW&SE ...9W—25,26N 45
Maywood Rd. N&S 10W—25N 45
McCormick Dr. E&W 9W—25N 45
McKinley Rd. N&S 10W—27N 45
Meadow Ln. N&S ..10W—27N 45
Meadowood Dr. N&S ...12W—26N 44
Melody Rd. E&W ...11,12W—26N 44,45
Michgame Ln. E&W ...11W—25N 45
Mickey Rd. N&S ...10W—25N 45
Milburne Rd. N&S .11W—23N 52
Mills Ct. E&W ...10W—27N 45
Minthaven Rd. N&S ...13W—24N 43,44
Monticello Cir. N&S ...12W—26N 44
Morningside Dr. E&W ...10W—24N 45
Mt. Vernon Av. N&S ...11W—24N 45
Negaunee Ln. N&S ...11W—25N 45
Newcastle Dr. NE&SW ...12W—25N 44
Niles Av. E&W ...10W—24N 45
Noble Av. E&W ...10W—27N 45
North Av. E&W ...11W—24N 45
North Cliff Way E&W ...12W—26N 44
North Gate Sq. E&W ...10W—26N 45
Northmoor Rd. E&W ...10W—25N 45
Oakdale Av. E&W .10W—24N 45
Oak Knoll Dr. N&S ...12W—23,24,25N 44,51
Oak Knoll Dr. N&S 12W—27N 44
Oakwood Av. N&S ...10W—26,27N 45
Old Barn Ln. N&S .13W—24N 43,44
Old Colony Rd. N&S ...11W—24N 45
Old Elm Rd. E&W ...10,11W—24N 45
O'Leary Ln. E&W ..12W—28N 37
Old Mill Rd. E&W ..11W—24N 45
Owentsia Rd. E&W 11W—25N 45
Overlook Dr. NW&SE ...9W—25N 45
Park Av. E&W ...10W—27N 45
Park Mead Ln. E&W ...12W—26N 44
Parliament Ct. E&W ...13W—23N 51
Pembroke Dr. E&W ...10W—26N 45
Pine Croft NE&SW 12W—25N 44
Pine Ln. E&W ...10W—27N 45
Polo Dr. N&S ...11W—24N 45
Poplar Rd. E&W ...11W—25N 45
Prairie Av. N&S ...11W—24N 45
Private Rd. E&W ...10W—27N 45
Private Rd. E&W ...11W—25N 45
Private Rd. E&W ...11W—26N 45
Private Rd. E&W ...11W—27N 45
Private Rd. E&W ...12W—26N 44
Private Rd. E&W ...12W—27N 44
Public Rd. E&W ...11W—27N 45
Quail Dr. E&W ...11W—25N 45
Ranch Rd. N&S ...13W—24N 43,44
Ravine Park Dr. E&W ...10W—27N 45
Ridge Ln. NE&SW 10W—26N 45
Ridge Rd. N&S .11W—25,26N 45
Ringwood Rd. E&W 9W—25N 45
Riparian Dr. NE&SW ...9W—25N 45

Page

Rockfeller Rd. N&S .9W—25N   45
Rosemary Rd. N&S
..................9,10W—26N   45
Rose Terr. E&W ....10W—27N   45
Rothesay Rd. E&W
..................12W—26N   44
Ryan Pl. NE&SW .10W—26N   45
Sandpiper Ln. E&W
..................11W—26N   45
Scott Av. E&W ....10W—27N   45
S. Gate Sq. E&W ..10W—26N   45
Shawford Way E&W
..................11W—23N   52
Shawnee Ln. N&S 11W—25N   45
Sheridan Rd. N&S
..........10W—25,26,27N   5
Skokie Hwy. N&S
..................11W—25,27N   45
Spring Ln. E&W ......9W—26N   45
Spruce Av. E&W ....10W—27N   45
Stone Av. E&W ....11W—24N   45
Stone Gate Ln. NE&SW
..................9W—26N   45
Stone Gate Rd. N&S
..................9W—26N   45
Stoneleigh Ct. E&W
..................13W—23N   51
Strafford Ct. E&W .13W—23N   51
Suffolk Ln. NE&SW
..................12W—26N   44
Summit Av. N&S ..10W—26N   45
Summit Pl. E&W ...10W—27N   45
Sunset Pl. E&W ...10W—26N   45
Surrey Rd. N&S ...11W—23N   52
Sussex Ln. NE&SW
..................12W—26N   44
Tanglewood Ct. N&S
..................12W—25N   44
Tara Ln. N&S ....11W—27N   45
Telegraph Rd. N&S 12W—23N 51,52
Thomas Pl. E&W ...11W—27N   45
Thorne Ln. NE&SW
..................10W—26N   45
Timber Ln. N&S 10W—24,25N   45
Townline Rd. E&W 10W—26N   45
Turicum Rd. E&W ...9W—25N   45
Valley Rd. N&S
..................10,11W—24,25N   45
Verda Ln. E&W ....12W—26N   44
Vine Av. E&W ......10W—26N   45
Walden Ln. E&W ....9W—26N   45
Warwick Rd. E&W .12W—26N   44
Washington Cir. NW&SE
..................10W—26N   45
Washington Rd. NW&SE
..................10W—26N   45
Waukegan Rd. N&S
..................12W—26N   44
Waveland Rd. N&S 10W—24N   45
Wedgewood Ct. NE&SW
..................13W—23N   51
Wedgewood Dr. NW&SE
..................13W—23N   51
Western Av. N&S
..................10W—25,27N   45
West Fork Dr. N&S 13W—24N 43,44
Westleigh Rd. E&W
..................9,11W—25N   45
Westminster Av. E&W
..................10,11W—26,27N   45
Westmoreland Rd. N&S
..................11W—26N   45
White Oak Rd. NE&SW
..................12W—24N   44
Wildwood Rd. N&SW
..................10W—26N   45
Wilson Dr. N&S ...13W—24N 43,44
Wild Rose Ln. E&W
..................12W—24N   44
Willshire Rd. E&W .10W—27N   45
Wimbleton Ct. E&W
..................13W—23N   51
Winston Rd. N&S ..10W—25N   45
Winthrop Ln. 10W—27N   45
Winwood Dr. E&W 12W—27N   44
Wisconsin Av. NE&SW
..................10W—27N   45
Woodbine Ln. E&W .9W—27N   45
Woodbine Pl. N&S 10W—27N   45
Wooded Ln. N&S ..10W—25N   45
Woodhill Ln. N&S .12W—24N   44
Woodland Rd. E&W
..................10W—27N   45
Woodlawn Av. E&W
..................10W—26N   45
Wynnfield Terr. E&W
..................10W—25N   45
Yore Rd. N&S ....12W—24N   44

Lake Villa Streets
Arapaho Trail E&W 22W—38N   16
Belmont Ave. E&W 22W—37N   16
Burnett Av. E&W ...23W—37N 15,16
Cedar Av. NE&SW 22W—38N   16
Central Av. NW&SE
..................22W—38N   16
Chelsea Cir. N&S ..22W—37N   16
Clayton Av. NW&SE
..................21W—38N   17

Page

Coventry Cove Ln. E&W
..................22W—37N   16
Cremin Dr. N&S ...22W—37N   16
Delwood Av. NW&SE
..................23W—37N 15,16
Grand Av. E&W ....22W—38N   16
Gurnett Av. E&W ..22W—37N   16
Kenz Ct. E&W ....22W—37N   16
Kevin Av. E&W .....22W—37N   16
Lake Av. NW&SE ..22W—38N   16
Lake Shore Dr. E&W
..................23W—38N 15,16
Laurie Ln. E&W ...23W—37N 15,16
McKinley Av. N&S .22W—37N   16
Milwaukee Av. NW&SE
..................22W—38N   16
Monica Dr. N&S ...22W—37N   16
N. Cedar Lake Ave. N&S
..................23W—38N 15,16
N. Shore Av. E&W .22W—37N 15,16
Oakwood Av. E&W 23W—37N 15,16
Oak Knoll Dr. N&S 23W—37N 15,16
Oak Knoll Ct. N&S 23W—37N 15,16
Park Pl. N&S ....22W—37N   16
Roselle Ct. ....22W—37N   16
Rosemont E&W
..................23W—38N 15,16
Sheehan Dr. N&S ..22W—37N 15,16
Sherwood Av. N&S 23W—38N 15,16
Shoshoni Trail E&W
..................22W—38N   16
Twin Oaks Dr. E&W
..................23W—37N 15,16
Villa Av. N&S ....22W—37N   16
Walden Ln. N&S ...23W—37N 15,16
Waterbury Cir. N&S
..................23W—37N 15,16
Wesley Av. E&W ..23W—38N 15,16
Wilton Av. E&S .....23W—38N 15,16
Woodhead Dr. N&S
..................21W—38N   17

Lake Zurich Streets
Aldine Rd. N&S ....24W—23N 47,48
Alpine Dr. E&W ....23W—23N   48
Andrew Ln. E&W ..22W—22N   48
Apache Ct. N&S ...22W—22N   48
Applegate Cir. E&W
..................24W—22N 47,48
Applegate Ln. E&W 24W—22N 47,48
Ash St. NE&SW ...23W—23N   48
Aspen Ln. N&S ....24W—22N 47,48
Bateau St. NW&SE
..................23W—23N   48
Bayview Dr. N&S ..22W—21N   48
Beach Rd. N&S ....24W—23N 47,48
Beaubien Ct. E&W 23W—23N   48
Beauteau St. NW&SE
..................23W—23N   48
Bech Rd. N&S ....24W—23N 47,48
Beechwood Dr. NW&SE
..................22W—22N   48
Berkley Rd. E&W ..22W—22N   48
Bern Ct. N&S ....23W—23N   48
Betty Dr. E&W ......24W—23N 47,48
Blacktwig St. N&S 22W—22N   48
Briar Point Ct. E&W
..................22W—22N   48
Bristol Trail Rd. N&S
..................22W—22N   48
Brookfield Ct. N&S 22W—22N   48
Browning Ln. E&W 22W—22N   48
Brush Hill Ln. E&W 22W—22N   48
Buffalo Creek Dr. E&W
..................22W—22N   48
Burr Oak Ct. NE&SW
..................23W—23N   48
Burr Oak Dr. N&S .22W—22N   48
Buesching Rd. N&S
..................22W—22N   48
Butera Ln. NW&SE 26W—24N 38,39
Butterfield Rd. E&W
..................24W—23N 47,48
Carolyn Ct. N&S ...23W—23N   48
Carriage Ln. E&W .24W—22N 47,48
Cedar St. E&W .....23W—22N   48
Centoni Dr. E&W ..24W—23N 47,48
Cheery St. NE&SW
..................23W—23N   48
Cherokee Rd. E&W
..................23W—22N   48
Cherry Ln. E&W ...23W—22N   48
Chris Ct. NW&SE ..24W—23N 47,48
Church St. NE&SW
..................23W—23N   48
Clearwater Ct. E&W
..................22W—21N   48
Clover Hill Ln. N&S,E&W
..................23W—23N 47,48
Clubhouse Ln. NW&SE
..................22W—22N 47,48
Coral Reef Way E&W
..................22W—21N   48
Cortland Cir. N&S ..24W—22N 47,48
Cortland Dr. N&S ..24W—22N 47,48
Country Club Rd. E&W
..................24W—23N 47,48
Craig Terr. N&S ....24W—23N 47,48
Crescent Rd. N&S .24W—23N 47,48
Cypress Bridge Rd. E&W
..................22W—21N   48

Page

Dan Vera Ln. NE&SW
..................24W—24N   48
Dearborn Ct. NE&SW
..................22W—22N   48
Deer Chase Rd. N&S
..................22W—21N   48
Deerpath Rd. N&S,E&W
..................23W—21,22N   48
Dogwood Ln. E&W 24W—22N 47,48
Eastman Rd. E&W 22W—22N   48
Eddy Ln. N&S ......22W—21N   48
Ela Rd. N&S ....24W—22N 47,48
Elm Pl. N&S ....23W—22N   48
E. Main St. E&W
..................22,23W—23N   48
Ensell Rd. E&W ....22W—23N   48
Evanston Terr. E&W
..................24W—21N 47,48
Evergreen St. NE&SW
..................23W—23N   48
Fairway Rd. N&S ..24W—23N 47,48
Fern Rd. N&S ....22W—22N   48
Fieldstone Cir. N&S
..................24W—21N 47,48
Florence Av. N&S ..23W—22N   48
Forest Av. NE&SW .23W—23N   48
Foxfire Dr. E&W ...23W—21N   48
Genesee St. E&W
..................23W—23N   48
Ginger Tr. E&W ....22W—22N   48
Glencoe Terr. E&W 24W—23N 47,48
Glen Farm Ln. N&S
..................22W—22N   48
Golf View Rd. NE&SW,E&W
..................24,25W—23N 47,48
Grand Av. E&W ....23W—23N   48
Grever Ct. E&W ....23W—22N   48
Grove Dr. NW&SE
..................23,24W—23N 47,48
Grove Rd. N&S .....24W—23N 47,48
Hapshire Ln. E&W 24W—24N 47,48
Harbor Dr. N. E&W 22W—21N   48
Harbor Rd. S. E&W
..................22W—21N   48
Harbor Rd. W. N&S
..................22W—21N   48
Harvest Dr. E&W ..22W—21N   48
Heartwood Ln. E&W
..................22W—22N   48
Hickory Rd. N&S ..24W—23N 47,48
Hillside Ct. N&S
..................23W—22N   48
Hobble Rush Dr. N&S
..................22W—22N   48
Holly Ct. Rd. N&S .24W—24N 47,48
Holly Ct. Terr. NE&SW
..................24W—23N 47,48
Honey Lake Rd. N&S
..................24W—23N 47,48
Hunters Ln. E&W ..24W—23N 47,48
Indigo Ct. N&S .....22W—22N   48
Interlaken Dr. N&S 23W—23N   48
Ironwood Ct. N&S 22W—22N   48
Ivy Ct. E&W ....22W—22N   48
Jean Terr. E&W ....24W—23N 47,48
Joan Rd. E&W ......24W—23N 47,48
Jonathan Rd. N&S
..................24,25W—23N 47,48
Joyce Ln. E&W .....24W—23N 47,48
June Terr. N&S .....23W—23N   48
Juneway Terr. N&S 24W—23N 47,48
Kenilworth Terr. E&W
..................24W—23N 47,48
Kim Tr. N&S ....24W—23N 47,48
Kingwood Ln. E&W
..................22W—22N   48
Knolwood Dr. E&W 24W—24N 47,48
Lake St. E&W ......23W—23N   48
Lakeview Pl. N&S .23W—22N   48
Lake Zurich Dr. N&S
..................23W—21N   48
Lake Zurich-Highwood E&W
..................24W—23N 47,48
Lancaster N&S .....24W—24N 39,40
Linden Ln. N&S ....24W—23N 47,48
Lions Dr. N&S ....23W—23N   48
Lorraine Ct. N&S ..23W—23N   48
Lucerne Dr. N&S ..23W—23N   48
Main St. E&W ....23W—23N   48
Main St. W. NE&SW
..................24W—24N 39,40
Manchester NE&SW
..................24W—24N 39,40
Manor Rd. N&S 24,25W—23N 47,48
Maple Av. N&S,E&W
..................22W—22N   48
Marble Hill Dr. E&W
..................22W—21N   48
March St. NW&SE 22W—24N 39,40
Meadow Ln. NW&SE
..................23W—23N   48
Meadowbrook Ct. N&S
..................22W—22N   48
Meadowbrook Ln. N&S
..................22W—22N   48
Millbrook Dr. E&W .22W—22N   48
Mionske Dr. NW&SE
..................23W—23N   48
Mohawk Tr. Rd. N&S
..................23,24W—22N 47,48

Page

N. Old Rand Rd. E&W
..................24W—23N 47,48
Northcrest Rd. N&S
..................24W—23N 47,48
Oak St. E&W ....23W—23N   48
Oakwood Rd. N&S, E&W
..................24W—23N   48
Old Mill Rd. N&S ..22W—22N   48
Old Rand Rd. N. NW&SE
..................24W—23N 47,48
Old Rand Rd. S. NW&SE
..................23W—22N   48
Pamela Rd. E&W ..24W—23N 47,48
Park Av. NW&SE ..22W—22N   48
Park Ln. N&S ....24W—23N 47,48
Partridge Ln. N&S,E&W
..................22W—22N   48
Parkway Av. NE&SW
..................23W—23N   48
Peachtree Ln. N&S 24W—22N 47,48
Pebblecreek Ct. N&S
..................22W—22N   48
Pheasant Ridge E&W
..................22W—22N   48
Pine Av. ....23,24W—23N 47,48
Pine Tree Row NE&SW
..................24W—23N 47,48
Pleasant Rd. N&S .24W—22N 47,48
Pohlman St. N&S .23W—23N   48
Poplar Ln. E&W ...22W—22N   48
Portree Ln. E&W ..22W—22N   48
Pottawatomi Tr. N&S,E&W
..................23W—22N   48
Prairie Ln. NW&SE 23W—22N   48
Prospect Rd. N&S .24W—23N 47,48
Public St. N&S ....23W—22N   48
Queen Ann Ln. N&S
..................23W—21N   48
Quentin Rd. N&S
..................21W—22,23N   48
Racine Ct. E&W ...23W—23N   48
Railway St. NE&SW
..................23W—22N   48
Ramblewood Ct. E&W
..................22W—22N   48
Ramblewood Ln. N&S
..................22W—22N   48
Rand Rd. N&S, NW&SE
..................23,24W—22,23N 47,48
Ravenswood N&S
..................22W—22N   48
Ravinia Terr. E&W
..................24,25W—23N 47,48
Red Bridge Ct. NW&SE
..................22W—22N   48
Red Bridge Rd. N&S
..................22W—22N   48
Red Haw Ln. E&W 22W—22N   48
Regent Ct. NE&SW
..................21W—22N   48
Ridgewood Ct. N&S
..................22W—22N   48
Riley Ln. NW&SE .22W—22N   48
Ripple Brook Ct. E&W
..................22W—21N   48
Robertson Av. NE&SW
..................23W—22N   48
Rose Rd E&W ......22W—23N   48
Rugby Rd. NE&SW
..................24W—23N 47,48
Russet Cir. NE&SW
..................22W—22N   48
Sandlewood Ct. E&W
..................22W—22N   48
Sandy Pass N&S
..................22,23W—21N   48
Schiller St. E&W ...23W—23N   48
Schuldt St. E&W ...23W—23N   48
Sebby Ln. N&S .....23W—23N   48
Shallow Cover Rd. E&W
..................22W—21N   48
Shoreview Ln. E&W
..................24W—22N 47,48
Silverwood Ct. N&S, E&W
..................22W—22N   48
Spruce St. NE&SW
..................23W—23N   48
Spring Ct. N&S .....22W—22N   48
South Shore Ln. N&S
..................22W—22N 47,48
S. Old Rand Rd. NW&SE
..................23W—22N   48
Stanton Pt. N&S ...22W—22N   48
Stillwater Ct. N&S
..................22,23W—22N   48
Sugar Tree Ct. E&W
..................22W—22N   48
Summit Dr. NW&SE
..................23W—23N   48
Summit Terr. NE&SW
..................24W—23N 47,48
Sunrise Ln. N&S
..................24W—23N 47,48
Sunset Ct. NE&SW
..................23W—23N   48
Sunset Tr. N&S .....24W—24N 39,40
Surryse Rd. E&W ..22W—22N   48
Telser Rd. N&S 22W—22,23N   48
Terrace Ln. E&W ..23W—22N   48
Thistle Ln. NW&SE 22W—22N   48

Page

Town Mall Dr. E&W 23W—22N   48
Trailside Dr. NW&SE
..................22,23W—22N   48
View Rd. N&S ......24W—23N 47,48
Vista Rd. N&S .....24W—23N 47,48
Waterbury Ct. NE&SW
..................24W—23N   48
White Birch Ln. E&W
..................22W—22N   48
Whitney Rd. NW&SE
..................24W—23N 47,48
Willow Terr. NW&SE
..................24W—23N 47,48
Wilmette Terr. E&W
..................23W—23N 47,48
Windermere Ln. E&W
..................22W—22N   48
Winnetka Terr. E&W
..................24,25W—23N 47,48
Woodbine Cir. NW&SE
..................22W—21N   48
W. Main St. N&S ..23W—22N   48

Libertyville Streets
Abby Ct. N&S ......17W—29N   34
Acorn Ln. E&W ....17W—28N   34
Alder Dr. E&W ..17,18W—30N   34
Ames St. N&S ......16W—28N   34
Amy Ct. E&W ....18W—30N   34
Amy Ln. N&S ....18W—30N   34
Anne Ln. N&S ......18W—30N   34
Appletree Ln. N&S 15W—27N   43
Appley Av. E&W ..16W—29N   34
Arbor Ct. NW&SE .16W—29N   34
Ardmore Terr. N&S 16W—28N   34
Aratus Pkwy. N&S,E&W
..................16W—27N   42
Arthur Av. N&S ....16W—28N   34
Ash St. N&S ....16W—28N   34
Austin Av. E&W ...16W—28N   34
Avalon Dr. N&S ...16W—29N   34
Bartlett Terr. N&S .16W—29N   34
Bedford Ln. N&S ..17W—28N   34
Big Oak Ln. ..15W—29N 35,36
Blackburn Cir. E&W
..................17W—29N   34
Blueberry Rd. N&S 17W—28N   34
Brainard Av. NE&SW
..................16W—29N   34
Briar Pl. E&W ......16W—28N   34
Briarwood Ln. E&W
..................16W—27N   42
Bridle Ct. E&W .....16W—27N   42
Broadway E&W ...16W—29N   34
Buckingham Pl. N&S
..................16W—28N   34
Buckley Rd. E&W
..................17,18W—30N   34
Burdick St. N&S ..16W—28N   34
Burridge Ct. E&W ..17W—28N   34
Butterfield Rd. N&S
..................17W—28N   34
Butterfield Rd. N&S
..................18W—29N   34
Cambridge Dr. N&S
..................16W—28N   34
Carter St. N&S .....17W—28N   34
Cass Ct. E&W ......17W—30N   34
Cass Dr. N&S ....17W—30N   34
Catalpa Ln. E&W ..16W—27N   42
Cedar Glen Dr. E&W
..................17W—30N   34
Chatham Ct. N&S .15W—27N   43
Church St. E&W ...16W—29N   34
Circle Dr. N&S ......16W—28N   34
Claridge Ct. N&S ..17W—29N   34
Cleveland Av. E&W
..................16W—28N   34
Concord Ln. N&S ..15W—27N   43
Cook Av. E&W .....16W—29N   34
Coolidge Av. E&W .16W—28N   34
Coolidge Pl. E&W .16W—28N   34
Country Club Dr. N&S
..................15W—28N 35,36
Crab Tree Ln. N&S 16W—27N   42
Crane Blvd. E&W ..17W—28N   34
Crestfield Av. E&W 17W—28N   34
Cypress Ln. E&W .16W—27N   42
Dawes St. N&S ....17W—27N   42
Deer Trail Ln. E&W
..................15W—28N 35,36
Douglas Av. N&S ..16W—29N   34
Dover Ct. N&S .17W—28N   34
Dowing Rd. E&W ..16W—27N   42
Downs Pkwy. N&S 15W—27N   43
Drake St. N&S .....16W—28N   34
Dymond Rd. N&S ..17W—28N   34
E. Ellis Av. E&W ..16W—29N   34
E. Park Av. E&W ..16W—28N   34
E. Winchester E&W
..................16W—29N   34
Eaton St. N&S ......15W—27N   43
Ellis Av. E&W ......16W—29N   34
Elm Ct. E&W ....16W—29N   34
Elm Dr. N&S ....16W—28N   34
Emerson Ln. N&S .15W—27N   43
Enterprise St. N&S 19W—30N   33
Evergreen Ct. E&W
..................16W—27N   42
Fairlawn Av. E&W .17W—28N   34

Page
Fairview Av. N&S ..16W—28N 34
Finstead Dr. E&W .16W—30N 34
Flamingo Pkwy. N&S
...........................16W—27N 42
Florence Ct. E&W .16W—28N 34
Florsheim Dr. E&W 16W—27N 42
Forest Ln. N&S .....16W—29N 34
Forever Av. N&S ....18W—30N 34
Fox Trail N&S ....15W—28N 35,36
Furlong Dr. N&S,E&W
...........................16W—27N 42
Garfield Av. N&S ...16W—28N 34
Garfield Av. NW&SE
...........................16W—27N 42
Garrison St. E&W .16W—29N 34
Glendale Rd. E&W 16W—28N 34
Golf Rd. E&W ...16,17W—28N 34
Gracewood Dr. E&W
...........................17W—28N 34
Grant Ct. E&W ......16W—29N 34
Greentree Ct. NW&SE
...........................16W—27N 42
Green Tree Pkwy. E&W
...........................16W—27N 42
Gulfstream Pkwy. E&W
...........................16W—27N 42
Hampton Terr. N&S
...........................16W—28N 34
Harding Av. N&S ...17W—28N 34
Harmis Av. E&W ...17W—28N 34
Harrison St. ....16W—28N 34
Harvard Ln. E&W ..16W—28N 34
Havenwood Ct. E&W
...........................17W—28N 34
Havenwood Dr. E&W
...........................17W—28N 34
Hayes Av. N&S ......16W—28N 34
Hemlock Ln. E&W .16W—27N 42
Hillcrest Dr. N&S ...17W—28N 34
Hollister Dr. N&S ...16W—26N 42
Homewood Dr. NW&SE
...........................16W—29N 34
Hunters Ln. E&W ..15W—27N 43
Hurlburt Ct. E&W ..16W—29N 34
Hyatt Dr. E&W ....16W—29N 34
Industrial Dr. NE&SW
...........................19W—30N 33
Innsbruck Ct. N&S 17W—29N 34
Interlaken Ct. E&W 17W—29N 34
Interlaken Ln. NW&SE
...........................17W—29N 34
Jackson Av. E&W ..16W—29N 34
Jeremy Ln. N&S ....17W—29N 34
Johnson Av. NE&SW
...........................16W—29N 34
Juliet Cir. NW&SE .18W—30N 34
Juniper Pkwy. N&S 16W—27N 42
Kenlock Av. N&S ...17W—28N 34
Kenwood Av. N&S .17W—28N 34
Lake St. E&W ...16,17W—29N 34
Lange Ct. N&S ......16W—29N 34
Laurel Av. E&W .....16W—29N 34
Liberty Bell Ct. NE&S
...........................15W—28N 35,36
Liberty Bell Ln. E&W
...........................16W—29N 34
Liberty Lake Dr. E&W
...........................15W—29N 35,36
Lilac Ct. N&S ....16W—27N 42
Lincoln Av. E&W ....16W—28N 34
Linden Ln. E&W ....16W—29N 34
Lothair Dr. N&S .....17W—28N 34
Magnolia Ln. NW&SE
...........................16W—27N 42
Manor Cir. E&W ....16W—29N 34
Maple Av. E&W .....16W—29N 34
Margate Ln. E&W .15W—28N 35,36
Mayfair Dr. N&S ....16W—27N 42
Maywood Ct. E&W 15W—27N 43
McKinley Av. E&W
...........................16W—28N 34
Meadow Ln. E&W .16W—28N 34
Merril Ct. NE&SW .16W—29N 34
Michaels Ln. N&S .16W—27N 42
Miller Ct. N&S ....16W—30N 34
Milwaukee Av. NW&SE
...........................16W—28N 34
Minear Dr. E&W ....16W—29N 34
Mullady Pkwy. NW&SE
...........................16W—27N 42
Newberry Av. E&W 16W—29N 34
Nita Ln. E&W ....16W—27N 42
Nordic Ct. E&W .....17W—28N 34
North Av. E&W ......15W—29N 35,36
Oaktrail Dr. E&W ...15W—27N 43
Oak St. N&S ....16W—27N 42
Oak Spring Rd. E&W
...........................15W—29N 35,36
Old Buckley Rd. NE&SW
...........................16W—30N 34
Old Hickory Ln. N&S
...........................15W—29N 35,36
Orchard Cir. NE&SW
...........................16W—29N 34
Oxford Ct. E&W ....17W—29N 34
Paddock Ct. N&S ..16W—27N 42
Paddock Ln. E&W .16W—27N 42
Paradise Ln. N&S .17W—29N 34
Park Av. E&W ...15,18W—28N 34,35
Park Pl. N&S ....16W—29N 34

Page
Parliament Ct. NW&SE
...........................16W—29N 34
Paul Revere Ln. NE&SW
...........................15W—28N 35,36
Pembroke Rd. E&W
...........................17W—28N 34
Pimlico Pkwy. E&W
...........................16W—27N 42
Pine Tree Ln. NE&SW
...........................17W—28N 34
Pond Ridge Rd. E&W
...........................17W—28N 34
Poplar Ct. E&W .....16W—27N 42
Prairie Av. N&S .....16W—28N 34
Quaker Hill N&S ....17W—29N 34
Red Top Dr. NE&SW
...........................16W—27N 42
Regency Ln. E&W .17W—28N 34
Ridgeway Ln. N&S 15W—28N 35,36
Ridgewood Ln. N&S
...........................17W—29N 34
Riverside Dr. N&S .15W—28N 35,36
Rockland Ln. E&W
...........................15,16W—28N 34,35
Romeo Cir. N&S ....18W—30N 34
Roosevelt Dr. N&S 17W—28N 34
Rosewood Terr. N&S
...........................16W—27N 42
Sandstone Dr. N&S
...........................16W—29N 34
Sandy Ct. E&W .....16W—27N 42
Sandy Ln. E&W .....16W—27N 42
Saxon Ln. N&S ......16W—28N 34
School St. E&W ....16W—29N 34
Scott Pl. N&S ....15W—28N 35,36
Sedgwick Dr. NE&SW
...........................17W—29N 34
Shari Ln. E&W ......17W—28N 34
Springhaven Dr. N&S
...........................17W—29N 34
Spruce Ct. N&S .....16W—27N 42
St. James Pl. E&W 17W—29N 34
Stewart Av. N&S
...........................16W—28,29N 34
Stevenson Dr. NW&SE
...........................17W—28N 34
Stonegate Ct. E&W
...........................17W—29N 34
Stonegate Rd. N&S, E&W
...........................17W—29N 34
Sunnyside Av. E&W
...........................16W—28N 34
Sunnyside Pl. E&W
...........................16W—28N 34
Sunset Dr. NE&SW
...........................16W—29N 34
Sussex Ln. N&S,E&W
...........................17W—29N 34
Tall Tree Terr. E&W
...........................16W—28N 34
Tamarack Ln. NW&SE
...........................16W—27N 42
Thomas Ct. E&W ..17W—29N 34
Thornapple Ln. NE&SW
...........................16W—27N 42
Thornbury Ln. E&W
...........................15W—29N 35 36
Tracy Ln. NW&SE .16W—27N 42
Trinity Pl. N&S,E&W
...........................17W—29N 34
Tyler Ct. E&W ......16W—28N 34
Valley Park Dr. E&W
...........................16W—28N 34
Victory Dr. E&W ....17W—28N 34
Virginia Av. N&S,E&W
...........................18W—30N 34
Walnut St. E&W ....16W—29N 34
Warwick Ln. N&S ..17W—28N 34
Wedgemere Pl. N&S
...........................16W—28N 34
Weeping Willow Ln. NW&SE
...........................16W—27N 42
Wellington Av. E&W
...........................17W—29N 34
West St. N&S ....16W—29N 34
W. Park Av. NE&SW
...........................17W—28N 34
Wexford Ct. N&S ...17W—28N 34
Wheeler Ct. N&S ...16W—29N 34
White Blvd. E&W ...19W—30N 33
Willard Av. N&S .....16W—29N 34
Willow Av. E&W .....17W—28N 34
Wilshire Ct. N&S ...17W—29N 34
Wilshire Dr. E&W ..17W—29N 34
Winchester Rd. E&W
...........................17,18W—29N 34
Windhaven Rd. N&S
...........................17W—29N 34
Windsor Terr. N&S 16W—28N 34
Winner's Cir. NE&SW
...........................16W—27N 42
Woodfield Ln. E&W
...........................15W—29N 35,36
Woodland Av. N&S 17W—28N 34
Wright Ct. N&S ......16W—29N 34
Wrightwood Terr. N&S
...........................16W—28N 34
Young Dr. NE&SW 17W—30N 34
1st St. N&S ....16W—29N 34
2nd Av. N&S .....16W—28,29N 34

Page
3rd St. N&S ....16W—29N 34
4th Av. E&W ....16W—28N 34
4th St. N&S ......16W—28,29N 34
5th Av. N&S ....16W—28N 34
5th St. N&S ....16W—28N 34
7th Av. N&S ....15W—28N 35,36

Lincolnshire Streets

Angelican Ln. E&W
...........................13W—22N 51
Barclay Blvd. N&S 15W—22N 50,51
Bedford Ct. N&S ...13W—22N 51
Berkshire Ln. N&S 13W—22N 51
Berwick Ct. N&S ...13W—22N 51
Brampton Ct. NE&SW
...........................13W—23N 51
Brampton Ln. NW&SE
...........................13W—23N 51
Bristol Ct. E&W ......13W—22N 51
Brunswick Ln. N&S 13W—22N 51
Buckingham Pl. E&W
...........................13W—22N 51
Burnham Ct. E&W 13W—22N 51
Buxton Ct. E&W ....13W—23N 51
Cambridge Ln. E&W
...........................14W—22N 51
Camden Ct. E&W .13W—22N 51
Canterbury Rd. N&S
...........................13W—22N 51
Cedar Ln. E&W .....14W—22N 51
Cold Stream Cir. E&W
...........................14W—22N 51
Cornell Ln. E&W ...13W—23N 51
Coventry Ln. E&W 14W—22N 51
Cumberland Dr. E&W
...........................14W—22N 51
Darby Ln. N&S ......14W—22N 51
Deer Run N&S ....13W—22N 51
Dover Dr. E&W ......14W—23N 51
Downing Sq. N&S .12W—22N 51,52
Dukes Cir. N&S .....13W—22N 51
Dukes Ct. N&S ......13W—22N 51
Dukes Ln. E&W .....13W—22N 51
Durham Ct. NE&SW
...........................13W—23N 51
Elmwood Ln. N&S .14W—23N 51
Elsinoor Dr. N&S ...14W—22N 51
Essex Ln. E&W .....14W—23N 51
Fairfax Ln. E&W ....13W—22N 51
Fox Tr. E&W ....13W—22N 51
Friar Truck Ct. E&W
...........................13W—23N 51
Grendier Ct. E&W .13W—22N 51
Hampshire Ct. E&W
...........................13W—22N 51
Hickory Ln. N&S ...14W—23N 51
Kensington Dr. N&S
...........................14W—22N 51
Kent NE&SW ....13W—22N 51
Keswick Ct. N&S ....13W—22N 51
Kings Cross Dr. E&W
...........................13W—22N 51
Knightsbridge Pkwy. E&W
...........................15W—22N 50,51
Lancaster Ln. N&S 14W—22N 51
Leeds Ct. NW&SE 13W—23N 51
Lincolnshire Dr. NE&SW
...........................14W—22N 51
Londonberry Ln. E&W
...........................14W—22N 51
Marrio Dr.E&W ......15W—22N 50,51
Mayfair Ln. E&W ...13W—23N 51
Melrose Ln. E&W ..14W—22N 51
Middlebury Ln. N&S
...........................13W—21N 51
Nottingham Dr. E&W
...........................13W—23N 51
Oakwood Ln. N&S 14W—23N 51
Oxford Dr. NW&SE 14W—22N 51
Park Pl. E&W ....16W—21N 50
Parton Ct. E&W ....13W—23N 51
Pembroke Dr. E&W
...........................13W—23N 51
Pembroke Ln. E&W
...........................14W—23N 51
Pheasant Row NE&SW
...........................13W—22N 51
Plymouth Ct. N&S .14W—22N 51
Portshire Dr. E&W .13W—22N 51
Queens Way E&W 13W—22N 51
Regent Ln. N&S ....13W—22N 51
Reliance N&S ....13W—22N 51
Rivershire Ln. E&W
...........................14W—22N 51
Riverside Dr. E&W 15W—23N 50,51
Riverside Rd. NW&SE
...........................15W—22N 50,51
Riverwoods Rd. N&S
...........................14W—22N 51
Robinhood Ct. E&W
...........................13W—23N 51
Royal Ct. E&W ......13W—22N 51
Schelter Rd. N&S ..15W—22N 50,51
Sheffield Ct. E&W .14W—22N 51
Sherwood Dr. N&S 13W—23N 51
Stafford Ct. N&S ...13W—23N 51
Stonegate Cir. N&S
...........................14W—23N 51
Suffield Sq. N&S ...13W—22N 51
Surrey Ct. E&W .....13W—23N 51

Page
Surrey Ln. N&S, E&W
...........................13W—23N 51
Sutton Ct. NW&SE 13W—22N 51
Victoria Ln. E&W ...14W—22N 51
Wellington Ct. N&S 13W—22N 51
Westminster Way NW&SE
...........................13W—22N 51
Westwood Ln. E&W
...........................13W—22N 51
Whitby Cir. N&S ....13W—22N 51
Whitby Ct. N&S ....13W—22N 51
William St. N&S .....15W—21N 50,51
Wiltshire Dr. E&W .14W—22N 51
Windsor Ct. N. N&S
...........................13W—22N 51
Windsor Ct. S. N&S
...........................13W—22N 51
Windsor Dr. E&W ..13W—22N 51
Yorkshire Dr. E&W 14W—22N 51

Lindenhurst Streets

Adams Dr. E&W ....19W—39N 9,17
Beck Rd. N&S ....20W—37N 17
Bonner Ln. NW&SE
...........................19W—37N 17
Briar Ln. E&W ....20W—37N 17
Brittany Ln. E&W ...20W—38N 17
Brook Ln. NE&SW 20W—38N 17
Burr Oak Ln. NW&SE
...........................20W—37N 17
Carriage Ln. E&W .20W—38N 17
Cherrywood Ln. NW&SE
...........................20W—38N 17
Chestnut Cir. N&S .20W—38N 17
Countryside Ln. NE&SW
...........................20W—37N 17
Crabtree Ct. NE&SW
...........................20W—37N 17
Deerpath Dr. E&W 19W—37N 17
Elm Tree Dr. E&W .19W—37N 17
Elmwood Dr. E&W 20W—38N 17
Fairfield Rd. N&S ..20W—38N 17
Federal Ct. N&S ....20W—39N 9,17
Federal Pkwy. N&S 20W—39N 9,17
Forest View Rd. N&S, E&W
...........................19W—38N 17
Glendale Ct. E&W .20W—37N 17
Grand Av. NW&SE 20W—37N 17
Grass Lake Rd. E&W
...........................20W—39N 9,17
Great Oak Dr. E&W
...........................19W—38N 17
Green Briar Ln. N&S
...........................19W—37N 17
Green Tree Ct. E&W
...........................20W—38N 17
Hawthorne Dr. N&S
...........................20W—38N 17
Hazelwood Dr. N&S
...........................20W—38N 17
Heron Dr. NW&SE 19W—38N 17
Hickory Ct. E&W ...20W—38N 17
Hickory Dr. N&S ....20W—38N 17
Highland Cir. NE&SW
...........................19W—37N 17
Highland Dr. E&W .19W—37N 17
Highpoint Dr. N&S,E&W
...........................20W—38N 17
Hillcrest Ln. N&S ...20W—37N 17
Honeysuckle Ct. NE&SW
...........................20W—37N 17
Jefferson Dr. E&W 20W—39N 9,17
Lake Shore Dr. N&S
...........................20W—38N 17
Laurel Dr. NW&SE 20W—37N 17
Lindenhurst Dr. N&S
...........................20W—37N 17
Long Meadow Dr. E&W
...........................20W—38N 17
Magnolia Ln. N&S .19W—37N 17
Mallard Dr. E&W ...19W—38N 17
Maplewood Ct. NE&SW
...........................20W—38N 17
Maplewood Dr. NW&SE
...........................20W—38N 17
Meadow Dr. E&W ..20W—38N 17
Monroe Dr. N&S ....19W—39N 9,17
Northgate Rd. N&S
...........................20W—38N 17
Old Elm Rd. NW&SE
...........................20W—37N 17
Orchard Ln. N&S ...19W—37N 17
Paine Av. N&S ....19W—39N 9 17
Penn Blvd. E&W
...........................19W—39N 9,17
Penn Ct. NE&SW ..19W—39N 9,17
Pheasant Ridge Ct. NW&SE
...........................19W—38N 17
Pinecrest Ln. E&W 20W—38N 17
Prospect Dr. NE&SW
...........................20W—38N 17
Red Bark Rd. NE&SW
...........................20W—38N 17
Ridge Ct. NE&SW .20W—38N 17
Ridgeland Dr. E&W
...........................20W—37N 17
Rolling Ridge Ln. N&S
...........................20W—38N 17
Rose Ln. E&W ......19W—38N 17

Page
Shagbark Ln. NW&SE
...........................20W—38N 17
Spring Hill Ln. E&W
...........................20W—38N 17
Sunset Ln. E&W ....20W—37N 17
Surrey Ln. NW&SE 20W—38N 17
Teal Rd. E&W ....19W—38N 17
Thornwood Dr. N&S, E&W
...........................20W—37N 17
Timber Ln. N&S ....19W—37N 17
Tree Ln. N&S ....19W—37N 17
Valley Dr. N&S ....20W—37N 17
Waterford Dr. NE&SW
...........................19W—38N 17
Whispering Pines Rd. NE&SW
...........................19W—38N 17
White Birch Rd. NE&SW
...........................19W—38N 17
White Oak Dr. N&S 20W—38N 17
Witchwood Ln. E&W
...........................20W—38N 17
Woodlane Dr. NW&SE
...........................20W—37N 17

Long Grove Streets

Antietam Dr. NW&SE
...........................18W—21N 50
Aptakisic Rd. E&W 17W—22N 50
Arlington Heights Rd. N&S
...........................18W—20N 50
Arrowhead Ct. N&S
...........................19W—25N 41
Bayberry Ln. E&W 19W—20N 49
Bernay Ln. E&W ....18W—20N 50
Bob-O-Link Ln. N&S
...........................18W—21N 50
Bordeaux Ln. N&S 18W—20N 50
Braeburn Rd. E&W 18W—25N 41,42
Briar Path Rd. E&W
...........................20W—21N 49
Brittany Ct. N&S ....18W—20N 50
Brittany Ln. E&W ...18W—20N 50
Brookhill Dr. NE&SW
...........................19W—23N 49
Brookside Ln. N&S 18W—20N 50
Cavalry Ct. ....19W—20N 49
Carriage Ct. N&S ..18W—20N 50
Checker Rd. E&W .19W—20N 49
Chickamuga Ln. N&S
...........................18W—20N 50
Coach Rd. N&S .....19W—20N 49
Country Ln. N&S ...19W—22N 49
Countryside Ln. N&S
...........................18W—20N 50
Creekside Dr. N&S 19W—25N 41
Crestview Dr. N&S 19W—22N 49
Cuba Rd. E&W ......19W—22N 49
Cumberland Cir. N&S
...........................19W—20N 49
Dawn Ct. E&W ......18W—20N 50
Diamond Lake Rd. N&S
...........................19W—24,25N 41
Driftwood Ln. NW&SE
...........................18W—22N 50
East Mardan Dr. N&S
...........................19W—21N 49
East Sheridan Dr. N&S
...........................19W—21N 49
Edgewood Ln. N&S
...........................18W—20N 50
Estate Ln. N&S ......19W—25N 41
Fairfield Dr. E&W ...18W—21N 50
Fairview Ln. N&S ...18W—21N 50
Federal Ct. E&W ....19W—20N 49
Fenview Ct. E&W ..17W—22N 50
Fenview Ln. E&W .17W—22N 50
Forest Ct. E&W .....17W—24N 42
Forest Way Dr. N&S
...........................17W—24N 42
Gilmer Rd. NW&SE
...........................18W—24N 41,42
Golf Ln. N&S ....18W—22N 50
Grant Ct. N&S ....18W—21N 50
Grant Pl. E&W ....18W—21N 50
Heather Knoll Ct. NW&SE
...........................18W—22N 50
Hedgewood Ct. NW&SE
...........................17W—22N 50
Heather Knoll Ct. E&W
...........................18W—22N 50
Hedge Apple Ct. NW&SE
...........................17W—22N 50
Hedge Apple Ln. E&W
...........................18W—22N 50
Hedgewood Ct. NW&SE
...........................17W—22N 50
Hickory Ct. E&W ...19W—23N 49
Hicks Rd. N&S ......19W—20N 49
High Meadow Ct. NW&SE
...........................18W—24N 41,42
Hilltop Rd. E&W ....18W—22N 50
Holly Ct. E&W ....18W—20N 50
Indian Creek Rd. E&W
...........................19W—25N 41
Indian Ln. E&W 18,19W—25N 41
Juniper Ln. E&W ...19W—20N 49
Knoll Ct. E&W ....20W—20N 49
Knoll Dr. N&S ....20W—20N 49
Knollwood Dr. E&W
...........................17W—21N 50

	Page
Krueger Ct. E&W ..19W—23N	49
Krueger Ln. E&W ..19W—23N	49
Lakeridge Ct. NW&SE	
...........................19W—25N	41
Lakeridge Dr. N&S 19W—25N	41
Lake Zurich Rd. E&W	
...........................18W—23N	50
Lexington Dr. E&W ..19W—20N	49
Lincoln Av. N&S ...19W—20N	49
Long Grove Rd. NE&SW	
.........18,19,20W—20,21N	49,50
Manassas Ln. NW&SE	
...........................18W—21N	49
Mardan Dr. N&S ...19W—21N	49
Mayflower Ln. E&W	
...........................19W—21N	49
Meadow Lark Dr. E&W	
...........................18W—20N	49
Meadow Knoll Ct. E&W	
...........................20W—20N	49
Meadow Knoll Ct. NE&SW	
...........................17W—22N	50
Merrimac Ln. E&W 19W—21N	49
Middlesax Dr. E&W	
...........................19W—21N	49
Millwood Farm Rd. NW&SE	
...........................19W—21N	49
Monitor Ln. E&W ...19W—21N	49
Monticello Ln. E&W	
...........................19W—21N	49
Mundelein Rd. N&S	
...........18W—21,24N	42,50
Newport Ct. N&S ..18W—21N	50
North Krueger Rd. N&S	
...........................19W—23N	49
Northridge Pl. E&W	
...........................18W—24N	41,42
Oak Grove Cir. E&W	
...........................17W—23N	50
Oak Grove Dr. E&W	
...........................17,18W—22N	50
Oak Forest Ln. NW&SE	
...........................17W—24N	42
Oak Grove Dr.E&W	
...........................17,18W—22N	50
Oak Hill Ln. N&S ...20W—21N	49
Oakwood Rd. E&W	
...........................18W—23N	50
Oldfield Ct. NE&SW	
...........................17W—22N	50
Oldfield Ln. E&W ...17W—22N	50
Oldfield Pl. E&W ...17W—22N	50
Old McHenry Rd. NW&SE	
...........................19W—22N	49
Oldwood Ln. NW&SE	
...........................17W—22N	50
Picardy Ct. N&S ...18W—20N	50
Picardy N. E&W ....20W—20N	50
Pine Ct. NE&SW ...19W—22N	49
Port Clinton Rd. E&W	
...........................17W—23N	50
Pottowatomie Ct. E&W	
...........................19W—21N	49
Prairie Crossing NW&SE	
...........................17W—22N	50
Prairiemoor Ct. E&W	
...........................17W—22N	50
Prairie Wind Rd. E&W	
...........................19W—22N	49
Prince Crossing NW&SE	
...........................17W—22N	50
Private Rd. N&S	
.........18,19,20W—21,22N	49,50
Pvt Rd. E&W ...18W—22,25N	42,50
Pvt. Ln. E&W ....19W—21N	49
Pvt. Ln. N&S,E&W 19W—20N	49
Red Oak Dr. N&S ..19W—23N	49
Roanoke Ct. A. E&W	
...........................18W—20N	50
Robert Parker Coffin Rd. E&W	
.........18,19W—21N	49,50
Robertson Blvd. E&W	
...........................20W—22N	49
Rolling Glen Dr. N&S	
...........................19W—22N	49
Saddle Ridge Ct. N&S	
.........18W—24N	41,42
Saddle Ridge Ln. E&W	
.........18W—24N	41,42
Salem Ct. NE&SW 18W—24N	41,42
Salem Lake Dr. N&S	
...........................20W—22N	49
Schaeffer Rd. N&S 18W—20N	50
Shagbark Ln. 19W—21N	49
Shaheen Ct. N&S ..19W—23N	49
Shenandoah Ln. N&S	
...........................19W—20N	49
Sheridan Ln. E&W .19W—21N	49
Shiloh Dr. E&W ....19W—21N	49
Sky Ln. N&S ......18W—22N	50
Stockbridge Ln. N&S	
.........18W—24N	41,42
Sumter Ct. NE&SW	
...........................18W—20N	50
Sumter Dr. E&W ...18W—20N	50
Sunshine Ln. E&W 18W—22N	50
Surrey Ln. E&W ...18W—22N	50
Three Lakes Ct. NE&SW	
...........................18W—21N	50

	Page
Three Lakes Dr. E&W	
...........................18W—21N	50
Tribal Ct. E&W ....19W—25N	41
Union Ct. E&W .....19W—20N	49
Walnut Ln. E&W ....19W—20N	49
Waterfowl Way N&S	
...........................19W—24N	41
Westmoreland Dr. E&W	
...........................18W—24N	41,42
West Mardan Dr. N&S	
...........................19W—21N	49
West Sheridan N&S	
...........................19W—21N	49
Willow Brook Rd. N&S	
...........................18W—22N	50
Willow Valley Rd. N&S	
...........................20W—21N	49
Willow Wood Ln. N&S	
...........................18W—21N	50
Windham Ct. N&S .18W—25N	41,42
Windham Ln. NW&SE	
...........................18W—25N	41,42
Wildwood Ln. N&W	
Woodbine Ln. N&S 19W—21N	50
Woodbine Ln. N&S 19W—21N	49
Woodview Ct. N&S 17W—22N	50

Metawa Streets

	Page
Bradley Rd. N&S ...14W—26N	43,44
Everett Rd. E&W ...14W—24N	43,44
Hawthorne Dr. E&W	
...........................13W—27N	43,44
Little St. Mary's Rd. Old Oak	
Hill Ln. N&S ....14W—27N	43,44
School Rd. E&W	
...........................14,15W—27N	43,44
Riverwoods Tri-State Tollway	
N&S ....13W—25,26N	43,44
St. Mary's Rd. N&S	
...........................15W—25,26N	43
Townline Rd. E&W 14W—26N	43,44

Mundelein Streets

	Page
Aberdeen Ln. NE&SW	
...........................19W—28N	33
Agnes Av. E&W ...18W—27N	41,42
Allanson Rd. E&W 18W—27N	41,42
Anthony Av. NW&SE	
...........................18W—27N	41,42
Appleby Cir. N&S ..19W—28N	33
Arbour Ct. E&W ...18W—28N	34
Archor Av. N&S ...18W—27N	41,42
Armour Blvd. E&W 17W—25N	42
Balmoral Dr. E&W .19W—27N	41
Banbury Rd. N&S	
...........................19W—28,29N	33
Banbury Rd. N&S .19W—28N	33
Baskin Rd. N&S ...17W—25N	42
Beach Rd. N&S ....19W—28N	33
Bedford Rd. E&W .17W—27N	42
Bishop Ct. N&S ...20W—28N	33
Bishop Wy NW&SE	
...........................20W—28N	33
Blue Spruce Ln. N&S	
...........................19W—28N	33
Bobby Ln. E&W ...19W—28N	33
Bonnie Brook Av. E&W	
...........................19W—28N	33
Braeburth Rd. E&W	
...........................19W—28N	33
Brice Av. N&S .....18W—27N	41,42
Bristol Ct. NE&SW 17W—27N	42
Buckingham Rd. E&W	
...........................20W—28N	33
California Av. N&S 19W—27N	41
Canterbury E&W ...17W—25N	42
Cardinal Pl. E&W ..19W—27N	41
Cedar St. N&S .....18W—27N	41,42
Chandler Dr. E&W .19W—28N	33
Charlotte Pl. E&W .18W—28N	34
Chestnut Av. N&S .18W—27N	41,42
Chicago Av. NW&SE	
...........................18W—27,28N	34,42
Churchill E&W .....17W—25N	42
Clearbrook Park Dr. NE&SW	
...........................18W—28N	41,42
Country Side Hwy. NE&SW	
...........................18W—27N	41,42
Courtland St. E&W	
.........18,19W—27N	41,42
Crane Av. E&W ...18W—26N	41,42
Crossmeadow Dr. N&S	
...........................18W—27N	41,42
Crystal St. E&W	
.........18,19W—27N	41,42
Dairy Ln. N&S ....19W—29N	33
Dalton Av. NW&SE 18W—27N	41,42
Dean Pl. E&W .....18W—27N	41,42
Deepwoods Dr. NE&SW	
...........................18W—26N	41,42
Division N&S ......18W—27N	41,42
Downing E&W .....17W—25N	42
Dublin Rd. E&W ...19W—28N	33
Dublin Rd. E&W ...19W—28N	33
Dunbar Ct. N&S ..19W—29N	33
Dunbar Rd. N&S ..19W—29N	33
Dunleer Dr. N&S ..19W—29N	33
East Greenview N&S	
...........................19W—27N	41

	Page
Edgar A. Poe Ln. N&S	
...........................18W—26N	41,42
Edgemont St. E&W	
...........................18W—28N	33
E. Garfield Av. N&S	
...........................19W—27N	41
Elm Av. E&W ......18W—26N	41,42
Emerald Av. N&S	
...........................19W—27,28N	33,41
Emerson Ln. E&W 18W—26N	41,42
Eton Way N&S ....17W—27N	42
Fairhaven Ln. E&W	
...........................18W—26N	34
Fairlawn Av. N&S	
...........................19W—27,28N	33,41
Firth Rd. N&S .....19W—28N	33
Forest Av. E&W ...18W—26N	41,42
French Ct. N&S ...18W—27N	41,42
French Dr. E&W ...18W—27N	41,42
Friars Ln. E&W ....20W—28N	33
Garfield Av. N&S ..19W—27N	1
George Dr. N&S ...18W—27N	41,42
Gifford Ct. NW&SE 18W—27N	41,42
Glendale Pl. E&W .18W—28N	34
Glenview Av. E&W 18W—28N	33
Goodwin Pl. NE&SW	
...........................18W—28N	34
Grace Av. NE&SW 18W—28N	34
Granville Av. N&S .18W—28N	33
Greenview Av. N&S	
.........18,19W—27,28N	33,41
Groveland Blvd. E&W	
...........................19W—27N	41
Grove St. E&W ....18W—27N	41,42
Hammond St. E&W	
...........................19W—27N	41
Hampton Ct. N&S .17W—27N	42
Hampton Ln. E&W 17W—27N	42
Hawley Ct. N&S ...19W—27N	41
Hawley St. E&W	
.........18,19W—28N	33,34
Hawthorne Blvd. E&W	
...........................18,19W—27N	41,42
Hickory Chestnut St. N&S	
...........................18W—27N	41,42
High St. E&W .....18W—27N	41,42
Highland Rd. N&S 19W—28N	33
Hillside Rd. E&W ..19W—27N	41
Holcomb Ct. N&S .18W—28N	34
Huntington Ct. NE&SW	
...........................17W—27N	42
Huntington Dr. E&W	
...........................17W—27N	42
Idlewild N. N&S	
.........17W—27,28N	34,42
James Av.N&S .18W—27,28N	34,42
Jeanette Pl. E&W ..18W—28N	34
Kari Ct. N&S ......18W—26N	41,42
Killarney Cir. E&W 19W—28N	33
Killarney Pass NW&SE	
...........................19W—28N	33
Kings Way E&W ...19W—28N	33
Knightsbridge Dr. N&S, E&W	
...........................17W—27N	42
Lake Av. N&S .19W—27,28N	33,41
Lake Av. NW&SE .18W—26N	41,42
Lake Shore Dr. E&W	
...........................18W—27N	41,42
Lake Terr. N&S ...18W—27N	41,42
Lake View Dr. E&W	
...........................19W—27N	41
Lange St. NE&SW 18W—27N	41,42
Laramie St. E&W ..19W—28N	33
Laurel Av. N&S ...18W—28N	34
Lawrence Dr. N&S 18W—26N	41,42
Leithon Rd. N&S ..17W—26N	42
Lincoln Av. N&S ...19W—27N	41
Lomond Dr. N&S,E&W	
...........................18W—28N	33
Londonderry Ct. NW&SE	
...........................18W—28N	33
Longfellow Ln. N&S	
...........................18W—26N	41,42
Longwood Terr. E&W	
...........................18W—26N	41,42
Lucerne Av. N&S .18W—28N	33
Lucerne Ct. E&W .19W—28N	33
Manor Ln. NE&SW 20W—28N	33
Maple Av. E&W	
.........17,18N—26,28N	34,42
Margaret Av. E&W 18W—27N	41,42
McCormick Av. N&S	
...........................17W—25N	42
McKinley Av. NE&SW	
...........................18W—27N	41,42
Midland Av. N&S ..18W—27N	41,42
Midlothian Av. N&S 19W—27N	41
Midlothian Rd. N&S	
...........................19W—28N	33
Midway Dr. E&W ..18W—27N	41,42
Morris Av. NW&SE 18W—28N	34
New Castle Ct. N&S	
...........................17W—27N	42
North Av. N&S ....18W—27N	41,42
N. Shore Dr. E&W .19W—27N	41
Norton Av. N&S ...18W—27N	41,42
Nottingham E&W ..17W—25N	42
Oak St. E&W .....18W—27N	41,42
Oakdale Av. E&W .18W—26N	41,42
Olga St. N&S .....18W—26N	41,42

	Page
Orchard Av. E&W ..18W—27N	41,42
Orchard St. E&W	
.........18,19W—27N	41,42
Park Av. E&W ....19W—28N	33
Park St. E&W ....19W—28N	33
Parliament Way N&S	
...........................17W—27N	42
Peramore Dr. N&S 19W—28N	33
Pershing Av. N&S .19W—27N	41
Pleasure Dr.E&W .18W—26N	41,42
Plymouth Farms Rd. E&W	
...........................17W—25N	42
Prairie Av. N&S 19W—27,28N	33,41
Prospect Av. NW&SE	
...........................18W—27N	41,42
Quigly Av. E&W ...19W—27N	41
Racine Pl. NE&SW 18W—28N	34
Raleigh Rd. N&S ..19W—28N	33
Rays Ln. E&W ....18W—26N	41,42
Reidel Dr. N&S ...17W—25N	42
Ridge Av. N&S ...18W—26N	41,42
Ridgemoor Av. N&S	
...........................19W—27,28N	33,41
Rotary Ct. N&S ...18W—28N	34
Rouse Av. NW&SE 18W—27N	41,42
Russell Pl. M&S ..18W—26N	41,42
Rye Rd. E&W .....19W—29N	33
Sandhurst Drd. E&W	
...........................17W—27N	42
Seymour Av. N&S .18W—27N	41,42
Shaddle Av. N&S ..18W—27N	41,42
Shady Ln. E&W W 18W—26N	41,42
Shady Dell Av. E&W	
...........................18W—26N	41,42
Shady Rest Ridge N&S	
...........................18W—26N	41,42
Sherwood Ct. NW&SE	
...........................17W—27N	42
Simpson Ln. E&W 18W—26N	41,42
S. Lake Shore Dr. E&W	
...........................18W—27N	41,42
S. Noel Dr. E&W ..18W—27N	41,42
South St. N&S .....18W—26N	41,42
Stratford Ln. E&W .18W—26N	41,42
Thomas Blvd. E&W	
...........................18W—27N	41,42
Thomas Rd. N&S ..18W—27N	41,42
Tower Rd. N&S ...18W—27N	41,42
Turret Ct. NE&SW .18W—26N	41,42
University Dr. N&S 18W—28N	34
Victoria Rd. E&W ..20W—28N	33
Wallcer Pl. E&W ..18W—28N	34
Walnut Ct. NE&SW 18W—27N	41,42
Walnut St. N&S ...18W—26N	41,42
Washington Blvd. N&S	
...........................18W—27N	41,42
Washington Ct. N&S	
...........................18W—27N	41,42
Wellington Av. E&W	
...........................19W—28N	33
Wellington Ct. N&S 19W—28N	33
West Greenview N&S	
...........................19W—27N	41
W. Garfield Av. N&S	
...........................19W—27N	41
Whitehall N&S ....17W—25N	42
Whittier Ln. E&W .18W—26N	41,42
Wilcox St. E&W ...18W—27N	41,42
Wildwood Av. N&S 18W—28N	34
Wilheim Rd. E&W .17W—25N	42
Wimpole E&W .....17W—25N	42
Windsor Pl. NE&SW	
...........................17W—27N	42
Winthrop Ct. E&W 18W—26N	41,42
Woodlawn Dr. E&W	
...........................19W—27N	41

North Barrington Streets

	Page
Ape Ct. N&S ....25W—23N	47
Biltmore Dr. N&S	
...........................25,26W—23N	47
Beachview Ln. N&S,E&W	
...........................25W—23N	47
Brookmont Ln. E&W	
...........................25W—23N	47
Brookside Rd. NE&SW, E&W	
...........................25,26W—23N	47
Carriage Rd. N&S .25W—24N	39
Castle View Ct. E&W	
...........................25W—23N	47
Cherry Hill Rd. E&W	
...........................26W—22N	47
Concord Ln. E&W .25W—23N	47
Crooked Ln. E&W .26W—23N	47
Drury Ln. N&S ....25W—23N	47
Duck Pond Ln. E&W	
...........................25W—23N	47
Essex Ln. N&S ...25W—23N	47
Eton E&W ....25W—23N	47
Eton Dr. NE&SW .26W—23N	47
Glen Circle Dr. NE&SW	
...........................26W—23N	47
Golfview Dr. NE&SW	
...........................25W—23N	47
Halcyon Ln. E&W .25W—23N	47
Hewes Dr. N&S ...25W—22N	47
Homewood Ln. N&S	
...........................25W—23N	47
Honey Lake Rd. N&S	
...........................25W—22N	47

	Page
Kathleen Ct. N&S ..25W—23N	47
Kimberly Rd. N&S .25W—23N	47
Lake Shore Blvd. N&S	
...........................26W—23N	47
Lakeview Rd. N&S 26W—23N	47
Mockingbird Ln. E&W	
...........................25W—23N	47
Mohawk Dr. N&S ..26W—22N	47
North Hill Dr. E&W 25W—23N	47
Old Oak Dr. N&*S .25W—22N	47
Onondaga Dr. E&W	
...........................26W—22N	47
Orchard Ct. N&S ..25W—23N	47
Osage Dr. N&S ...26W—22N	47
Ottawa Dr. N&S ...26W—22N	47
Oxford Rd. NW&SE	
...........................25W—23N	47
Pheasant Run Trail N&S	
...........................25W—23N	47
Pinewoods Dr. E&W	
...........................25W—22N	47
Pook's Hill Rd. NE&SW	
...........................25W—22N	47
Randolph Ct. NW&SE	
...........................25W—22N	47
Rugby Rd. E&W ...25W—23N	47
Saddle Tree Ln. N&S	
...........................25W—22N	47
Seminole Dr. N&S .26W—22N	47
Shady Ln. N&S ...25W—23N	47
Signal Hill Rd. N&S,E&W	
...........................26W—22N	47
Sioux Dr. E&W ...26W—22N	47
Thomas Dr. E&W .25W—22N	47
View Ct. N&S .....25W—23N	47
Woodbine Pl. NW&SE	
...........................25W—23N	47
Wooded Ln. N&S ..26W—23N	47
Woodland Dr. NW&SE	
...........................25W—23N	47

North Chicago Streets

	Page
Adams St. N&S ...10W—31N	29
Argonne Dr. E&W	
...........................11,12W—31N	37
Arlington Av. E&W .11W—32N	29
Beechnut Av. N&S 12W—32N	29
Beetnoven St. E&W	
...........................12W—31N	37
Birch Av. N&S ....12W—32N	29
Broadway Av. NE&SW	
...........................11W—31N	37
Carver Av. E&W ..11W—32N	29
Common Wealth Av. N&S	
...........................11W—31N	37
Davis St. N&S .....11W—31N	37
Dickey Av. N&S ...11W—32N	29
Dickey St. N&S ...11W—32N	29
Dougdale Rd. N&S 11W—31N	37
Elizabeth Av. N&S 11W—32N	29
Evergreen Av. N&S 12W—32N	29
Fairway Ln. N&S ..12W—32N	29
Fellows Pl. NE&SW	
...........................10W—31N	37
Foss Park Av. E&W	
...........................10W—32N	29
Glen Dr. N&S ...11W—31,32N	29,37
Green Bay Rd. N&S	
...........................12W—32N	29
Greenfield Av. N&S	
...........................11W—31,32N	29,37
Greenwood Av. N&S	
...........................12W—32N	29
Grove Av. N&S .11W—31,32N	29,37
Hervey Av. N&S 11W—31,32N	29,37
Hickory Av. N&S ..12W—32N	29
Hillcrest Av. N&S .12W—32N	29,37
Honore St. N&S ...11W—31N	37
Jackson St. N&S ..10W—31N	29,37
Jones Dr. E&W ...11W—32N	29
Kemble Av. N&S	
...........................11W—31,32N	29,37
Kennedy Dr. N&S ..11W—31N	37
Kristan Av. N&S 11W—31,32N	29,37
Lakeside Av. NE&SW	
...........................10W—32N	29
Lenox Av. N&S ....10W—32N	29
Leona Av. E&W ...11W—31N	37
Lewis Av. N&S ....11W—31N	37
Lincoln St. N&S ...10W—31N	37
Main St. NE&SW ..10W—31N	37
Maple Av. N&S ....12W—32N	29
Marquette St. N&S 10W—31N	29
McAlister Av. N&S 10W—32N	29
McAree Rd. N&S ..12W—32N	29
Meadow Ln. N&S .12W—31N	37
Morrow Av. NE&SW	
...........................11W—31N	37
Neil Ln. E&W .....11W—31N	37
Northern Av. N&S .12W—32N	29
Oak Av. N&S .....12W—32N	29
Park Av. N&S .....10W—32N	29
Prospect Av. N&S	
...........................11W—31,32N	29,37
Renken Av. N&S ..11W—32N	29
Seymour Av. N&S	
...........................11W—31,32N	29,37
Sheridan Rd. NE&SW	
...........................10W—31,32N	29,37

Page

Sherman Av. N&S
..........11W—31,32N 29,37
Victoria St. N&S ....10W—32N 29
Wadsworth Av. N&S
..........10W—32N 29
Wallace St. N&S ....11W—31N 37
Willow Av. N&S ....12W—32N 29
Winter Av. N&S ....11W—31N 37
Wright St. N&S ....11W—31N 37
11th St. E&W ....10W—32N 29
12th St. E&W ....10W—32N 29
13th St. E&W ...10,12W—32N 28,29
14th Pl. E&W ......12W—32N 28,29
14th St. E&W ...10,12W—32N 28,29
15th Pl. E&W ......12W—32N 28,29
15th St. E&W ......12W—32N 28,29
16th Pl. E&W . 10 .12W—32N 28,29
17th Pl. E&W ......12W—32N 28,29
17th St. E&W ...10,12W—32N 28,29
18th St. E&W ...10,12W—32N 28,29
19th St. E&W ......12W—32N 28,29
20th Pl. E&W ......12W—32N 28,29
20th St. E&W ...11,12W—32N 28,29
21st Pl. E&W ......12W—32N 31 37
21st St. E&W ...10,12W—32N 37
22nd Pl. E&W ......12W—31N 37
22nd St. E&W ......11W—31N 37
23rd Pl. E&W ......12W—31N 37
23rd St. E&W ......12W—31N 37
24th Pl. E&W ......12W—31N 37
24th St. E&W ...11,12W—31N 37
25th St. E&WW .....11W—31N 37

Old Mill Creek Streets
Hunt Club Rd. N&S
..........17W—38,40N 10,18
Kelly Rd. E&W ......16W—40N 10
Milburn Rd. E&W ..18W—38N 18
Wadsworth Rd. E&W
..........17W—39N 19

Park City Streets
Bedford Ct. N&S ...13W—33N 27,28
Birch Av. N&S ....12W—33N 28
Bryn Mawr Av. N&S
..........13W—33N 27,28
Cambridge Dr. E&W
..........13W—33N 27,28
Cornell Av. N&S ...13W—33N 27,28
Devonshire Av. E&W
..........13W—33N 27,28
Dixie Av. E&W ......12W—33N 28
Docs Ln. E&W ......12W—33N 28
Dorset Ct. NE&SW ...13W—33N 27,28
Dromey Av. N&S ...12W—33N 28
Fredson Rd. N&S ...13W—33N 27,28
Greenview Av. N&S
..........13W—33N 27,28
Gulf Pl. N&S ......13W—33N 27,28
Harwick Ln. E&W ...13W—33N 27,28
Hood Av. N&S ......12W—33N 28
Judy Ln. E&W ......12W—33N 28
Kehm Blvd. E&W ...13W—33N 27,28
Lake Park Av. E&W
..........13W—33N 27,28
Mobile Blvd. E&W ...12W—33N 28
Noll Dr. E&W ......12W—33N 28
Pace Av. N&S ......12W—33N 28
Rosedale Av. N&S 13W—33N 27,28
Staben Av. N&S ...12W—33N 28
Sussex Ct. E&W ...13W—33N 27,28
Sutherland Dr. N&W
..........13W—33N 27,28
Telegraph Rd. N&S 13W—33N 27,28
Teske Blvd. N&S ...13W—33N 27,28
Thorndale Av. N&S 13W—33N 27,28
Winthrop Av. N&S .13W—33N 27,28
7th St. E&W ......12W—33N 28
8th St. E&W ......12W—33N 28
9th St. E&W ......12W—33N 28

Riverwoods Streets
Arrow Ln. E&W ....12W—21N 51,52
Arrow Wood Tr. E&W
..........13W—20N 51
Big Oak Ln. E&W .12W—21N 51,52
Blackhawk Ln. N&S
..........13W—21N 51
Blackheath Ln. N&S
..........12W—21N 51,52
Blackhorn Rd. E&W
..........14W—20N 51
Braeburn Ct. NW&SE
..........12W—21N 51,52
Braeburn Dr. E&W 12W—22N 51,52
Braeburn Ln. N&S .13W—21N 51
Burr Oak Tr. E&W .13W—21N 51
Calvin Ct. N&S ...13W—22N 51
Cherokee Ln. E&W 13W—21N 51
Chianti Tr. E&W ...13W—20N 51
Chippewa Pthwy. N&S
..........13W—21N 51
County Line Rd. E&W
..........13W—20N 51
Crestwood Ct. E&W
..........13W—21N 51
Crestwood Ln. E&W
..........13W—21N 51
Daquiri Dr. E&W ...13W—20N 51

Page

Deepwood Tr. E&W
..........13W—20N 51
Deerfield Rd. E&W 14W—21N 51
Dell Ln. E&W ......13W—22N 51
Dubonnet N&S ......13W—20N 51
Duffy Lane E&W ...13W—22N 51
East Course Dr. NW&SE
..........12W—21N 51,52
Edgewood Ln. N&S
..........13W—22N 51
Farner Ct. E&W ...13W—22N 51
Forest Glen Ct. NE&SW
..........13W—21N 51
Forest Glen Trail E&W
..........13W—21N 51
Gemini Ln. E&W ...13W—20N 51
Glendenim Ln. N&S
..........13W—21N 51
Greenbrier Ln. E&W
..........13W—20N 51
Hazel Nut Ln. E&W
..........13W—20N 51
Hiawatha Ln. N&S .13W—21N 51
Hill Ln. E&W ....12W—22N 51,52
Hoffman Ln. N&S ...13W—21N 51
Indian Trail Dr. N&S
..........13W—21N 51
Julie Ln. E&W ......13W—22N 51
Juneberry Rd. N&S
..........14W—20N 51
Kenilwood Ct. N&S 13W—21N 51
Kenilwood Ln. N&S
..........13W—21N 51
Kenwick Ct. N&S ..13W—22N 51
Kenwick Pl. N&S ..13W—22N 51
Kingswood Ct. NE&SW
..........13W—21N 51
Knollwood Way E&W
..........13W—21N 51
Lyndale Ln. N&S
..........13W— 20,21N 51
Lyngby Ct. N&S ...13W—21N 51
Meredith Dr. E&W .13W—20N 51
Oakhurst Ln. NE&SW
..........12W—21N 51,52
Oak Ln N&S ....12W—21N 51,52
Orange Brace Rd. E&W
..........13W—20N 51
Pine Tree Ln. NE&SW
..........13W—21N 51
Portwine Rd. N&S .13W—20N 51
Pvt Rd. E&W ......13W—22N 51
Ringland Ln. E&W 13W—20N 51
Riverwoods Ct. E&W
..........13W—21N 51
Robinhood Ln. N&S
..........13W—22N 51
Saunders Rd. N&S 12W—21N 51,52
Scotch Ln. E&W ...13W—20N 51
Shawnee Tr. N&S .13W—21N 51
Sherry Ln. NW&SE
..........13W—20N 51
Strenger Ln. N&S ..13W—22N 51
Studio Ln. N&S ...13W—21N 51
Sunset Tr. E&W
..........14W—20N 51
Thornmeadow Rd. N&S
..........14W—20N 51
Thornwood Ln. N&S
..........13W—22N 51
Timberleaf Ln. E&W
..........13W—21N 51
Timberline Ln. E&W
..........14W—21N 51
Timber Trail N&S ...13W—20N 51
Timberwood Ln. N&S
..........14W—21N 51
Treasure Ln. N&S .13W—20N 51
Trillium Ln. N&S ...13W—22N 51
West Course Dr. N&S
..........12,13W—22N 51,52
Whigam Ln. E&W ..13W—21N 51
Whigham Rd. N&S 13W—21N 51
White Oak Ln. N&S
..........13W—20N 51
Windlake Tr. N&S ..12W—22N 51,52
Woodland Ct. E&W 13W—21N 51
Woodland Ln. West E&W
..........13W—21N 51
Woodland Ln. N&S 13W—20N 51

Round Lake Streets
Alma Cir. E&W ......24W—34N 23,24
Alma Ct. N&S ......24W—34N 23,24
Alpine Dr. NE&SW 23W—33N 23,24
Amtakes Cir. N&S ..23W—33N 23,24
A-Ok Ct. N&S ......24W—34N 23,24
Apollo Ct. N&S ....24W—34N 23,24
Avilon Av. E&W ...23W—33N 23,24
Avilon Ct. N&S ...23W—33N 23,24
Belvidere Rd. NE&SE
..........23W—32N 23,24
Bimini Bay NW&SE
..........23W—33N 23,24
Capri Ct. E&W ......23W—33N 23,24
Capri Dr. N&S ......23W—33N 23,24
Catalpa Dr. N&S ...23W—34N 23,24
Cedar Crest Ct. NW&SE
..........23W—33N 23,24
Cedar Lake Rd. N&S
..........23W—32N 23,24

Page

Crest Ct. E&W ....23W—33N 23,24
Dorothy Ct. NE&SW
..........23W—34N 23,24
Forest Av. N&S ....23W—33N 23,24
Garden Cr. N&S ...23W—33N 23,24
Goodnow Blvd. N&S
..........23W—33N 23,24
High Point Dr. N&S 24W—33N 23,24
High School Av. N&S
..........23W—34N 23,24
Hillandale Av. N&S .23W—33N 23,24
Hillside Dr. N&S ...23W—33N 23,24
Lake Dr. E&W ......23W—33N 23,24
Lakeview Dr. NE&SW
..........23W—33N 23,24
Lakewood Dr. E&W
..........23W—33N 23,24
Laurel Av. N&S ...23W—33N 23,24
Lawn Terr. NE&SW 23W—33N 23,24
Lem Drt. E&W ......24W—34N 23,24
Lincoln Av. N&S ...23W—33N 23,24
Linden Dr. N&S ...23W—33N 23,24
Long Lake Rd. NW&SE
..........23W—34N 23,24
Lunga Ct. N&S ....24W—34N 23,24
Lunga Dr. N&S ....24W—34N 23,24
Macalls Dr. N&S ...23W—33N 23,24
Magna Dr. N&S ...23W—33N 23,24
Maple Ln. NE&SW 23W—33N 23,24
Moon Rover Dr. N&S, E&W
..........24W—34N 23,24
Nippersink Rd. E&W
..........23W—33N 23,24
N. Bernice Ct. E&W
..........23W—34N 23,24
N. Rosedale Ct. N&S
..........23W—34N 23,24
Orbiter Dr. E&W ...24W—34N 23,24
Orchard St. N&S ...23W—33N 23,24
Park Av. E&W ......23W—33N 23,24
Park Rd. N&S,E&W
..........23W—33N 23,24
Pineview Dr. NW&SE
..........23W—33N 23,24
Railroad Rd. NW&SE
..........23W—34N 23,24
Ravine Av. E&W ...23W—33N 23,24
Ridgewood Dr. N&S
..........23W—34N 23,24
Roberta Cr. NE&SW
..........23W—34N 23,24
Spanky Ct. N&S ...23W—34N 23,24
S. Bernice Ct. E&W
..........23W—34N 23,24
S. Rosedale Ct. E&W
..........23W—34N 23,24
Sunset Dr. N&S ....23W—34N 23,24
Sycamore Dr. NE&SW
..........24W—34N 23,24

Round Lake Beach Streets
Apache Trail N&S .23W—35N 23,24
Ardmore Dr. N&S ..23W—35N 23,24
Barberry Ln. N&S ..24W—34N 23,24
Bayview Dr. NW&SE
..........23W—34N 23,24
Beachview Dr. E&W
..........23W—34N 23,24
Beverly Dr. N&S ...24W—35N 23,24
Bonnie Brook Ln. NE&SW
..........24W—34N 23,24
Brentwood Dr. N&S
..........23W—34N 23,24
Briar Ln. NW&SE ..23W—34N 23,24
Buena Vista Ct. N&S
..........23W—34N 23,24
Central Park Dr. E&W
..........24W—34N 23,24
Cedar Lake Rd. N&S
..........23W—35N 23,24
Channel Dr. N&S ..23W—35N 23,24
Cherokee Dr. N&S 24W—35N 23,24
Chestnut Dr. N&S ..23W—35N 23,24
Clarendon Dr. E&W
..........22W—35N 24
Clarendon Dr. N&S 23W—34N 23,24
Clover Av. N&S ...22W—35N 24
Cohona Ct. E&W ..24W—34N 23,24
Comanche Trail N&S
..........23W—35N 23,24
Crescent Ct. N&S ..24W—34N 23,24
Daisy Ct. N&S .....22W—35N 24
Dakota Ct. N&S ...23W—35N 23,24
Diana Ct. NW&SE .22W—35N 24
Eagle Creek Dr. E&W
..........23W—35N 23,24
East End Av. N&S .22W—35N 24
Edgewater Ct. N&S
..........23W—34N 23,24
Elm Av. N&S ......22W—35N 24
Fairfield Terr. N&S .24W—34N 23,24
Fairview Pkwy. E&W
..........23W—35N 23,24
Ferndale Dr. E&W .23W—34N 23,24
Geneva Terr. N&S .23W—35N 23,24
Glenwood Dr. E&W 23W—34N 23,24
Goldenwood Terr. N&S
..........23W—35N 23,24
Golfview Ct. E&W .23W—35N 23,24

Page

Golfview Dr. E&W .23,24W—35N 23,24
Grove Dr. N&S ....23W—35N 23,24
Hainesville Rd. NE&SW
..........22W—35N 24
Hather Terr. E&W ..22W—35N 24
Hawthorne Dr. NE&SW
..........22,23W—34,35N 23,24
Hickory Av. N&S ...23W—35N 23,24
Hickory St. N&S ...22W—34N 24
Highland Pkwy. NW&SE
..........23W—35N 23,24
Highland Terr. E&W
..........23W—35N 23,24
Hillside Av. E&W ..24W—35N 23,24
Hillside Dr. N&S ...23W—35N 23,24
Hillwood Cir. N&S .24W—34N 23,24
Idlewild Dr. N&S ...23W—35N 23,24
Ivy Ct. E&W ....22W—35N 24
Juneway Terr. N&S 23W—35N 23,24
Juniper Terr. E&W .23W—35N 23,24
Kenilworth Dr. N&S 23W—35N 23,24
Kenmore Av. N&S .22W—35N 24
Kildeer Dr. N&S ...24W—35N 23,24
Lagoon Terr. E&W 23W—35N 23,24
Lake Av. E&W ......22W—34N 24
Lake Shore Dr. NW&SE
..........23W—34,35N 23,24
Lakewood Pkwy. NE&SW
..........23W—35N 23,24
Laurel Ct. E&W ...23W—35N 23,24
Leslie Av. N&S ...22W—35N 24
Lilac Ct. E&W ......22W—35N 24
Lilac Ln. N&S .....22W—35N 24
Lotus Dr. N&S ....24W—35N 23,24
Lotus Ln. N&S ....24W—34N 23,24
Maple Dr. N&S ....23W—35N 23,24
Mayfield Dr. NW&SE
..........23W—35N 23,24
Meadowbrook Dr. N&S
..........23W—35N 23,24
Meadowbrook Dr. NW&SE
..........23W—35N 23,24
Meadow Green Ln. E&W
..........23W—35N 23,24
Melrose Av. N&S ..22W—35N 24
Morningside Dr. E&W
..........23W—35N 23,24
North Av. N&S ....22W—35N 24
N. Channel Dr. E&W
..........23W—34N 23,24
Oak Av. N&S ......22W—35N 24
Orchard Ct. E&W ..23W—35N 23,24
Park Dr. N&S .....23W—35N 23,24
Partridge Ct. N&S .23W—35N 23,24
Pheasant Dr. E&W 23W—35N 23,24
Pine Grove Av. N&S
..........22W—35N 24
Pleasant Dr. N&S ..23W—35N 23,24
Poplar Av. N&S ...22W—35N 24
Redwing Dr. E&W .22W—35N 24
Ridgeway Av. N&S 23W—35N 23,24
Ridgeway Av. N&S 22W—35N 24
Rollins Rd. E&W ...23W—35N 23,24
Ronald Terr. NW&SE
..........24W—34N 23,24
Round Lake Dr. N&S
..........23W—35N 23,24
Sauk Ct. E&W ......23W—35N 23,24
Shady Ln. N&S ....23W—34N 23,24
Shady Ln. Ct. N&S 23W—34N 23,24
Shoreland Dr. N&S 23W—34N 23,24
S. Channel Dr. N&S
..........23W—34N 23,24
Southmoor Ln. E&W
..........24W—34N 23,24
Sunnyside Dr. NW&SE
..........23W—35N 23,24
Sunset Dr. NW&SE
..........23W—35N 23,24
Turnbull Dr. N&S ..24W—35N 23,24
Villa Vista N&S ....24W—34N 23,24
Vine Av. NE&SW ..22W—35N 24
Walnut Dr. N&S ...23W—35N 23,24
West End Dr. N&S 22W—35N 24
Wildwood Dr. E&W
..........22,24W—34N 23,24
William Av. NE&SW
..........22W—35N 24
Witchwood Ln. NW&SE
..........23W—34N 23,24
Woodbine Dr. N&S 23W—35N 23,24
Woodland Dr. N&S 24W—34N 23,24
Woodmere Dr. E&W
..........24W—34N 23,24
Woodridge Dr. N&S
..........24W—35N 23,24

Round Lake Heights Streets
Arrowhead Dr. E&W
..........23W—35N 23,24
Brentwood Dr. N&S
..........23W—35N 23,24
E. Cedarwood Cir. N&S
..........23W—35N 23,24
Flintwood Dr. N&S .23W—35N 23,24
Hiawatha Tr. N&S .24W—35N 23,24
Lotus Dr. N&S ....24W—35N 23,24
Mohawk Dr. E&W .23W—35N 23,24

Page

N. Cedarwood Cir. E&W
..........23W—35N 23,24
N. Summit Ct. N&S 23W—35N 23,24
Pontiac Dr. N&S ...23W—35N 23,24
S. Cedarwood Cir. N&S
..........23W—35N 23,24
Summit Ct. N&S ...23W—35N 23,24
Tomahawk Tr. E&W
..........34W—35N 23,24
Turkey Run Dr. E&W
..........23W—35N 23,24
Warrior Dr. N&S ...24W—35N 23,24
W. Cedarwood Cir. N&S
..........24W—35N 23,24

Round Lake Park Streets
Alleghany Rd. N&S 21W—31N 33
Arbor Dr. N&S .....23W—34N 24
Beechwood Dr. N&S
..........23W—33N 23,24
Bellvue Dr. N&S ...22W—33N 24
Briar Hill Dr. N&S .22W—33N 24
Cedar Mound Rd. NE&SW
..........23W—33N 23,24
Clifton Dr. N&S ...22W—33N 24
Elder Dr. N&S .....22W—33N 24
Elm Av. N&S ......22W—34N 24
Fairlawn Dr. N&S ..22W—33N 24
Forest Glen Dr. N&S
..........23W—33N 24
Grandview Dr. N&S
..........23W—33N 24
Greenwood Rd. N&S
..........23W—33N 24
Harris Rd. N&S 19W—31,32N 25,33
Highmoor Dr. N&S 22W—33N 24
Hillcrest Terr. N&S .22W—33N 24
Indian Tr. E&W ...22W—34N 24
Ivanhoe Rd. N&S .20W—31N 33
Kenwood Dr. N&S .22W—33N 24
Knollwood Dr. NE&SW
..........22W—34N 24
Lake Shore Dr. E&W
..........22W—33N 24
Locust Dr. E&W ...22W—33N 24
Lyle Av. E&W ......22W—33N 24
Main St. NW&SE ..23W—33N 23,24
Maple Av. E&W ...22W—34N 24
Mayflower Terr. E&W
..........22W—34N 24
Midland Dr. E&W ..22W—33N 24
Parkview Ct. E&W 22W—33N 24
Pawnee Dr. NW&SE
..........23W—33N 24
Peterson Rd. E&W
..........20,21W—30N 33
Pine View Dr. NW&SE
..........22W—33N 24
Prospect Dr. N&S 22W—33N 24
Ravine Dr. N&S ...22W—33N 24
Sylvan Dr. E&W ...22W—34N 24
Washington St. NW&SE
..........23W—33N 23,24
Willow Rd. E&W ...22W—33N 24

Third Lake Streets
Brigantine Ln. E&W
..........18W—35N 26
Clipper Ct. NE&SW
..........18W—35N 26
Hickory Av. N&S ...19W—35N 25
Lake Av. E&W ......19W—35N 25
Lakeview Dr. E&W 19W—35N 25
Linden Av. N&S, E&W
..........19W—34,35N 25
Mainsail N&S ......18W—35N 26
Seafarer Dr. N&S ..18W—35N 26
Sunshine Av. E&W 19W—05N 25
Windjammer Ct. NE&SW
..........18W—35N 26

Tower Lakes
Abbul Pl. N&S .....26W—25N 38,39
Barsumian Dr. N&S
..........27W—25N 38
Bays Pl. N&S ......26W—25N 38,39
Blue Stem Cr. N&S 26W—24N 38,39
Bridge Ln. E&W ...26W—25N 38,39
Cambridge Dr. E&W
..........26W—25N 38,39
Circle Dr. N&S,E&W
..........26W—25N 38,39
Devonshire Rd. N&S
..........26W—25N 38,39
East Dr. N&S ......26W—25N 38,39
Edward Ln. N&S ...26W—25N 38,39
Essex Pl. E&W ....26W—25N 38,39
Esther Dr. E&W ...28W—25N 38
Fenview Dr. E&W ..27W—24N 38
Gateway Dr. E. N&S
..........26W—25N 38,39
Indian Grass Ct. E&W
..........26W—24N 38,39
Indian Trail NW&SE
..........26W—25N 38,39
Kelsey Rd. NE&SW
..........27W—24N 38
Lake Shore Dr. E. N&S, E&W
..........26W—25N 38,39

Page

Lake Shore Dr. N. E&W ....26W—25N 38,39
Lake Shore Dr. W. N&S ....26W—25N 38,39
Lake Shore Terr. N&S ....26W—25N 38,39
Leon Dr. E&W ....26W—25N 38,39
Marion Ct. N&S .....26W—25N 38,39
Medinah Ln. NW&SE ....25W—25N 39
Melrose Dr. E&W ...26W—25N 38,39
Murray Rd. E&W ...27W—25N 38
Nooding Flower Ct. NE&SW ....26W—24N 38,39
Oak St. NW&SE ....26W—25N 38,39
Oriole Rd. E&W .....27W—25N 38
Oxford Rd. N&S ....26W—25N 38,39
Pebblecreek Dr. E&W ....26W—25N 38,39
Raleigh Pl. N&S ....26W—25N 38,39
Robin Rd. E&W .....27W—25N 38
Rolling Green Dr. N&S ....25W—25N 39
Rose Terr. E&W ....26W—25N 38,39
Rooosyln Pl. E&W .26W—25N 38,39
Scenic Dr. N&S .....26W—25N 38,39
South Dr. NE&SW .26W—24N 38,39
South Hills Dr. E&W ....26W—25N 38,39
Stonehenge Ln. E&W ....25W—25N 39
Summit Dr. E&W ...25W—25N 39
Tomahawk Ln. N&S ....26W—25N 38,39
Tower Dr. E. E&W .26W—25N 38,39
Tower Dr. W. N&S .26W—25N 38,39
Warwick Rd. N&S ..26W—25N 38,39
West Dr. N&S ....26W—25N 38,39
Wren Rd. N&S ......27W—25N 38

Vernon Hills Streets

Abbey Ln. E&W ....17W—25N 42
Abilene Ln. N&S,E&W ....16W—25N 42
Adair Ct. E&W ......17W—25N 42
Adams Ct. N&S ......17W—26N 42
Albany Ln. N&S .....17W—25N 42
Albert Dr. NW&SE .17W—25N 42
Albright NW&SE ....17W—25N 42
Alexandria Dr. N&S 17W—25N 42
Alice Ct. E&W ....17W—25N 42
Allentown Ct. N&S 16W—25N 42
Almond Ct. N&S .....17W—25N 42
Alpine Dr. E&W .....17W—25N 42
Altoona Ct. E&W ...16W—25N 42
Amber Ln. E&W .....17W—25N 42
Amherst Ct. N&S ...16W—25N 42
Angela Ct. N&S .....17W—25N 42
Ann Ct. E&W ....17W—25N 42
Annapolis Dr. NW&SE ....17W—25N 42
Appian Way NW&SE ....17W—25N 42
Appleton Dr. N&S ..17W—25N 42
Apollo Ct. E&W ......17W—25N 42
April Av. N&S ....17W—25N 42
Aqua Ct. NE&SW ..17W—25N 42
Ardmore Ct. N&S ...17W—25N 42
Arlington Ct. NW&SE ....17W—25N 42
Arron Ct. E&W ......17W—25N 42
Ashland Ct. N&S ......17W—25N 42
Ashville Ct. N&S ....16W—25N 42
Ashwood Ct. NE&SW ....17W—25N 42
Aspen Dr. N&S .17W—25,26N 42
Astoria Ct. NW&SE ....16W—25N 42
Athens Ct. E&W ...16W—25N 42
Atlantic Dr. E&W ....17W—25N 42
Auburn Ct. N&S ....17W—25N 42
Augusta Dr. E&W ..17W—25N 42
Augusta Dr. E&W .17W—25N 42
Aurora Ct. NW&SE 16W—25N 42
Austin Ct. NE&SW 17W—25N 42
Autumn Ln. N&S ...17W—25N 42
Avon Ct. NW&SE ..17W—25N 42
Basswood Dr. NW&SE ....17W—25N 42
Birchwood Ct. NE&SW ....17W—25N 42
Birmingham Pl. N&S ....16W—25N 42
Brandywine Ct. E&W ....17W—26N 42
Briarwood Ct. NE&SW ....17W—25N 42
Brookwood Ct. NW&SE ....17W—25N 42
Browning Ct. N&S .17W—26N 42
Bryant Pl. NE&SW 17W—26N 42
Buchanan Ct. E&W ....17W—26N 42
Burnside Ct. E&W .17W—26N 42
Burr Oak Dr. N&S .17W—24N 42
Butterfield Rd. N&S ....17W—25N 42
Caldwell Ln. E&W .17W—24N 42
Castlegate Ct. E&W ....16W—25N 42

Page

Cedar Ct. NE&SW 17W—26N 42
Center Dr. E&W ....16W—26N 42
Centurion Ln. N&S 17W—26N 42
Chatham Ct. N&S .17W—26N 42
Cherokee Rd. E&W ....16W—25N 42
Cherry Valley Rd. E&W, N&S ....17W—24N 42
Cherrywood Ct. NE&SW ....17W—25N 42
Chesapeake Ct. E&W ....17W—26N 42
Chestnut Ct. NE&SW ....17W—26N 42
Clairmont Ct. NE&SW ....17W—24N 42
Cleveland Ct. NW&SE ....17W—26N 42
Collins Dr. N&S .....17W—26N 42
Colony Ct. E&W ....17W—26N 42
Commonwealth Ct. N&S,E&W ....17W—26N 42
Constitution Ct. N&S ....17W—26N 42
Country Club Ln. NE&SW ....17W—24N 42
Court Of Ash NE&SW ....17W—24N 42
Court Of Elm NE&SW ....17W—24N 42
Court Of Shorewood E. W. S. N&S, E&W ....18W—24N 41,42
Court Of Spruce E&W ....17W—24N 42
Court Of Birch E&W ....17W—24N 42
Coventry Cir. N&S,E&W ....16W—26N 42
Crabtree Ln. N&S .16W—25N 42
Creekside Dr. NW&SE ....17W—25N 42
Crestview Ln. E&W ....17W—26N 42
Cromwell Ct. N&S .16W—26N 42
Cumberland Ct. N&S ....17W—26N 42
Darby Ct. E&W ......17W—24N 42
Debill Ct. E&W ....16W—24N 42
Deerpath Dr. N&S .17W—24N 42
Deerpath Dr. E. N&S ....16W—25N 42
Dickinson Ct. NE&SW ....17W—26N 42
Dirksen Dr. NW&SE ....17W—26N 42
Dogwood Ln. NW&SE ....17W—25N 42
Dover Ct. N&S ......17W—26N 42
Echo Ct. E&W ....17W—26N 42
Edgewood Rd. E&W ....16W—25N 42
Eisenhower Ct. NW&SE ....17W—26N 42
Elm Tree Ln. NE&SW ....16W—25N 42
Emerson Pl. NW&SE ....17W—26N 42
Evergreen Dr. N&S 17W—24N 42
Exeter Pl. NW&SE 16W—25N 42
Farmington Ln. E&W ....17W—25N 42
Farmingdale Cir. N&S ....17W—25N 42
Faulkner Pl. N&S ..17W—26N 42
Fernwood Cr. NE&SW ....17W—25N 42
Forest Hill Ct. NE&SW ....17W—24N 42
Forest Way Ct. NW&SE ....17W—24N 42
Forest Way Dr. NE&SW ....17W—24N 42
Franklin Pl. NW&SE ....17W—26N 42
Gladstone Dr. N&S 17W—26N 42
Grant Pl. NW&SE .17W—26N 42
Greenbriar Ln. N&S ....17W—24N 42
Greenleaf Dr. NE&SW ....17W—26N 42
Greenvale Rd. NE&SW ....16W—25N 42
Hackberry Dr. NE&SW ....17W—24N 42
Hamilton Pl. NE&SW ....17W—26N 42
Hampton Pl. E&W .17W—26N 42
Hanover Pl. E&W ..17W—26N 42
Harding Ct. E&W ...17W—26N 42
Harrison Ct. E&W .17W—26N 42
Harvest Ct. NE&SW ....17W—25N 42
Hastings Ct. E&W .17W—26N 42
Hawthorne Ct. E&W ....16W—25N 42
Hawthorne Pkwy. E&W ....17W—26N 42
Hayes Ct. NW&SE 17W—26N 42
Hemingway Ct. E&W ....16W—26N 42

Page

Hughes Pl. N&S ....17W—26N 42
Hyannis Ct. E&W ..17W—24N 42
Indianwood Dr. N&S ....17W—26N 42
Jackson Ct. N&S ...17W—26N 42
Jamestown Ct. NW&SE ....17W—24N 42
Jefferson Ct. E&W 17W—26N 42
Kennedy Pl. NE&SW ....17W—26N 42
Keswick Ln. E&W .16W—25N 42
Kingston Ct. N&S ..17W—26N 42
Knollwood Ln. N&S ....16W—25N 42
Lafayette Pl. N&S .17W—26N 42
Lakeside Dr. N&S ....17,18W—24N 41,42
Lakeside Dr. E. N&S ....17W—24N 42
Lakeside Dr. N. E&W ....17W—24N 42
Lakeview Pkwy. N&S ....16W—26N 42
Lancaster Pl. E&W 17W—26N 42
Larchmont Ln. N&S ....16W—25N 42
Lexington Dr. E&W 16W—25N 42
Lincroft Ln. E&W ...17W—24N 42
Lindenwood Ct. NW&SE ....17W—25N 42
Lindon Ln. E&W ....16W—24N 42
Lowell Pl. NE&SW 17W—26N 42
Mac Arthur Ct. NW&SE ....17W—26N 42
Mallard Ct. E&W ...17W—25N 42
Malvern Ln. E&W ..16W—25N 42
Manchester Ln. N&S ....17W—24N 42
Marimac Ln. N&S ..17W—24N 42
Marinewood Dr. NW&SE ....17W—25N 42
Market Ct. E&W ....17W—26N 42
Marlowe Pl. NW&SE ....17W—26N 42
Martin Dr. N&S ......17W—24N 42
Mayflower Rd. NE&SW ....16W—25N 42
Meadow Ct. E&W .17W—25N 42
Melody Ln. N&S ....16W—25N 42
Memphis Pl. E&W .17W—24N 42
Meredith Pl. NE&SW ....17W—26N 42
Michigan Ct. E&W .17W—26N 42
Midway Ln. NE&SW ....16W—24N 42
Monroe Ct. N&S ....17W—26N 42
Montauk Ln. N&S ..17W—24N 42
Montebello Dr. N&S ....17W—24N 42
Monterrey Dr. N&S 17W—24N 42
Montgomery Ln. N&S ....17W—24N 42
Murwood Ct. NE&SW ....17W—25N 42
Mystic Pl. N&S ......17W—25N 42
Onwentsia Rd. N&S ....16W—25N 42
Oxford Rd. E&W ...16W—25N 42
Parkside Ct. E&W .17W—26N 42
Peachtree Ct. E&W ....17W—26N 42
Phillip Rd. E&W .....17W—25N 42
Pierce Ct. NE&SW 17W—26N 42
Plumwood Ln. NE&SW ....17W—25N 42
Plymouth Farms Rd. E&W ....17W—25N 42
Polk Ct. NW&SE ...17W—26N 42
Princeton Ct. N&S .17W—26N 42
Redwood Ct. NW&SE ....17W—25N 42
Regency Ct. N&S ..16W—26N 42
Revere Pl. NW&SE ....17W—26N 42
Roosevelt Dr. NW&SE ....17W—26N 42
Russet Way NE&SW ....17W—25N 42
St. Ives Ln. E&W ...16W—25N 42
Saratoga Ct. E&W 17W—26N 42
Southwick Ct. E&W ....16W—26N 42
Spring Ln. S. N&S 16W—25N 42
Stevenson Pl. NE&SW ....17W—26N 42
Stockton N&S ....17W—26N 42
Sullivan Dr. NW&SE ....17W—25N 42
Sutton Ct. N&S ......16W—26N 42
Swinburne Pl. NW&SE ....17W—26N 42
Tally Ho Dr. E&W ..17W—24N 42
Tanglewood Ct. NE&SW ....17W—25N 42
Tanwood Ln. NW&SE ....17W—25N 42
Taylor Ct. NE&SW 17W—26N 42
Televista Ct. NW&SE ....17W—24N 42
Tennis Ln. E&W ....18W—24N 41,42

Page

Tennyson Pl. NW&SE ....17W—26N 42
Timber Ln. E&W ....17W—26N 42
Towine Rd. E&W ...17W—26N 42
Tyler Ct. NE&SW ..17W—26N 42
Van Buren Ct. N&S 17W—26N 42
Vernon Ct. N&S ....17W—26N 42
Vernon Ln. N&S ....17W—26N 42
Victoria Dr. N&S,E&W ....17W—24N 42
Wadsworth Pl. NW&SE ....17W—26N 42
Warrington Rd. NE&SW ....16W—25N 42
Washington Ct. E&W ....17W—26N 42
Waterview Cir. E&W ....18W—24N 41,42
Webster Pl. E&W ..17W—26N 42
Wentworth Ct. N&S ....16W—26N 42
West End Ct. N&S 17W—26N 42
West End Ln. NW&SE ....17W—26N 42
Westmoreland Dr. E&W,N&S ....18W—24N 41,42
Westwood Ct. NE&SW ....17W—25N 42
Whiting Ct. E&W ...17W—26N 42
Whitman Pl. NW&SE ....17W—26N 42
Whitney Pl. N&S ...17W—26N 42
Wildwood Ct. NE&SW ....17W—25N 42
Wilshire Ct. E&W ..17W—26N 42
Windsor Dr. E&W ..17W—26N 42
Wine Ct. N&S ....17W—25N 42
Woodbine Pl. NW&SE ....16W—25N 42

Wadsworth Streets

Anna Dr. N&S, E&W ....15W—37N 19
Bryn Mawr N&S ....13W—38N 19,20
Burr Oak Ln. N&S 14W—38N 19,20
Cashmore Rd. N&S ....14W—38N 19,20
Chaplin St. E&W . 13W—38N 19,20
Country Lane Dr. E&W ....14W—38N 19,20
Elm Ln. E&W ....13W—38N 19,20
Golf Lane Dr. N&S 14W—38N 19 20
Hansen Rd. E&W ..15W—37N 19
Highview Rd. E&W 14W—39N 19 20
Jody Ln. E&W ....14W—39N 19,20
Kilbourne Rd. N&S 14W—39N 19,20
McCarty Rd. N&S .15W—38N 19
Meadow Ln. N&S ..14W—39N 19,20
Mulberry Ln. E&W .16W—37N 18
Northwoods Dr. N&S ....14W—38N 19,20
Oak Knoll Rd. E&W ....14W—39N 19,20
Pickford St. E&W ..13W—38N 19,20
Red Oak Terr. N&S 14W—38N 19,20
Rosedale Av. N&S 13W—38N 19,20
Sandy Ct. E&W .....15W—38N 19
Schlosser Ct. E&W 15W—38N 19
Schlosser Rd. N&S 15W—38N 19
Shagbark Ln. N&S 14W—38N 19,20
Sheryl Lynn Dr. E&W ....14W—39N 19,20
Skokie Hwy. N&S ..16W—40N 11
Thornapple Ln. E&W ....15W—37N 19
Valleyview Rd. N&S ....15W—37N 19
Wadsworth Rd. E&W ....14W—39N 12
Willow Ln. N&S .....15W—37N 19
Winchester Rd. N&S ....13W—39N 12

Wauconda Streets

Adams Av. N&S .....25W—28N 31
Bangs St. NE&SW 26W—27N 38,39
Barbara Ln. NW&SE ....25W—28N 31
Briar Rd. NW&SE .26W—28N 30,31
Brown St. N&S .26W—27,28N 30,38
Church St. E&W ....26W—27N 38,39
Clover Rd. E&W ....25W—28N 31
Cook St. E&W ....26W—28N 30,31
Crescent Terr. NW&SE ....26W—28N 30,31
Daniel Av. N&S ......26W—27N 38,39
Dato Ln. N&S ....26W—28N 30,31
Delta Dr. N&S ....25W—27N 39
Dunbar Rd. N&S ...26W—27N 38,39
Earls Ct. N&S ....25W—28N 31
Edgewater Pkwy. E&W ....25W—28N 31
Edward Pl. N&S ....25W—28N 31
Foster Av. N&S ......25W—27N 39
Francis St. N&S ....26W—27N 38,39
George Av. E&W ...26W—27N 38,39
Grant Pl. E&W ......25W—28N 31
Hammond St. N&S 25W—27N 39
Harrison Av. N&S ..25W—28N 31
Helena Av. E&W ....26W—27N 38,39

Page

Highland Av. E&W .25W—27N 39
High St. N&S ....25W—26N 39
Hill St. N&S ....25W—27N 39
Hubbard Ct. E&W .26W—27N 38,39
Jackson Av. N&S ...25W—28N 31
Jackson Ct. E&W ..25W—28N 31
James Av. NE&SW 25W—28N 31
Kent Av. E&W ....25W—26N 39
Kimball Av. E&W ...25W—27N 39
Lake St. N&S ....25W—27N 39
Lakedale Row N&S ....26W—28N 30,31
Lake Shore Blvd. N&S ....25W—27,28N 31,39
Lake Shore Dr. N&S ....25W—28N 31
Lakeview Av. N&S,E&W ....25W—27N 39
Larkdale Row N&S 26W—27N 38,39
Laurel Av. E&W .....26W—28N 30,31
Lewis Av. E&W .....26W—27N 38,39
Liberty St. E&W ....26W—27N 38,39
Lincoln Av. NE&SW ....25W—28N 31
Lotus St. N&S ....25W—27N 39
Madison Av. N&S ..25W—28N 31
Main St. N&S ....26W—27N 38,39
Maple Av. E&W .....26W—27N 38,39
Marine Rd. E&W ...26W—28N 30,31
Mill St. NE&SW .....26W—27N 38,39
Minerva Av. E&W ..26W—27N 38,39
Monroe Av. N&S ...25W—28N 31
Nancyu Ct. NE&SW ....25W—28N 31
Neil Ct. NE&SW ....25W—28N 31
North Av. E&W ......26W—27N 38,39
North Shore Ct. NW&SE ....25W—28N 31
North Shore Dr. E&W ....25W—28N 31
Oak Dr. E&W ....25W—28N 31
Oakdale Av. E&W .25W—28N 31
Oaks Av. E&W .25,26W—27N 38,39
Oakwood Rd. N&S 26W—27N 38,39
Orton Av. NW&SE, E&W ....26W—27N 38,39
Osage St. N&S, E&W ....26W—27N 38,39
Osage Terr. NE&SW ....26W—28N 30,31
Pamela Ct. NE&SW ....25W—28N 31
Park Av. NE&SW ....25W—27,28N 31,39
Park Pl. E&W ....25W—28N 31
Park St. NE&SW ...26W—27N 38,39
Pershing Dr. E&W .25W—28N 31
Pleasant View Av. E&W ....25W—28N 31
Rand Rd. N&S, NW&SE ....26W—27,28N 31,39
Ridge Av. N&S ......25W—28N 31
Ridge Ct. E&W ......25W—27N 39
Ridge St. N&S ....25W—27N 39
Road Way NE&SW 26W—27N 38,39
Roosevelt Av. E&W ....26W—27N 38,39
Ross St. E&W ....26W—27N 38,39
Sheila Ct. E&W .....25W—28N 31
Sheridan Dr. E&W .25W—28N 31
Sky Hill Rd. N&S ...25W—27N 39
Slocum Lake Rd. E&W ....26W—27N 38,39
South St. E&W ......25W—27N 39
Summit Av. NW&SE ....25W—28N 31
Sunnyside Av. E&W ....25W—27N 39
Surf Terr. N&S ......26W—28N 30,31
Thomas Ct. N&S ...26W—27N 38,39
Van Buren Av. N&S ....25W—28N 31
Walnut Rd. E&W ...26W—28N 30,31
Washington Av. N&S ....25W—28N 31
Wauconda Rd. E&W ....25W—27N 39
Willow Rd. N&S .....26W—27N 38,39
Woodland Rd. N&S ....25W—28N 31

Waukegan Streets

Abington Ct. N&S ..14W—36N 19,20
Adams St. N&S .....10W—33N 29
Alexander Ct. N&S 10W—35N 29
Alta Vista Dr. NE&SW ....9W—36N 21
Apache Rd. N&S ...11W—36N 20,21
Apple Av. E&W ......12W—33N 28,29
Archer Av. N&S .....10W—33N 29
Arizona Av. E&W ...12W—36N 20
Armory Pl. E&W ....11W—35N 29
Arthur Ct. NE&SW 12W—34N 28,29
Arthur Dr. E&W .....11W—38N 20,21
Ash St. N&S .....10W—34,36N 21,29
Atlantic Av. E&W ....10,11W—35N 29
Auston Av. N&S ....12W—34N 28,29
Bank Ct. SE&NW ..10W—38N 21

Page

Baldwin Av. N&S
..............12W—34,35N 28,29
Ballentine St. E&W 11W—37N 20,21
Barnot At. E&W .....12W—35N 28,29
Batberry Ct. NE&SW
..............14W—32N 27,28
Beech Av. E&W ...10W—36N 21
Belevidere St. E&W
..............10,12W—33N 28,29
Benny Av. N&S ....11W—33N 29
Berry Ct. E&W ......11W—35N 29
Berwick Blvd. N&S
..............11W—34,35N 29
Bexley Pl. N&S ......10W—33N 29
Birch Av. E&W ......10W—36N 21
Birch Av. N&S ....12W—33N 28,29
Blanchard Rd. E&W
..............11W—36N 21
Blanchard Rd. E&W
..............14W—37N 19,20
Blossom Av. E&W .14W—37N 19,20
Bluff Ct. N&S ....10W—34N 29
Bluff St. E&W ....10W—34N 29
Boardman St. E&W
..............11W—37N 20,21
Bob O'Farrell Ln. E&W
..............10W—38N 21
Bonnie Brook Ln. E&W
..............11W—37N 20,21
Brentwood Ln. E&W
..............14W—36N 19,20
Briar Ln. N&S ......11W—36N 20,21
Brighton Av. E&W .10W—33N 29
Bristol Rd. N&S ....11W—37N 20,21
Brookside Av. E&W
..............11,12W—34N 28,29
Browne Ct. E&W ..10W—39N 21
Browning Av. E&W 10W—33N 29
Buck Av. E&W ..10,11W—36N 20,21
Buckingham Rd. E&W
..............11W—37N 20 21
Burris Av. E&W ...12W—36N 28,29
Burr Oak Dr. N&S 14W—37N 19,20
Burton Av. E&W ...11W—34N 29
Butrick St. N&S 11W—34,37N 21,29
Carnation Ct. N&S 10W—34N 29
Carney Av. N&S
..............11W—32,33N 29
Caroline Pl. N&S ..10W—33N 29
Carriage Ln. E&W .12W—34N 28,29
Caryn Ln. E&W ...12W—34N 28,29
Cashmoro Rd. N&S
..............14W—37N 19,20
Casimer Puaski Dr. NE&SW
..............13W—32N 27,28
Castle Ct. N&S .....11W—37N 20,21
Castle Rd. NW&SE
..............11W—38N 20,21
Catalpa Av. E&W ..11W—34N 29
Cedar Av. N&S .11W—32,34N 29
Celand Ct. SE&NW
..............14W—32N 27,28
Center St. E&W .....10W—35N 29
Central Av. E&W ...12W—34N 28,29
Chapel St. N&S ....10W—34N 28,29
Charleston Rd. N&S
..............11W—37N 20,21
Charron Ln. E&W ..11W—34N 29
Chatham Rd. N&S
..............11W—37,38N 20,21
Cherokee Rd. N&S 11W—36N 20,21
Cherry Tree Ct. E&W
..............14W—37N 19,20
Chestnut St. N&S
..............10W—34,36N 21,29
Cheyenne Rd. N&S
..............11,12W—36N 20,21
Chinook Rd. E&W .11W—36N 20,21
Chippewa Rd. N&S
..............11W—36N20 21
Choctaw Rd. E&W 11W—36N 20,21
Clearview Av. E&W
..............11W—35N 29
Clark Av. E&W ......10W—33N 29
Clarkson St. N&S ..11W—34N 29
Clayton St. E&W ...10W—34N 29
Clinton St. NS& ...10W—33N 29
Colbert Rd. E&W ..12W—34N 28,29
Coller Ct. N&S .....11W—32N 29
Colorado Av. E&W 12W—36N 19,20
Colville Pl. E&W ...10W—36N 21
Commanche Ct. E&W
..............11W—36N 20,21
Commonwealth Av. N&S
..............11W—33N 29
Continental Dr. E&W
..............14W—36N19 20
Cook Ct. E&W ......11W—33N 29
Cornelia Av. E&W .11W—34N 29
Cornelia Av. E&W .12W—34N 28,29
Cornell Rd. N&S ...11W—37N 20,21
Corona Rd. NE&SW
..............10W—36N 21
Cory Av. N&S ....10W—34N 29
County St. N&S .....10W—34N 29
Creek Rd. E&W ....11W—36N 20,21
Crescent Av. E&W 11W—35N 20,21
Crest Ct. N&S ....10W—34N 29
Crest St. E&W ....14W—37N 19,20

Page

Cummings Av. E&W
..............10W—33N 29
Cypress St. N&S ..10W—33N 29
Dady Pl. N&S ......10W—33N 29
Dahringer Rd. E&W, N&S
..............9W—35N 29
Dakota Rd. E&W ..11W—36N 20,21
Dale Ln. E&W ......11W—36N 20,21
Dana Av. E&W .....12W—36N 20
Darrow Ln. E&W ..12W—33N 28,29
Delaware Rd. N&S 11W—36N 20,21
Devonshire Rd. E&W
..............11W—37N 20,21
Dickinson St. E&W 11W—37N 20,21
Dilger Av. N&S ....12W—33N 28,29
Dodge Av. E&W ...11W—33N 29
Dorchester Av. E&W
..............12W—34N 28,29
Dorchester Ct. N&S
..............11W—34N 29
Dorothy Ct. E&W .14W—37N 19,20
Douglas Av. E&W .10W—35N 21
Douglas Cir. N&S .12W—34N 28,29
Douglas Ct. N&S ..10W—35N 29
Dover Rd. E&W ....11W—37N 20,21
Dugan St. N&S ....10W—34N 29
Dugdale Rd. NE&SW
..............11W—33N 29
Dunlay Ct. N&S ....11W—34N 29
East Dr. NW&SE ..12W—34N 27,28
East Bonnie Brook Ln. N&S
..............11W—36N 20,21
East End Av. E&W .12W—34N 28,29
Eastview Dr. N&S ..12W—35N 29
Eastwood Ct. E&W 14W—37N 19,20
Edison Ct. N&S .....11W—34N 29
Edwards St. E&W .10W—34N 29
Ellis Av. E&W ......12W—34N 28,29
Elizabeth Av. NS& .11W—32N 29
Elm St. E&W ....10W—33N 29
Elmwood Av. N&S
..............11W—32,34,36N 20,29
Emanuel Av. N&S .12W—38N 20
Ernie Krueger Cir. N&S
..............13W—36N 19,20
Evergreen Av. N&S
..............12W—33,34N 28,29
Evergreen Ct. N&S 12W—34N 28,29
Fairfield Cir. E&W .11W—35N 29
Fairfield Ct. E&W ..10W—35N 29
Ferry St. E&W ......11W—37N 20,21
Fields Terr. E&W ..11W—36N 20,21
Florence Av. E&W .12W—34N 28,29
Florida Av. E&W ...12W—36N 20
Flossmoor Av. N&S
..............11W—35N 29
Forest Av. E&W ....10W—33N 29
Forest Ct. N&S ....10W—35N 29
Forest Ln. N&S ....11W—37N 20,21
Forest St. N&S .....10W—35N 29
Franklin St. E&W ..10W—34N 29
Frazier At. E&W ...11W—37N 20,21
Frolic Av. N&S ..12W—34,36N 20,21
Fulton Av. N&S .11W—32,33N 29
Gallagher Rd. E&W
..............10W—36N 21
Garden Pl. E&W ...11W—35N 29
Gennessee St. N&S
..............10W—33,34N 29
Gent Dr. E&W .....14W—37N 19,20
George Av. E&W ..10W—33N 29
George St. E&W ..12W—34N 28,29
Georgetown Av. E&W
..............11W—36N 20,21
Gillette Av. E&W ..10W—34N 29
Gladstone Av. N&S 11W—33N 29
Gladys Ct. E&W ...10W—39N 21
Glen Ct. E&W ......10W—33N 29
Glen Dr. N&S ......11W—32N 29
Glenden N&S ....10W—36N 21
Glen Flora Av. E&W
..............9,10,11W—35N 28,29
Glen Rock Av. NE&SW
..............10W—35N 29
Glenwood Av. N&S 11W—33N 29
Golf Rd. NW&SE ..11W—36N 20,21
Golfmoor Av. E&W 12W—36N 20
Grand Av. E&W ...12W—35N 28,29
Graham Ln. E&W ..10W—38N 21
Gray Ct. E&W .....12W—33N 28,29
Greenbay Pl. E&W 12W—33N 28,29
Greenbay Rd. N&S 12W—34N 28,29
Greenfield Av. N&S 11W—32N 29
Greenwood Av. E&W
..............10,11W—36N 20,21
Gretta Av. N&S .11W—33,34N 29
Griffith Av. N&S ....10W—38N 21
Grove Av. E&W 10,12W—35N 28,29
Grove St. E&W .....10,12W—35N 29
Hamilton St. E&W .11W—34N 29
Harbor Pl. N&S ....9W—34N 29
Harding Av. E&W
..............10,11W—35N 29
Harper Rd. E&W ..11W—37N 20,21
Harrison Av. E&W 11,12W—35N 28,29
Hawthorne Ct. E&W
..............13W—36N 19,20
Hawthorne Ln. E&W
..............11W—37N 20,21
Hazel Ct. N&S ......10W—34N 29

Page

Hemholz Av. E&W .10W—33N 29
Hendee Av. E&W ..11W—37N 20,21
Henry Pl. N&S ......10W—35N 29
Herbert Dr. E&W ..11W—38N 20,21
Hickory Hills Rd. N&S
..............14W—36N 19,20
Hickory St. N&S
..............10W—34,36N 21,29
Highland Av. E&W
..............10,11W—35N 29
Highland Av. E&W 11W—38N 20,21
Highland Cir. E&W 10W—35N 29
Hill St. N&S ....10W—33N 29
Hillside Av. E&W ..12W—34N 28,29
Hilman Ct. E&W ...11W—34N 29
Hollis Av. N&S .....12W—34N 28,29
Home Av. E&W .....10W—33N 29
Hull Ct. E&W ....10W—35N 29
Huron Terr. E&W ..11W—36N 20,21
Hyde Park Av. E&W
..............12W—34N 28,29
Illini Rd. E&W ......12W—36N 20
Indian Rd. N&S ....12W—36N 20
Indiana Rd. N&S ..12W—36N 20
Iroquois Rd. E&W .12W—36N 20
Irving Pkwy. E&W .11W—38N 20,21
Jackson Ct. NE&SW
..............10W—34N 29
Jackson St. N&S
..............10W—33,35N 29
James Ct. N&S ....10W—35N 29
Jaquelyn Ln. E&W 12W—36N 20
Jefferson Av. N&S .11W—34N 29
Jenkinson Ct. E&W
..............11W—34N 29
Jolley Av. E&W ....12W—34N 28,29
Judge Av. E&W ..11W—34,36N 21,29
Judge Pl. N&S .....11W—35N 29
Julian St. E&W .....10W—34N 29
Juniper St. N&S ...10W—34N 29
Kathy Ln. E&W ....12W—34N 28,29
Keith Av. E&W .....11W—34N 29
Keller Av. N&S .....11W—35N 29
Kellogg Av. N&S ..11W—36N 20,21
Kennard St. N&S ..10W—33N 29
Kingston Rd. E&W 11W—37N 20,21
Lake Ct. E&W ......10W—33N 29
Lake St. E&W ......10W—34N 29
Lakehurst Rd. N&S 13W—33N 27,28
Lakeview Av. E&W 10W—33N 29
Lakewood Av. N&S 12W—34N 28,29
Laurel Av. E&W ...10W—34N 29
Laurel Ln. N&S ....11W—36N 20,21
Lawn Ct. E&W .....10W—34N 29
Lebaron St. N&S ..12W—34N 28,29
Lenox Av. N&S ....11W—34N 29
Leo Singer Ct. SE&NW
..............10W—38N 21
Leth Av. N&S ....11W—34,35N 29
Lewis Av. N&S ....11W—33,35N 29
Lewis Pl. N&S ......10W—35N 29
Liberty St. E&W ...10W—35N 29
Lincoln Av. N&S ..10W—33N 29
Linden Av. N&S 10W—35,36N 21,29
Lindsay Av. E&W ..10W—33N 29
Little Fort Rd. N&S 12W—36N 20
Lizabeth Ln. E&W .11W—37N 20,21
Lloyd Av. E&W ....11W—33N 29
Longview Rd. E&W
..............10W—36N 21
Loraine Av. N&S
..............11W—34,36,37N 21,29
Loraine Pl. N&S ...11W—35N 29
Lorene Ct. NE&SW
..............11W—38N 20,21
Low Av. NW&SE ..10W—34N 29
Lucia Av. N&S .11,12W—33N 28,29
Lydia St. E&W .....11W—34N 29
Lynn Terr. E&W ...11W—34N 29
Lyons Av. N&S .....11W—32N 29
Madison St. E&W ..10W—34N 29
Maple Av. N&S ....11W—33N 29
Maple Tree Ln. N&S
..............14W—37N 19,20
Marian Ct. E&W ...10W—33N 29
Mariposa Av. N&S 10W—36N 21
Market St. N&S ....10W—33N 29
Marshall St. E&W .10W—33N 29
Martin Av. N&S 11W—32,34N 29
Mary Jane Ln. E&W
..............10W—38N 21
Massena Av. E&W 10W—35N 29
May St. E&W ....10W—33N 29
McKay St. E&W ..11W—37N 20,21
McKinley Av. N&S 10W—35N 29
McAlaster Av. N&S 10W—33N 29
McAree Av. N&S
..............12W—34,36N 20,28
McArthur Dr. E&W 11W—37N 20,21
Meadow Lark Ln. N&S
..............11W—37N 20,21
Melrose Av. E&W ..11W—33N 29
Menominee Rd. E&W
..............12W—36N 20
Merton Av. N&S ...12W—36N 20
Metropolitan Av. N&S
..............12W—34,36N 20,28
Miami Rd. N&S ...12W—36N 20
Michigan Rd. NS& 12W—36N 20
Midlane Dr. N&S ..14W—37N 19,20

Page

Mill Ct. NW&SE .....10W—34N 29
Mini Dr. N&S ....14W—37N 19,20
Minoque Av. N&S ..12W—33N 28,29
Miraflores Av. NW&SE
..............10W—36N 21
Mobile Blvd. E&W .12W—33N 28,29
Mohawk Rd. E&W .12W—36N 20
Monroe St. E&W ...11W—34N 29
Monroe St. E&W ...12W—34N 28,29
Morrs Ct. E&W .....10W—38N 21
Montesano Av. E&W
..............11W—36N 20,21
Muirfield Av. N&S ..11W—35N 29
Muncey Av. N&S ...9W—35N 29
Myrtle St. N&S .....10W—35N 29
Navajo Rd. E&W ..12W—36N 20
N. Butrick St. N&S
..............11W—34,36N 21,29
Nemery Ct. N&S ..11W—35N 29
Nemesis Av. N&S ..12W—36N 20
Newcastle Rd. N&S
..............11W—37N 20,21
New York St. N&S
..............11W—35,36N 21,29
Ning Pl. N&S ....10W—36N 21
Niva St. E&W ....11W—36N 20,21
N. Jackson St. N&S
..............10W—34N 29
Noll Dr. E&W ....12W—33N 28,29
Noll St. N&S ....12W—34N 28,29
Nordigan Dr. E&W .10W—36N 21
Norma Ln. NE&SW
..............12W—34N 28,29
North Av. N&S .10W—34,36N 21,29
Northfield Av. E&W 12W—36N 20
Northmoor Av. E&W
..............11W—35N 29
Northpark Av. N&S 10W—34N 29
Northwest St. N&S 10W—34N 29
N. Utica St. N&S ...10W—34N 29
Oak St. N&S E&W
..............10W—33,34N 29
Oakland Av. E&W .12W—35N 28,29
Oakley Av. N&S ...10W—35N 29
Oak Tree Ln. E&W 14W—37N 19,20
Oakwood Av. N&S 12W—34N 28,29
Orchard Av. N&S ..11W—34N 29
Orchard Av. N&S ..12W—35N 28,29
Osage Cir. E&W ...12W—36N 20
Otto E&W ....10W—38N 21
Ottowa Rd. N&S ...12W—36N 20
Pacific Av. E&W ...10W—35N 29
Palmer Pl. N&S ....10W—35N 29
Parmalee Pl. E&W 10W—36N 21
Partridge St. E&W .11W—37N 20,21
Paul St. E&W ....11W—34N 29
Pawnee Rd. E&W .12W—36N 20
Pearsall St. E&W ..11W—33N 29
Pershing Rd. N&S
..............10W—34,35N 29
Phillipa Av. N&S ...10W—34N 29
Piccadilly Ct. N&S .10W—34N 29
Pidgen Av. NW&SE
..............12W—34N 28,29
Pikus Ctr. NW&SE 12W—34N 28,29
Pine St. N&S ....11W—34,36N 21,29
Pioneer Ct. N&S ...12W—34N 28,29
Pioneer Rd. N&S
..............12W—33,35N 28,29
Poplar St. N&S .10W—34,36N 21,29
Porter St. NW&SE 10W—34N 29
Powell Av. N&S ...10W—33N 29
Prairie Av. N&S ...12W—34N 28,29
Presscott St. N&S .10W—33N 29
Prospect St. N&S ..10W—34N 29
Public Service Av. N&S
..............12W—34N 28,29
Ravine Av. E&W ...10W—33N 29
Rice St. E&W ....11W—37N 21
Ridge Av. E&W ....12W—33N 28,29
Ridgeland Av. N&S
..............10,12W—35N 28,29
Roberts Av. N&S ..12W—37N 20
Rock Pkwy. NW&SE
..............11W—38N 21
Rogers Ct. NW&SE
..............10W—34N 29
Roger Edwards Av. E&W
..............11W—35N 29
Rudd Ct. NE&SW .14W—32N 27,28
Rugby St. N&S ....11W—37N 21
Runyard Pl. N&S ..11W—37N 21
Salem Av. N&S ....11W—34N 29
S. Bonnie Brook Ln. E&W
..............11W—36N 21
Sea Horse Dr. E&W 9W—34N 29
Seminole Rd. N&S 12W—36N 20
Sequoit Rd. E&W ..11W—36N 21
S. Fullerton Av. N&S
..............11W—33N 29
Shawnee Rd. N&S 12W—36N 20
Sheller Av. E&W ..12W—34N 28,29
Sheridan Ct. East E&W
..............10W—35N 29
Sheridan Rd. N&S
..............9,10W—33,36N 21,29
Sherman St. E&W .10W—34N 29
Shoshone Pl. E&W
..............12W—36N 20
Sioux Rd. E&W ....11W—36N 21

Page

S. Orchard N&S ....11W—35N 29
South Av. E&W ....10W—33N 29
Spaulding Av. E&W
..............12W—34N 28,29
Spitz Dr. N&S ......11W—38N 21
Spring St. N&S .....10W—34N 29
Spruce Av. E&W ..10W—36N 21
Staben Av. N&S ...12W—33N 28,29
Stanley Av. E&W ..10W—35N 29
Steele Ct. N&S .....10W—34N 29
Stewart Av. E&W ..10W—34N 29
Stonegate Rd. N&S
..............11W—37,38N 21
St. James St. N&S 10W—34N 29
Stripe Ct. N&S .....10W—34N 29
Sumac Av. N&S 11W—33,34N 29
Sunderlin St. .10W—33N 29
Sunset Av. E&W ...10W—36N 21
Sunset Rd. (Bonnie Brook Rd.)
E&W ....13W—36N 19,20
Sunset Rd. E&W ..11W—36N 20,21
Tanahill Dr. E&W ..13W—36N 19,20
Tamara St. E&W ..11W—34N 29
Taxter Av. N&S ....12W—33N 28,29
Ten Pin Ln. E&W ..10W—38E 21
Terrace Av. N&S ..10W—35N 29
Tewes Ln. E&W ....10W—38N 21
Theresa Av. E&W .12W—33N 28,29
Thompson Av. N&S .9W—36N 21
Thornberry Ct. N&S
..............14W—32N 27,28
Tobin Ct. N&S ......11W—32N 29
Twyford Rd. N&S .11W—37N 20 21
University Av. E&W 11W—34N 29
Utica St. N&S ....10W—33N 29
Varonen Av. E&W .12W—36N 20
Vermont Av. N&S ..12W—36N 20
Victory St. N&S .....10W—33N 29
Wadsworth Av. N&S
..............10W—33N 29
Walker Av. N&S .....9W—36N 21
Wall Av. E&W ......12W—36N 20
Walnut St. N&S 10W—35,36N 21,29
Wainlow Av. N&S ..10W—33N 29
Washington St. E&W
..............10,12W—34N 28,29
Washington Park N&S
..............11W—32,33N 29
Washington Terr. N&S
..............12W—34N 28,29
Water St. E&W .....10W—34N 29
Waverly Pl. E&W ..11W—35N 29
W. Bonnie Brook Ln. N&S
..............11W—36,37N 20,21
West Dr. N&S ......12W—34N 28,29
Western Av. N&S ..11W—36N 20,21
Westmoreland Av. N&S
..............11W—34,35N 29
West Waukee Rd. N&S
..............12W—34N 28,29
Wetzel Ct. E&W ...11W—34N 29
Whidden Av. N&S .11W—33N 29
Whitney St. E&W ..11W—37N 20,21
Willamsburg Av. E&W
..............11W—36N 20,21
Willow Av. N&S ...12W—33N 28,29
Willow Ct. N&S ...12W—34N 28,29
Willow Dr. E&W ..10W—36N 21
Wilson Av. E&W ..11W—36N 20,21
Winnebago Rd. N&S
..............12W—36N 20
Witchwood Ln. N&S
..............11W—37N 20,21
Wisconsin Av. N&S 11W—33N 29
Winhaven Dr. NE&SW
..............11W—38N 20,21
Wood Av. E&W ...12W—33N 28,29
Woodlawn Av. F&W
..............10W—35N 29
Woodlawn Cir. E&W
..............10W—35N 29
Worack Pl. N&S ...11W—34N 29
Yeoman St. N&S
..............11W—36,37N 20,21
Yorkhouse Rd. E&W
..............10,11W—37N 20,21
Zepher St. E&W ...12W—38N 20
1st St. E&W ....10W—34N 29
2nd St. E&W ....10W—34N 29
3rd St. E&W ....9W—36N 21
4th St. E&W ....10W—34N 29
4th St. E&W ....9W—36N 21
5th St. E&W ....9W—36N 21
6th St. E&W .....11,12W—33N 28,29
7th St. E&W ....12W—33N 28,29
8th St. E&W .....10,12W—33N 28,29
9th St. E&W .....10,12W—33N 28,29
10th Ct. E&W ....11W—32N 29
10th St. E&W ...10,11W—33N 29
11th Ct. E&W ....11W—32N 29
11th St. E&W ....11W—32N 29
11th St. E&W ....11W—32N 29
12th St. E&W ....11W—32N 29
13th St. E&W ....11W—32N 29
14th St. E&W ....11W—32N 29

Winthrop Harbor Streets
Adams Av. N&S ...10W—42N 13
Aiken Ct. N&S ....9W—41N 13
Alison St. E&W .....8W—42N 13
Alton Ct. N&S ....10W—42N 13

	Page
Beckett St. E&W .....8W—42N	13
Ben Ct. N&S ...10W—41N	13
Berong Av. NS& ...10W—42N	13
Burke Dr. E&W ...10W—41N	13
Cavin Av. N&S ...10W—42N	13
Cedar Ct. E&W ....9W—43N	13
Charles Av. N&S ...10W—42N	13
Chestnut Cir. N&S ...9W—43N	13
Clearwear Ct. NE&SW	
.............11W—43N	12,13
College Av. N&S ....9W—42N	13
Deerpath Cir. E&W .9W—42N	13
Deerpath Dr. E&W ...9W—42N	13
East Broadway Av. N&S	
.............10W—41N	13
Ellis Av. N&S ...10W—42N	13
English Ln. N&S ...10W—42N	13
Franklin Av. N&S ....9W—42N	13
Franklin St. N&S ...10W—41N	13
Frans Ct. NE&SW .10W—42N	13
Fulton Av. N&S ....9W—42N	13
Fundebark Dr. E&W	
.............10W—41N	13
Funderburk Av. ...10W—42N	13
Garnett Av. N&S ...10W—42N	13
Geddes Av. N&S ...10W—42N	13
Harbor Ln. NE&SW	
.............10W—42N	13
Highland Ct. E&W .10W—42N	13
Holdridge Av. N&S 10W—42N	13
Irene Av. N&S ...9W—42,43N	13
James Av. NW&SE 10W—42N	13
Judith Ct. N&S, E&W	
Kellogg Ct. N&S ...10W—42N	13
Kirkwood Av. N&S ...10W—42N	13
Lake Shore Rd. N&S	
.............8W—42N	13
La Lor Ct. E&W ....9W—42N	13
Landon Av. N&S ....9W—42N	13
Laurie Av. N&S ......9W—42N	13
Laurence St. E&W ..8W—43N	13
Linda St. E&W ......8W—43N	13
Madison Av. N&S ..10W—42N	13
Mae Ct. E&W ......10W—41N	13
Main Av. N&S ...9,10W—42N	13
Marion St. NS& ....8W—42N	13
Mary Av. N&S ......10W—42N	13
Meadow Ct. N&S ..11W—42N	13
Meadow Ln. N&S ..11W—42N	13
Monroe Av. N&S ...10W—41N	13
North Ave. N&S ...10W—42N	13
North Park Av. NW&SE	
.............9W—42N	13
Oakdale Av. N&S ...9W—43N	13
Park Av. N&S ......9W—42N	13
Potash St. E&W .....8W—42N	13
Prairie Av. N&S ...11W—43N	13
Ravine Av. N&S .....9W—42N	13
Roberts Rd. N&S ..10W—42N	13
Runyard Av. N&S ...9W—43N	13
Russell Av. N&S ...10W—42N	13
Sheridan Pl. E&W .10W—43N	13
Sheridan Rd. N&S ..9W—42N	13
Shields Av. N&S ...10W—42N	13
South Park Av. N&S	
.............10W—42N	13
Steven St. E&W ......8W—43N	13
Thompson Av. N&S	
.............10W—42N	13
Vista Rd. N&S ....8W—42N	13
Washington Av. N&S	
.............10W—42N	13
West Broadway Av. N&S	
.............11W—41N	13
Whitney Av. N&S ....9W—42N	13
Wilson Av. N&S ......9W—43N	13
2nd St. E&W ...9,10W—43N	13
3rd St. E&W ....9,10W—43N	13
4th St. E&W ....9,10W—43N	13
5th St. E&W ...10,11W—43N	13
6th St. E&W ......10W—42N	13
8th St. E&W ......10W—42N	13
9th St. E&W ...9,11W—42N	13
10th St. E&W ...9,11W—42N	13
11th St. E&W ...9,11W—42N	13
12th St. E&W ...9,11W—42N	13
13th St. E&W ...9,11W—42N	13
14th St. E&W ...9,11W—42N	13
15th St. E&W ...9,11W—42N	13

Zion Streets

Barnhart Av. E&W .10W—41N	13
Bethany Av. NE&SW	
.............10W—40N	13
Bethel Blvd. N&S	
.............10W—39,40N	13
Bethesda Blvd. N&S	
.............10W—40N	13
Bethlehem Av. NW&SE	
.............11W—41N	13
Caledonia Av. NW&SE	
.............9,10W—39,40N	13
Calvary Ln. N&S ...11W—40N	13
Carmel Blvd. E&W	
.............9,10W—39N	13
Champart St. E&W 11W—41N	13
Clover Ln. N&S ....10W—39N	13
Deborah Av. N&S ....9W—40N	13
Douglas Dr. E&W ..12W—42N	12
Eden Av. N&S ......9W—40N	13

	Page
Edina Blvd. N&S 9W—39,40N	13
Eli Av. N&S ....9W—40N	13
Elisha Av. N&S .10W—39,40N	13
Elizabeth Av. N&S	
.............9W—39,40N	13
Elm Av. N&S ...10W—39,40N	13
Elijah Av. N&S .10W—39,40N	13
Emmaus Av. N&S	
.............10W—39,40N	13
Enoch Av. N&S ....10W—40N	13
Eshcol Av. N&S 10W—39,40N	13
Ezekiel Av. N&S 10W—39,40N	13
Ezekiel Pl. N&S ...10W—39N	13
Ezra Av. N&S ...10W—39,40N	13
Fleming Av. N&S ..11W—41N	13
Franklin Ct. NW&SE	
.............12W—42N	12
Franklin St. N&S	
.............12W—42N	12
Gabriel Av. N&S 10W—39,40N	13
Galilee Av. N&S 11W—39,40N	13
Gideon Av. N&S 10W—39,40N	13
Gilboa Av. N&S 10W—39,40N	13
Gilead Av. N&S 10W—39,40N	13
Gregory Dr. NW&SE	
.............12W—42N	12
Hebron Av. N&S ..11W—40N	13
Hermon Av. N&S ..11W—40N	13
Hillside Av. N&S ....9W—41N	13
Hilltop Av. N&S ...11W—41N	13
Horeb Av. N&S ...11W—40N	13
Industrial Av. N&S .11W—40N	13
Jethro Av. N&S ...11W—40N	13
Joanna Av. N&S ...11W—40N	13
Joppa Av. N&S ...11W—40N	13
Jordan Av. N&S ...11W—40N	13
Leah Av. N&S ....11W—40N	13
Lear Av. N&S .....11W—40N	13
Lebanon Av. NE&SW	
.............11W—39N	13
Lorlei Av. N&S ...12W—42N	13
Lowery Ct. N&S ...11W—40N	13
Luckie Ct. NW&SE 12W—42N	12
Lydia Av. N&S ..11W—40,41N	13
Lydia Pl. N&S .....11W—40N	13
Mary-Kay Ln. N&S 10W—39N	13
Salem Blvd. E&W .11W—40N	13
Shiloh Blvd. E&W .10W—40N	13
Stella Ct. E&W ...11W—40N	13
Thompson Av. N&S	
.............10W—41N	13
Timothy St. NW&SE	
.............12W—42N	12
Willow Ln. E&W ...11W—41N	13
Wilson Ct. E&W ...10W—41N	13
Yale Av. E&W ....10W—39N	13
Yale Ct. E&W ....10W—39N	13
16th St. E&W ...9,11W—41N	13
17th St. E&W ...9,11W—41N	13
20th St. E&W ..10,11W—41N	13
23rd St. E&W ...9,11W—40N	13
24th St. E&W ..10,11W—40N	13
25th St. E&W ....11W—40N	13
26th St. E&W ....11W—40N	13
27th St. E&W ..10,11W—40N	13
28th St. E&W ...9,11W—40N	13
29th St. E&W ....11W—40W	13
30th St. E&W ..10,11W—39N	13
31st St. E&W ..10,11W—39N	13
32nd St. E&W ....11W—39N	13
33rd St. E&W ..10,11W—39N	13
34th St. E&W ....10W—39N	13

Lake County Un-Inc.
Antioch Twp. Streets

Ackerma Rd. N&S .26W—38N	14 15
Adams Cr. N&S ...22W—40N	8
Addison Ln. N&S ..25W—42N	7
Ainsley St. E&W ...23W—41N	7,8
Ann Pl. E&W .....28W—38N	14
Arbor Ln. N&S ...26W—43N	6,7
Ashbury Av. N&S .20W—39N	7,15
Ashland Av. N&S ..27W—38N	14
Ash St. N&S ......26W—43N	6,7
Banyan Av. E&W ..24W—40N	7,8
Beach Av. E&W .24W—34N	23,24
Beach Dr. N&S ...22W—40N	8
Beach Dr. E&W ...24W—43N	7,8
Beach Rd. NE&SW	
.............27W—42N	6
Beach St. E&W ...26W—42N	6,7
Beachlane Dr. N&S	
.............22W—40N	8
Beachview Dr. N&S	
.............26W—42N	6,7
Beachview Dr. E&W	
.............22W—40N	8
Bayview Dr. E&W .22W—40N	8
Bayview Rd. E&W .23W—41N	7,8
Beechwood Av. N&S	
.............28W—38N	14
Belden Av. E&W ..27W—38N	14
Benes Rd. N&S .26W—38N	14,15
Birch Av. E&W ...26W—42N	6,7
Bittersweet Pl. N&S	
.............27W—38N	14
Bluff Lake Rd. N&S	
.............25W—40N	7
Bluff Ln. E&W ....25W—40N	7
Bolton Pl. N&S .26W—38N	14,15

	Page
Briar Rd. E&W ....27W—38N	14
Briar Terr. E&W ...23W—41N	7,0
Broadway Av. N&S 26W—38N	14,15
Brown Av. N&S ....25W—41N	8
Buck Ln. NW&SE .26W—41N	6,7
Buena Terr. E&W ..23W—41N	7,8
Bunham Ct. N&S ..22W—40N	8
Burr Hollow Dr. E&W	
.............19W—41N	9
Burton Av. E&W ...28W—38N	14
Calvin Rd. E&W ...22W—40N	8
Catalpa Av. E&W ..26W—43N	6,7
Catherine Av. N&S	
.............25W—42,43N	7
Cedar Crest Ln. N&S	
.............25W—38,39N	15
Cedar Pl. NW&SE 22W—40N	8
Cedar St. E&W ...26W—42N	6,7
Center Dr. N&S ...22W—42N	8
Circle Dr. N&S	
.............25,26W—40,41N	6,7
Circle Dr. NE&SW .27W—38N	14
Channel Av. E&W .26W—40N	6,7
Channel Dr. E&W ..24W—40N	7,8
Channel Ln. E&W .26W—39N	14,15
Channel St. N&S ..28W—38N	14
Channelview Dr. N&S	
.............25W—39N	15
Chase St. N&S ...26W—42N	6,7
Cherry St. E&W ...26W—42N	6,7
Chestnut St. NW&SE	
.............26W—42N	6,7
Clara Av. N&S ....26W—41N	6,7
Claridan St. E&W .25W—42N	7
Clubhouse Rd. N&S	
.............26W—41N	6,7
Converse Rd. N&S 28W—42N	6
Crescent Av. E&W 25W—42N	7
Darrow Dr. N&S ...22W—40N	8
Dawn Cir. E&W, N&S	
.............27W—38N	14
De Coven Ct. E&W 22W—40N	8
Deer Ridge Ln. E&W	
.............24W—42N	7,8
Dell Ln. N&S .....22W—40N	8
Dewes St. E&W ...23W—40N	7,8
Diemer St. E&W ...24W—40N	7,8
Dogwood Cir. NE&SW	
.............24W—40N	7,8
Donald Dr. N&S ...22W—40N	8
Dot Av. N&S .....26W—41N	6,7
Dressels Rd. E&W 25W—40N	7
Drexel Blvd. N&S .26W—38N	14,15
East Av. E&W ....25W—41N	7
East Channel Av. E&W	
.............26W—39N	14,15
East Shore Dr. NE&SW	
.............23W—40N	7,8
Echo Dr. N&S ....25W—40N	7
Echo Rd. N&S ....25W—40N	7
Edgewood Av. E&W	
.............26W—43N	6,7
Edwards Rd. E&W 19W—42N	9
Elimie Rd. N&S ...25W—40N	7
Elm Av. E&W ....24W—39N	15,16
Elm St. N&S ......26W—42N	6,7
Elm Tree Td. E&W 26W—39N	14,15
Emerson Av. NW&SE	
.............26W—38N	14,15
Esther St. N&S ...26W—40N	6,7
Estor St. E&W ...26W—38N	14,15
Evergreen Av. N&S 26W—42N	6,7
Fairview Dr. E&W .22W—40N	8
Fairview St. N&S ..25W—40N	7
Florence Av. E&W .25W—40N	7
Forest Av. N&S ...26W—41N	6,7
Forest Av. N&S ...26W—38N	14,15
Forest Dr. N&S ...22W—42N	8
Forest Dr. N&S ...25W—39N	15
Forest Dr. N&S ...25W—43N	7
Forest Ln. NW&SE 27W—42N	6
Fox Av. E&W ....24W—42N	7,8
Fox Dr. N&S .....21W—40N	9
Fox St. N&S 26W—38N	14,15
Frederick Ct. E&W 25W—42N	7
Golfview Dr. E&W .28W—39N	14
Grimm Rd. E&W ..23W—41N	7,8
Grace Ln. E&W ...25W—40N	7
Grand Av. N&S ...25W—40N	7
Grapevine Ave E&W	
.............26W—42N	6,7
Grass Lake Rd. N&S	
...23,24W—40N & 26W—39N	7,14
Greenleaf Pl. E&W 26W—39N	14,15
Greenview Av. E&W	
.............25W—39N	15
Groveland Av. E&W	
.............27W—38N	14
Haling Rd. E&W ..26W—39N	14,15
Harlem Av. E&W ..26W—38N	14,15
Harloff Rd. E&W ..25W—40N	7
Harold Pl. NE&SW 28W—38N	14
Haskel St. E&W ..28W—38N	14
Hawthorne Av. E&W	
.............25W—39N	15
Hawthorne Ln. E&W	
.............24W—41N	7,8
Heart O Lakes Blvd. E&W	
.............25W—40N	7
Herman Av. E&W .25W—39N	15

	Page
Hickory Av. N&S ...25W—39N	15
Hickory Ln. N&S ...25W—43N	7
Hickory St. N&S ...25W—41N	7
Hickory St. N&S ...28W—39N	14
High St. N&S .....26W—38N	14,15
Highland Av. E&W	
.............25,26W—38,39N	14,15
Highview Dr. N&S .25W—39N	15
Highview Rd. E&W 24W—42N	7,8
Highwood Av. E&W	
.............24W—39N	15,16
Hillandale Dr. E&W 27W—38N	14
Hillcrest Av. E&W	
.............25,26W—40,42N	6,7
Hilldale Av. E&W ..25W—39N	15
Hill Dr. E&W .....27W—39N	14
Hillside Av. N&S ..27W—38N	14
Hillside Av. NW&SE	
.............26W—39N	14,15
Hillside Ln. N&S ..25W—41N	8
Hilltop Av. NE&SW 26W—38N	14,15
Hook Cir. NW&SE 25W—41N	8
Island Dr. E&W ...24W—43N	7,8
Jackson Dr. N&S ..27W—39N	14
James Av. N&S ...26W—41N	6,7
James Rd. N&S ...28W—41N	6
Janette St. N&S ...25W—41N	7
Judson St. N&S ...28W—38N	14
Julia Ct. N&S .....23W—41N	7,8
Kairys St. N&S ....23W—43N	7,8
Karen Ct. N&S ....23W—41N	7,8
Kathryn Dr. E&W .23W—41N	7,8
Kenmore Rd. E&W 26W—38N	14,15
Klondike Av. E&W .26W—36N	14,15
Lagoon Ct. N&S ...25W—41N	7
Lake Av. N&S ...25,26W—42N	6,7
Lake Av. E&W ...26W—39N	14,15
Lake Av. NW&SE .25W—40N	7
Lake Blvd. NW&SE	
.............25W—40N	7
Lake Ct. E&W ....22W—40N	8
Lake Dr. N&S ....25W—42N	7
Lake Rd. NW&SE .22W—40N	8
Lake Rd. NE&SW .26W—39N	14,15
Lake Bluff Dr. N&S 22W—40N	8
Lake Center Blvd. N&S	
.............25W—39N	15
Lake East Dr. N&S 25W—40N	7
Lake Shore Dr. E&W	
.............23W—40N	7,8
Lake Shore Dr. E&W	
.............27W—38N	14
Lake Shore Dr. N&S	
.............25W—40N	7
Lakeside Pl. N&S .26W—38N	14,15
Lake St. N&S ..25,26W—42N	6,7
Lake St. N&S ....27W—38N	14
Lakeview Av. E&W	
.............25W—40,43N	7
Lakeview Av. N&S .25W—40N	7
Lakeview Ct. N&S .22W—40N	8
Lakeview Dr. E&W 23W—40N	7,8
Lakeview Dr. E&W 23W—40N	7,8
Lakeview Av. N&S .22W—40N	8
Lakeview Rd. N&S 26W—39N	14,15
Lakeview Terr. N&S	
.............23W—41N	7,8
Lake Vista Av. E&W	
.............23W—41N	7,8
Lanet Ct. N&S ....25W—39N	15
Lawson Av. E&W ..27W—42N	6
Lee Dr. E&W .....25W—40N	7
Leland Av. E&W ..26W—38N	14,15
Lilac Pl. N&S .....24W—40N	7,8
Lilian Av. E&W ....25W—43N	7
Lillian Pl. N&S ....22W—41N	8
Lincoln Av. N&S ..27W—38N	14
Lincoln Dr. N&S ..22W—41N	8
Linden Ln. E&W ..25W—43N	7
Linden Ln. N&S ...25W—42N	7
Linden Rd. E&W ..25W—43N	6,7
Little Silver Lake Re. N&S	
.............22W—40N	8
Lolcott Ln. E&W ..24W—40N	7,8
Loon Dr. E&W ....22W—40N	8
Loon Lake Rd. E&W	
.............22W—40N	8
Lotus Av. E&W ...27W—38N	14
Lotus Av. N&S ...26W—41N	6,7
Lotus Ln. E&W ...26W—39N	14,15
Lotus Rd. N&S, E&W	
.............26W—39N	14,15
Madison Av. N&S .22W—41N	8
Magnolia Dr. N&S .24W—40N	7,8
Mallard Dr. N&S ..26W—40N	6,7
Maple Av. E&W ...26W—42N	6,7
Maple Dr. N&S ...25W—43N	7
Maple Ln. N&S ...25W—42N	7
Maple Ln. NE&SW 22W—40N	8
Marcus Av. N&S ..25W—40N	7
Marcus Rd. N&S ..25W—40N	7
Margaret St. N&S .26W—40N	6,7
Margate Terr. E&W 23W—41N	7,8
Marie Av. E&W	
.............25,26W—41,42N	6,7
Marie Av. NW&SE .26W—41N	6,7
Mary Av. N&S ....25W—43N	7
Maryann Rd. E&W 26W—41N	6,7
Masaryk Rd. N&S .24W—40N	7,8

	Page
May St. E&W .....25W—41N	
May St. NW&SE ..28W—38N	14
McMillan Rd. N&S .23W—41N	7,8
Meadow Ln. E&W .24W—41N	
Meadow Ln. N&S .24W—42N	6,7
Melva Av. N&S ...25W—43N	7
Michele Ln. E&W .21W—40N	9
Michigan Blvd. E&W	
.............26W—38N	14,15
Mildred Av. N&S ..25W—43N	7
Miller Rd. E&W ...20W—40N	9
Mills N&S ....26W—40N	6,7
Mill St. N&S .....26W—42N	6,7
Milwaukee Av. N&S	
.............23W—41N	7,8
Mitchell Ln. N&S ..22W—40N	8
Montrose Rd. E&W 26W—38N	14,15
Morley Rd. N&S ..24W—43N	7,8
Mound Av. N&S ..27W—39N	14
Muriel Rd. E&W ..28W—38N	14
Nevelier Dr. N&S .24W—40N	7,8
New Venice Way N&S	
.............24W—43N	7,8
Nippersink N&S 28W—38N	14
North Av. E&W .21,22W—40N	8,9
North Av. E&W ...24W—43N	7,8
North Av. E&W ...25W—42N	7
Norman Dr. E&W .25W—39N	15
North Dr. E&W ...22W—40N	8
North Rd. E&W ...24W—39N	15,16
North St. E&W ...23W—40N	7,8
Northview Ln. E&W	
.............26W—42N	6,7
North Way N&S ..26W—42N	14,15
Oak Av. N&S .....24W—39N	15,16
Oak Av. E&W ....26W—40N	6,7
Oak Av. 24,25W—39,40N	15,16
Oak Dr. N&S .....24W—39N	15,16
Oak Dr. N&S .....25W—43N	7
Oak Ln. E&W ....25W—43N	7
Oak Ln. N&S .....26W—42N	6,7
Oakland St. E&W .27W—38N	14
Oak Lang Dr. E&W 22W—40N	8
Olive Ct. N&S ....25W—41N	7
Orchard Av. E&W .26W—42N	6,7
Orchard Ln. N&S .25W—42N	7
Orchard Ln. E&W .22W—40N	8
Park Av. N&S ....22W—40N	8
Park Av. E&W .24W—39,42N	7,8
Park Av. N&S .26,28W—38N	14,15
Park Av. N&S ....27W—38N	6
Park Blvd. N&S ...26W—40N	7
Park Ct. E&W ....25W—42N	7
Park Dr. E&W ....22W—40N	8
Park Dr. E&W ....25W—43N	7
Park Ln. N&S ....25W—42N	7
Park Ln. E&W ....22W—40N	8
Park Pl. NW&SE .26W—42N	6,7
Park St. N&S ....25W—43N	7
Park St. N&S ....26W—38N	14,15
Park Terr. E&W	
.............22,23W—40,41N	7,8
Park Terr. N&S ...25W—43N	7
Parkview Dr. NW&SE	
.............26W—41N	6,7
Pauline St. N&S ..26W—39N	14,15
Pearl Rd. N&S ...26W—39N	14,15
Pearl St. E&W ...28W—38N	14
Pederson Dr. E&W 19W—41N	9
Pederson Dr., S. N&S	
.............19W—41N	9
Petite Av. E&W ...25W—42N	7
Petite Ct. E&W ...24W—39N	15,16
Petite Pass N&S ..25W—39N	15
Petite Terr. N&S ..24W—39N	15,16
Pine Ln. E&W ....25W—43N	7
Pine St. E&W ....26W—42N	6,7
Pineview Dr. E&W 22W—40N	8
Point Rd. N&S ...23W—41N	7,8
Poplar Av. N&S ..25W—42N	6,7
Poplar Ct. N&S ..26W—42N	6,7
Prairie Av. N&S ..25W—42N	7,8
Primrose Ln. N&S .27W—38N	14
Prospect Av. E&W 26W—42N	6,7
Ravine Av. E&W ..24W—39N	15,16
Ravine Ct. NW&SE	
.............24W—39N	15,16
Ravine Dr. E&W ..27W—39N	14
Ravine Dr. E&W ..24W—39N	15,16
Rowe Av. E&W ...26W—38N	14,15
Regina Rd. N&S ..21W—40N	9
Rena Av. N&S ....25W—39N	15
Resthaven E&W ..25W—39N	15
Richmond Av. E&W	
.............25W—39N	15
Richmond Rd. NE&SW	
.............26W—41N	6,7
Ridge Dr. N&S ...22W—42N	8
Riverside Rd. E&W 25W—41N	8
Riverview Dr. E&W 26W—41N	6,7
Riverview Pl. NW&SE	
.............26W—41N	6,7
Sarana Dr. E&W ..22W—40N	8
Savage Rd. N&S ..20W—40N	9
Shady Ln. N&S ...25W—40N	8
Sherwin Av. E&W 26W—38N	14,15
Shore Av. NE&SW 26W—39N	14,15
Shannon Dr. E&W .26W—42N	6,7
Sibley Dr. N&S ...25W—40N	7

	Page
Silver Lake Av. E&W ....22W—42N	8
Simon Dr. E&W ...25W—39N	15
South Dr. N&S ......24W—39N	15,16
South Dr. E&W ......22W—40N	8
Spring Av. E&W ....27W—42N	6
Spring Grove Rd. NE&SW ....26W—42N	6,7
Spring Well Av. E&W ....26W—39N	14,15
Spruce Dr. E&W ...22W—40N	8
Spruce St. E&W ...26W—42N	6,7
Stanton Rd. E&W ..22W—40N	8
............19W—43N	9
State Park Rd. N&S, E&W ....28W—39N	14
Sterling Av. E&W ..28W—38N	14
Stewart Av. NW&SE ....27W—38N	14
St. James St. E&W 28W—38N	14
Stonegate Av. NW&SE ....27W—38N	14
Stonegate Dr. E&W ....27W—38N	14
Summerside Dr. N&S ....25W—39N	15
Sunker Ct. E&W ...22W—41N	8
Sunset Av. E&W ...27W—38N	14
Sunset Ct. E&W ...24W—40N	7,8
Sunset Dr. E&W ...24W—40N	7,8
Sunset Rd. E&W ...26W—43N	6 7
Suraya Dr. N&S ...23W—41N	7 8
Sycamore Av. E&W ....26W—43N	6 7
Sylvan Dr. E&W ...25W—43N	7
Sylvan Woods Dr. E&W ....25W—43N	7
Sylvan Woods Rd. E&W ....24W—43N	7,8
Tammi Terr. NW&SE ....19W—41N	9
Taylor Ct. E&W ...22W—41N	8
Terry Ln. NW&SE ..24W—40N	7,8
Tiffany Rd. N&S ...24W—42N	7,8
Town Line Rd. E&W ....24W—40N	7,8
Tracy Ln. NW&SE ..24W—40N	7,8
Trevor Rd. E&W ...24W—43N	7,8
Trinity Ln. NE&SW 24W—40N	7,8
Trillium Pl. N&S ...27W—38N	14
Venetian Dr. N&S .24W—43N	7,8
Venn Rd. NW&SE ..25W—41N	7
Vinena Av. N&S ...25W—40N	7
Villa Rica Rd. E&W 22W—40N	8
Villa Rica Rd. NE&SW ....23W—40N	7,8
Vine St. E&W ......26W—38N	14,15
Vineland Av. N&S .27W—38N	14
Virell Dr. E&W ....22W—40N	8
Washington Av. N&S ....27W—38N	14
Washington St. E&W ....22W—41N	8
Watts Av. NE&SW .28W—38N	14
Wedgewood Dr. E&W ....22W—40N	8
West End Av. N&S 27W—39N	14
West Lake Av. N&S ....25W—41N	7
West Shore Av. N&S ....23W—40N	7,8
White Rd. NE&SW 21W—40N	9
Whitehall Ct. E&W 25W—41N	9
Willow Av. N&S ...25W—43N	7
Willow Rd. N&S ...25W—42N	7
Willow St. NE&SW 26W—39N	14,15
Wilmot Rd. E&W ....26,27W—43N	6,7
Winsor Terr. E&W .23W—41N	7,8
Wilson Rd. E&W ..26W—38N	14,14
Woodbine Av. E&W ....26W—42N	6,7
Woodbine Av. N&S 26W—42N	6,7
Wood Cir. E&W ...25W—42N	7
Wood Dr. N&S ....25W—42N	7
Woodland Av. E&W ....25W—39,40N	7,15
Woodland Av. N&S ....27W—38N	14
Woodland Pl. NW&SE ....27W—42N	6
Woodlawn Av. E&W ....25W—43N	7
Woodmere Terr. NW&SE ....19W—41N	9
Woodside Av. N&S 25W—39N	15
1st St. E&W ....25W—43N	7
1st St. N&S ....25W—42N	7
1st Av. N&S ....27W—38N	14
2nd St. E&W ....25W—42N	7
2nd St. E&W ....25W—42N	7
2nd St. N&S ....23W—41N	7,8
2nd Av. N&S ....27W—38N	14
3rd St. E&W ....25W—42N	7
3rd St. N&S ....23W—41N	7,8
3rd St. N&S ....27W—38N	14
3rd Av. N&S ....27W—38N	14
4th St. N&S ....25W—42N	7
4th Av. N&S ....27W—38N	14

	Page
5th Av. N&S ....27W—38N	14
6th Av. N&S ....25W—42N	7
6th Av. N&S ....28W—38N	14
7th St. N&S ....25W—42N	7
7th Av. N&S ....28W—38N	14
8th St. N&S ....28W—38N	14
9th St. N&S ....28W—38N	14
10th Av. N&S ....28W—38N	14
11th Av. N&S ....28W—38N	14

Avon Twp. Streets

	Page
Acre Ct. E&W ......22W—35N	24
Alleghany Rd. N&S 21W—33N	25
Atkinson Rd. N&S .20W—33N	25
Bacon Rd. N&S ....24W—32N	23,24
Beech Ct. E&W ....22W—34N	24
Belvidere Rd. E&W 19W—32N	25
Brae Loch Rd. E&W ....19W—33N	25
Brobson Av. E&W .24W—35N	23,24
Cedar Av. N&S ....22W—34N	24
Cedar Ln. N&S ....22W—34N	24
Center St. E&W ...19W—33N	25
Clinton Av. N&S ..24W—35N	23,24
Curran Rd. N&S,E&W ....24W—32N	23,24
East End Av. N&S .22W—34N	24
Eldor Av. E&W .....21W—34N	25
Fairfield Rd. N&S .24W—32N	23,24
Forest Av. E&W ...24W—35N	23,24
Garfield Blvd. N&S 20W—32N	25
Gerwal Av. N&S ...24W—34N	25
Grand Av. NW&SE 19W—32N	17
Harrison Av. N&S .24W—34N	23,24
Harris Rd. N&S ...19W—32N	25
Hart Rd. E&W .....24W—34N	23,24
Hauge St. N&S ....24W—35N	23,24
Hawthorne Dr. E&W ....24W—35N	23,24
Hendee Av. N&S ..22W—34N	24
Hickory Av. N&S .22W—34N	24
Hickory Ln. N&S ....21,22W—34N	24,25
Hickory Ln. E&W ..24W—35N	23,24
Hickory St. E&W ..24W—35N	23,24
Hillside Av. N&S ..24W—35N	23,24
Ivanhoe Rd. N&S .20W—32N	25
Lake Av. N&S .....22W—34N	24
Lake Av. N&S .....21W—34N	25
Lake Ct. E&W .....22W—34N	24
Lake Dr. E&W .....24W—35N	23,24
Lake Park Av. E&W ....22W—34N	24
Lake Shore Dr. N&S ....21,22W—34N	24,25
Lake Shore Dr. NW&SE ....24W—35N	23,24
Lakeview Av. E&W 22W—34N	24
Lilac Av. N&S .....22W—34N	24
Luther Av. E&W ...24W—35N	23 24
McKinley Av. N&S .20W—32N	25
Merriwood Ln. E&W ....22W—34N	24
Michigan Av. E&W 24W—35N	23,24
Nielson Av. N&S ..24W—35N	23,24
Norelius Av. N&S .24W—35N	23,24
N. Circle Dr. N&S .22W—34N	24
Oak Av. N&S ......22W—34N	24
Oak Ct. N&S,E&W 19W—35N	25
Oak St. E&W ......24W—35N	23,24
Old Rollins Rd. NW&SE ....19W—35N	25
Orchard Ln. N&S .22W—35N	24
Orchard Pl. E&W ..24W—35N	23,24
Passavant Av. E&W ....24W—35N	23,24
Poplar St. E&W ...24W—35N	23,24
Rollins Rd. NW&SE ....19W—35N	25
Ross Av. N&S .....24W—34N	23,24
Round Lake Rd. NW&SE ....24W—35N	23,24
Shorewood Dr. E&W ....22W—34N	24
Shorewood Rd. E&W ....21W—35N	25
Shorewood Rd. N&S ....20W—35N	25
S. Circle Dr. NW&SE ....22W—34N	24
Stub Av. E&W .....24W—35N	23,24
Summit St. N&S ..24W—35N	23,24
Sunset Dr. E&W ...23W—34N	23,24
Terri Ln. E&W .....20W—35N	25
Thompson St. N&S 24W—35N	23,24
Todd Dr. E&W .....20W—35N	25
Tyler Dr. E&W .....24W—34N	23,24
Wabash Av. N&S ....24W—35N	23,24
Washington St. E&W ....19,21W—34N	25
Wilmar Av. E&W ..21W—34N	25
Wilson Blvd. N&S .24W—35N	23,24

Benton-Zion Twp. Streets

	Page
Adelphi Av. N&S ....12W—38,39N	12,20
Ames Av. E&W ...10W—39N	13,21
Ash Ct. E&W ......12W—40N	12
Barnhart Ct. E&W .9W—41N	13

	Page
Beach Pl. E&W .....10W—38N	21
Beach Rd. E&W .9,11W—38N	20,21
Bernice Terr. N&S .11W—39N	13,21
Block Ln. E&W .....11W—43N	12,13
Bowling Av. N&S ..12W—39N	12,20
Brockway Av. N&S ..9W—40N	13
Broecker Av. N&S .11W—42N	12,13
Burnett Av. N&S ....8W—40N	13
California Av. E&W 10W—39N	13,21
Carnahan Av. E&W ....11W—38N	20,21
Cedar Av. N&S ....11W—38N	20,21
Center St. E&W 10,12W—38N	28,29
Chaney Av. E&W ..10W—38N	21
Chaney St. E&W ..12W—38N	20
Chaplin Av. E&W ..12W—38N	21
Chaplin St. E&W ..12W—38N	20
Chicago Av. E&W .10W—39N	13,21
Chicago Ln. N&S ...9W—41N	13
Circle Dr. E&W ...10W—39N	13,21
Clarendon Rd. E&W ....12W—38N	20
Coolidge Av. N&S .10W—38N	21
Coral Ln. NW&SE .11W—39N	13,21
Cornell St. N&S ...12W—40N	12
Crissy Av. E&W ...10W—38N	21
Delores Av. E&W ..12W—38N	20
Dewoody Dr. N&S 11W—38N	20,21
Dodson St. E&W ..11W—42N	12,13
Douglas St. E&W ..12W—38N	20
Dowie Memorial Dr. NW&SE ....10W—38N	13
Edward St. E&W ..11W—42N	12,13
Emmanuel Av. N&S ....12W—38N	20
E. Ravine Dr. NE&SW ....10W—41N	13
Everett Rd. E&W ..11W—38N	20,21
Evergreen Av. E&W 12W—38N	20
Fago Av. N&S ...11W—42,43N	12,13
Fairbanks Av. E&W 10W—38N	21
Ford Av. E&W .....10W—38N	21
Ford St. E&W .....12W—38N	20
Forman Dr. E&W,N&S ....12W—42N	12
Fossiands Av. N&S ....11W—42,43N	12,13
Frolic Av. E&W ...12W—39N	12,20
Fulton Av. N&S ....8W—40N	13
Garnett Av. N&S ....10W—38,39N	13,21
Geneva Ln. N&S ..11W—39N	13,21
Geraghty Av. N&S .10W—38N	21
Gilbert Av. E&W ..10W—38N	21
Gish Av. N&S .....10W—38N	21
Glendale Rd. N&S 11W—40N	12,13
Green Av. N&S ...12W—39N	12,20
Green Bay Rd. N&S ....12W—36,39N	12,20
Harding St. N&S ..10W—38N	21
Hart Av. E&W .....10W—38N	21
Hart St. E&W .....12W—38N	20
Hanks Av. N&S 11W—42,43N	12,13
Hickory Ln. E&W ..12W—38N	20
Hickory Rd. E&W .11W—38N	20,21
Holridge Av. N&S .10W—38N	21
Howard St. E&W ....10,12W—38N	20,21
Howland Av. N&S ..9W—40N	13
Illinois Av. E&W 10,12W—39N	12,13
Illinois St. N&S ...10W—41N	13
Jensen Av. N&S ..11W—43N	12,13
Johnson Rd. E&W .11W—39N	20,21
Joyce Av. N&S ....10W—38N	21
Kedron Blvd. E&W 10W—41N	13
Kenosha Rd. N&S ....11,12W—40,42N	12,13
Lake St. E&W ....9W—38N	21
Lake Front Dr. N&S 11W—38N	13
Lakeside Av. N&S ..9W—40N	13
Lakeview Av. N&S ....9W—38,41N	13,21
Loland Av. E&W ...11W—38N	20,21
Lewis Av. N&S ....11W—43N	12,13
Liberty Av. E&W ..10W—39N	13,21
Liberty Ct. E&W ..10W—38N	21
Lincoln Av. N&S ..10W—38N	21
Linden Av. N&S ...11W—38N	20,21
Logan Ct. E&W ..9,10W—41N	13
Lone Oak Rd. N&S 12W—40N	12
Lybach Av. E&W ..12W—38N	12,20
Lynn Dale Dr. N&S 12W—43N	12
Major Av. E&W ...12W—38N	12,20
Major Av. N&S ...12W—39N	12,20
Maplewood Rd. E&W ....12W—39N	12,20
Marguerite Rd. N&S 10W—38N	21
Marguérite Ln. E&W 9W—38N	21
Mather Av. N&S ..11W—42N	12,13
McAree Av. N&S ..12W—38N	20
McAree Rd. NE&SW ....11W—38N	20,21
Metropolitan Av. N&S ....12W—39N	12,20
Michigan Blvd. E&W 9W—38N	21
Mills Av. N&S .....8W—40N	13
Minturn Av. E&W .12W—38N	20
Morse Av ... N&S ..9W—40N	13
Morse Av. N&S ...12W—38N	20
New York Av. N&S 11W—38N	20,21

	Page
Noble Av. N&S .....12W—38N	20
North Av. N&S ..10W—38,39N	13,21
Northern Av. N&S .12W—38N	20
North Shore Av. N&S ....10W—38N	21
Oak Av. E&W .....11W—38N	20,21
Oak Ln. E&W .....11W—43N	12,13
Oakcrest Av. N&S .12W—43N	12
Oakforest Dr. E&W .9W—38N	21
Orbers Av. N&S ...12W—38N	20
Park Av ..... N&S ..9W—38N	21
Parkview Av. N&S ..9W—40N	13
Paxton Av. N&S ...9W—39N	13,21
Peacock Rd. E&W 12W—39N	12,20
Pearsal Av. N&S ...9W—40N	13
Pickford Av. N&S .12W—38N	20
Pickford St. E&W .12W—38N	20
Pine Av. N&S .....11W—38N	20,21
Pine Ct. E&W .....12W—40N	12
Prairie Av. N&S ...11W—43N	12,13
Princeton Av. E&W 12W—39N	12,20
Prospect Av. E&W .12W—40N	13
Ravine Av. E&W ..10W—41N	12,13
Reiner Pl. E&W ...12W—38N	21
Reiner St. E&W ...12W—38N	20
Richard Pl. E&W ..11W—39N	13,21
Rita Av. E&W .....12W—40N	13
Russell Av. N&S ..10W—38N	21
Ruth Av. N&S .....12W—38N	20
Sheridan Pl. N&S .10W—38N	21
Sheridan Rd. N&S .9W—38N	21
Short Av. N&S .....8W—40N	13
Stewart Av. N&S ..10W—38N	21
Strong Av. N&S ....9W—40N	13
Suddard Pl. E&W ..9W—38N	21
Suddard St. E&W .12W—38N	20
Talmadge Av. E&W 10W—38N	21
Tewes Ct. N&S ....10W—38N	21
Thorpe Av. N&S ..11W—42N	12,13
Transportation Av. N&S ....9W—40N	13
Wadsworth Rd. E&W ....10W—39N	13,21
Waldo Av. E&W 10,12W—39N	12,13
Wilmont Av. N&S ..9W—40N	13
Wilson Ct. E&W ...11W—39N	13
Winthrop Ct. E&W ....9,10W—41N	13
Winthrop Harbor Rd. E&W ....12W—42N	12
Woodland Av. E&W ....10W—38N	21
Wyer St. E&W .10,12W—38N	20
Zepher St. E&W ..12W—38N	20
3rd St. E&W ......11W—43N	12,13
4th St. E&W ......11W—43N	12,13
5th St. E&W ......11W—43N	12,13
9th St. E&W ......11W—42N	12,13
10th St. E&W .....11W—42N	12,13
11th St. E&W .....11W—42N	12,13
12th St. E&W .....11W—42N	12,13
13th St. E&W .....11W—42N	12,13
17th St. E&W ...10,11W—41N	12,13
18th St. E&W .....9,10W—41N	13
19th St. E&W .....9,10W—41N	13
20th St. E&W .....9W—41N	13
21st St. E&W .....9W—41N	13
22nd St. E&W .....9W—40N	13
22nd St. E&W .....9W—40N	13
27th St. E&W .....12W—40N	12
28th St. E&W .....12W—40N	12
29th St. E&W .....12W—40N	12
32nd St. E&W .....12W—39N	12,20
33rd St. E&W .....12W—39N	12,20

Cuba Twp. Streets

	Page
Apple Tree Ln. E&W ....26W—22N	47
Arrowhead Ln. N&S ....25W—24N	39
Barrington Rd. N&S ....26W—21N	47
Beach Dr. E&W ..28W—24N	38
Beech Way NW&SE ....28W—24N	38
Bertha Ln. N&S ...26W—22N	47
Bloners Dr. E&W ..28W—24N	38
Bluff Ln. E&W ....28W—23N	46
Border Rd. N&S ..25W—22N	47
Brant Rd. E&W ...26W—21N	47
Broken Bow Pass NW&SE ....26W—24N	38,39
Canyon Creek Ct. N&S ....26W—25N	38,39
Chamberlain Dr. E&W ....28W—23N	46
Chatham Rd. E&W 25W—21N	47
Church Rd. N&S ...28W—23N	46
Columbus Dr NE&SW ....25W—21N	47
Country Estates Rd. E&W ....26W—21N	47
Countryside Ln. N&S ....26W—22N	47
County Line Rd. N&S ....28W—22,23N	46
Craft Ct. NE&SW .26W—21N	47
Crestview Dr. N&S,E&W ....25W—21N	47
Cuba Rd. E&W 26,27W—21N	46,47

	Page
Drake Rd. E&W ...25W—21N	47
East Dr. N&S ......28W—23N	46
Edgemond Ln. E&W ....26W—22N	47
Edgewood Av. E&W ....28W—24N	38
Elizabeth Ln. N&S .25W—21N	47
Falkirk Cir. E&W ...26W—21N	47
Fairhaven Dr. NE&SW ....25W—21N	47
Flint Creek Dr. N&S ....27W—23N	46
Fox River Dr. NE&SW ....28W—24N	38
Fox River Rd. E&W ....28W—24N	38
Glenbarr Ln. NW&SE ....26W—21N	47
Fox St. E&W ....28W—23N	46
Grand View Dr. NE&SW ....25W—24N	39
Grant St. E&W .....27W—21N	46
Greenwood Ln. N&S ....25W—25N	39
Hanover Hill NW&SE ....25W—21N	47
Hart Rd. N&S .....26W—21N	47
Hess Dr. N&S .....28W—23N	46
High Ridge Rd. E&W ....25W—21N	47
Hillcrest Av. E&W .28W—24N	38
Hillside Rd. N&S ..28W—23N	46
Hipplers Rd. E&W .25W—21N	47
Holly Dr. N&S .....28W—24N	38
Hough Rd. N&S ...25W—20N	47
Jensen Av. NW&SE ....28W—24N	38
Kelsey Av. N&S ...28W—23N	46
Kelsey Ct. E&W ...28W—23N	46
Kelsey Rd. N&S ...28W—23N	46
Knollwood Dr. N&S 25W—25N	39
Kristy Ln. N&S ....28W—24N	38
Lagoon Dr. N&S ..27W—24N	38
Lakeshore Dr. E&W ....25W—21N	47
Lake Shore Dr. NW&SE ....25W—25N	39
Lakeview Pkwy. N&S, E&W ....25W—25N	39
Lake Zurich Rd. N&S ....25W—21N	47
Laurine Dr. E&W ..25W—21N	47
Lincoln St. E&W ..27W—21N	46
Lindbergh Dr. E&W ....28,29W—23N	46
Main St. NE&SW ..28W—24N	38
Meadow Ln. N&S .28W—23N	46
Merton Rd. E&W ..26W—20N	47
Midway St. E&W ..28W—23N	46
North Dr. E&W ...28W—23N	46
North Oaks Ct. N&S ....25W—25N	39
Northwest Hwy. NW&SE ....28W—22N	46
Oak Creek Cir. NE&SW ....25W—25N	39
Oakland Av. N&S .28W—24N	38
Oakridge Rd. E&W 25W—25N	39
Oakwood Dr. NE&SW ....25W—25N	39
Oakwood Dr. E. N&S ....25W—25N	39
Park Dr. E&W .....28W—23N	46
Park St. E&W .....28W—23N	46
Pepper Rd. E&W ..28W—23N	46
Pioneer Grove Rd. E&W ....28W—23N	46
Pitner Av. E&W ...28W—24N	38
Prestick Dr. N&S ..26W—21N	47
Providence Rd. E&W ....25W—21N	47
Ravine Dr. E&W ..28W—23N	46
Redwing Ln. N&S .25W—25N	39
River Rd. NE&SW .28W—23N	46
Rivershore Dr. N&S ....27W—24N	38
Riverside Dr. NE&SW ....28W—24N	38
River St. N&S .....28W—23N	46
Roslyn Rd. E&W ..26W—20N	47
Rustic Ln. E&W ...28W—24N	38
Scott Rd. E&W .25,27W—22N	46,47
Short St. N&S .....28W—24N	38
South St. E&W ....28W—23N	46
Spring Dr. N&S ...28W—23N	46
Summit Dr. N&S ..28W—23N	46
Sunset Ln. E&W ..28W—24N	38
Sunset Ln. E&W ..25W—21N	47
Sunset Rd. E&W ..25W—21N	47
Sylvester St. NW&SE ....28W—24N	38
Tara Dr. E&W .....25W—25N	39
Taylor Rd. N&S ...26W—20N	47
Timber Canyon Creek Ct. N&S ....26W—25N	38,39
Timberlake Pkwy. ....25W—25N	39
Timberlake Rd. E&W ....25W—25N	39

Page

Wagon Wheel Ct. N&S
..............25W—25N   39
West Oakwood Dr. N&S
..............25W—25N   39
Wildwood Dr. E&W 25W—25N   39
Woodland Av. N&S 25W—21N   47
17th St. N&S ....26W—21N   47
18th St. N&S ....26W—21N   47
19th St. N&S ....26W—21N   47
20th St. N&S ....26W—21N   47
21st St. N&S ....27W—21N   46
22nd St. N&S ......27W—21N   46
23rd St. N&S ....27W—21N   46
24th St. N&S ....27W—21N   46
25th St. N&S ...27,28W—21N   46

Ela Twp.

Anna Ct. N&S ...24W—25N 39,40
Arrowhead Dr. N&S
..............19W—25N   41
Aspen Dr. E&W ...19W—25N   41
August Ln. E&W ...24W—25N 39,40
Bagpipe Ct. E&W .23W—25N 39,40
Bonnyrigg Ct. E&W
..............23W—25N 39,40
Border Rd. N&S ...26W—21N   47
Briggs Dr. NE&SW 23W—23N   48
Buckeye Rd. N&S, E&W
..............23W—20N   48
Cabriel Ct. E&W ...22W—24N   40
Cabriel Dr. N&S ...22W—24N   40
Cattail Ln. E&W ...23W—20N   48
Cedar Ln. E&W ....23W—23N   48
Cedar St. E&W ....23W—22N   48
Cherry Ln. E&W ...23W—23N   48
Clover Hill Ln. N&S, E&W
..............23W—23N   48
Columbia Ct. E&W 21W—25N   41
Crestwood Ln. E&W
..............23W—23N   48
Deerpath Rd. N&S ...23W—21N   48
Driftwood Dr. (Pvt. Rd.)
NW&SE ....19W—22N   49
Eagle Dr. N&S ....19W—25N   41
East Ln. N&S ......23W—23N   48
Echo Lake Rd. NE&SW
..............23W—23N   48
Echo Ln. N&S .....23W—23N   48
Ellrie Terr. N&S ...24W—25N 39,40
Fairfield Rd. NW&SE
..............22W—25N   40
Florence Av. N&S .23W—22N   48
Grand Av. ....23W—22N   48
Grand Av. E&W ...23W—22N   48
Grever Ct. E&W ...23W—22N   48
High Ridge Rd. N&S
..............23W—23N   48
Hillcrest Dr. E&W ..23W—23N   48
Indian Trails Rd. NW&SE
..............24W—24N 39,40
Ivy Ln. N&S ....21W—25N   41
June Terr. N&S ....23W—22N   48
Juniper Ln. NW&SE
..............23W—20N   48
Kyle Ct. N&S, NW&SE
..............22W—25N   40
Lakewood Dr. S. E&W
..............23W—23N   48
Lakewood Ln. N. E&W
..............23W—23N   48
Libertyville Rd. N&S
..............23W—24N 39,40
Lochanora Dr. N&S, E&W
..............23W—25N 39,40
Lonetree Ln. E&W .23W—23N   48
Mable Av. N&S ....23W—22N   48
Mary Dale Av. E&W
..............24W—25N 39,40
Middle Fork Rd. E&W
..............24W—21N 47,48
Midlothian Rd. NE&SW
..............22W—24N   40
Miller Rd. N&S .23,24W—24N 39,40
North Ln. E&W ....23W—23N   48
Orchard Ln. N&S ..24W—21N 47,48
Plum Pl. NW&SE ..23W—20N   48
Public Rd. N&S ...19W—23N   49
Rand Rd. N&S ....24W—24N 39,40
Ravine Ct. NE&SW
..............24W—25N 39,40
Ravine Ln. N&S ...24W—25N 39,40
Redwing Pl. NE&SW
..............23W—20N   48
Rose Av. E&W ....24W—25N 39,40
Shagbark Dr. N&S ..23W—24N   40
Somerset Ct. N&S .23W—25N   40
South Ln. E&W ...23W—23N   48
Stone Marsh Ln. E&W
..............24W—25N 39,40
Stoney Kirk Ct. N&S
..............23W—25N   40
Strum St. ....22W—20N   48
Summit Terr. NW&SE
..............23W—23N   48
Sunset Dr. NW&SE
..............23W—23N   48
Tahoe Ct. NE&SW 19W—25N   41
Tahoe Dr. E&W ...19W—25N   41
Timberlake Dr. E&W
..............24W—25N 39,40

Page

Virginia Av. N&S ...24W—25N 39,40
West Ln. N&S ....23W—23N   48
Wildrose Dr. ..23W—20N   48
Woodbury Ct. E&W
..............21W—25N   41
14th St. N&S ....26W—21N   47
15th St. N&S ....26W—21N   47
16th St. N&S ....26W—21N   47

Freemont Twp.

Alleghany Rd. N&S 21W—31N   33
Bacon Ln. N&S ....23W—31N 31,32
Baker Ln. NW&SE ..24W—29N 31,32
Barnswallow Ln. NE&SW
..............23W—27N 39,40
Bitter Sweet Dr. E&W
..............21W—26N   41
Bonner Rd. E&W ..24W—28N 31,32
Briar Ter. N&S .....21W—26N   41
Buckthorn Ct. E&W
..............21W—26N   41
Buena Ter. N&S ...21W—26N   41
Cambridge Rd. E&W
..............19W—29N   33
Cardinal Ct. NE&SW
..............24W—28N 31,32
Casey Rd. E&W ...18W—31N   34
Chardon Rd. E&W
..............23,24W—30N 31,32
Cherokee Tr. E&W 24W—31N 31,32
Chevy Chase Rd. N&S,
NE&SW ....21W—27N   41
Countryside Lake Dr. N&S
..............20W—26N   41
Countryside Valley Dr. E&W
..............21W—26N   41
Crescent Dr. E. N&S
..............21W—26N   41
Crescent Dr. N. E&W
..............21W—26N   41
Crescent Dr. S. E&W
..............21W—26N   41
Crescent Dr. W. E&W
..............21W—26N   41
Driftwood Ct. E&W 20W—26N   41
Erhart Rd. E&W ...23W—29N 31,32
Fairfield Rd. N&S
..............24W—28,29,31N 31,32
Freemont Center Rd. N&S
..............22W—28N   32
Freemont Rd. E&W 23W—30N 31,32
Gilmer Rd. NW&SE
..............22,23W—27,28N 32,40
Greeleaf Rd. N&S .21W—26N   41
Hackberry Rd. N&S
..............20W—26N   41
Harris Rd. N&S 19W—30,31N   33
Harvard Rd. E&W .19W—29N   33
Hawley Rd. E&W ..22W—27N   40
Hawley St. N&S ...20W—27N   41
Hawtha Terr. N&S .21W—26N   41
Heather Ln. E&W .21W—26N   41
Hickory Rd. E&W .21W—26N   41
Highland Dr. N&S .20W—26N   41
Hillside Ln. E&W ..21W—26N   41
Hilltop Terr. N&S ..22W—28N   32
Horizon Spur E&W 23W—26N 39,40
Imperial Ct. N&S ...23W—30N 31,32
Ivanhoe Ct. N&S ..23W—27N 39,40
Ivanhoe Ln. NE&SW
..............20W—28N   33
Ivanhoe Rd. N&S
..............20W—28,31N   33
Ivanhoe Terr. E&W 20W—28N   33
Jack Pine Ct. NE&SW
..............20W—26N   41
Jackson Av. NW&SE
..............25W—29N   31
Lake Field Ln. E&W
..............24W—29N 31,32
Lakeview Pkwy. E&W
..............20,21W—26,27N   41
Lexington Ct. N&S 20W—28N   33
Liberty St. N&S ....18W—31N   34
Maple Av. E&W ....20W—28N   33
Maple Rd. N&S ....20W—26N   41
Maple Terr. N&S ...21W—26N   41
Marion Av. NW&SE
..............20W—28N   33
Meadow Ln. E&W .24W—31N 31,32
Milton Rd. NE&SW
..............23,24W—26N 39,40
North Rd. E&W ....21W—27N   41
Northwest Pkwy. NW&SE
..............20W—27N   41
Oak Leaf Ln. E&W .21W—27N   41
Oak Terr. N&S .....21W—27N   41
Old Oak Dr. E&W ..24W—28N 31,32
Owens Rd. N&S
..............22,23W—26,27N 39,40
Oxford Dr. N&S ....19W—29N   33
Park Av. E&W ......20W—28N   33
Peterson Rd. E&W
..............18,22W—30N 32,34
Pheasant Run NW&SE
..............22W—26N   40
Pierre St. N&S .....19W—26N   41
Pon Dr. E&W ......23W—26N 39,40
Ranch Rd. N&S ...18W—31N   34

Page

Red Pine Ct. NE&SW
..............20W—26N   41
Rosewood Rd. E&W
..............21W—26N   41
Russell Ln. E&W ...24W—29N 31,32
Schank Rd. NE&SW
..............20W—28N   33
Scherman Rd. N&S
..............22,23W—26N 39,40
Shady Ln. NW&SE 21W—26N   41
Spring Ct. NW&SE 24W—28N 31,32
St. Andrews Dr. N&S
..............18W—30N   34
Steger Rd. E&W ...18W—31N   34
Sunny Ct. E&W ...19W—26N   41
Sunset Ct. NE&SW
..............24W—29N 31,32
Sylvan Dr. N. E&W 21W—26N   41
Sylvan Dr. S. E&W 21W—26N   41
Taylor Lake Ct. E&W
..............19W—26N   41
Thorntree Rd. N&S 21W—27N   41
Valley View Terr. NE&SW
..............21W—26N   41
Wauconda Rd. E&W
..............24W—27N 39,40
Wild Flower Terr. E&W
..............21W—26N   41
Winchester Rd. N&S
..............20W—30N   33
Yale Ct. N&S ....19W—29N   33

Fremont Twp. Diamond Lake Streets

Acorn Ln. N&S ....19W—26N   41
Circle Dr. N. NW&SE
..............19W—26N   41
Circle Dr. S. NE&SW
..............19W—26N   41
Elmwood Av. NW&SE
..............19W—26N   41
Fairview Dr. N. NE&SW
..............19W—26N   41
Fairview Dr. S. NE&SW
..............19W—26N   41
Forest Ln. N. NW&SE
..............19W—26N   41
Forest Ln. S. NW&SE
..............19W—26N   41
Hickory Av. NE&SW
..............19W—26N   41
Hoag Ct. NW&SE .19W—26N   41
Iride Dr. NE&SW ..19W—26N   41
Kenmore Av. E&W 19W—26N   41
Krueger Ct. NW&SE
..............19W—26N   41
Lakeview Av. E&W 19W—26N   41
Maple Av. NE&SW 19W—26N   41
Martin Dr. NE&SW 19W—26N   41
Oak Av. NE&SW ...19W—26N   41
Oakdale Ln. N. NW&SE
..............19W—26N   41
Oakdale Ln. S. NE&SW
..............19W—26N   41
Prospect Dr. NW&SE
..............19W—26N   41
Ridge Ct. N&S .....19W—26N   41
Sunny Ct. E&W ...19W—26N   41
Taylor Lake Ct. E&W
..............19W—26N   41
Trinity Dr. NE&SW .19W—26N   41
University Dr. E&W 19W—26N   41
Walnut Av. NE&SW
..............19W—26N   41
Weich Rd. E&W ...19W—26N   41
West Shore Dr. NE&SW
..............19W—26N   41
Willow Av. N&S ....19W—26N   41

Grant Twp. Streets

Anchorage E&W ...27W—35N   22
Andrew Ct. NW&SE
..............25W—36N   15
Ash St. N&S ....25W—35N   23
Augustana Av. N&S
..............25W—35N   23
Bachman Rd. E&W
..............26W—37N 14,15
Bayview Av. E&W .25W—35N   23
Bayview Dr. E&W ..27W—35N   22
Beach Park NW&SE
..............27W—35N   22
Bellevue Pl. N&S ..26W—34N 22,23
Belevidere Rd. NE&SW
..............25W—32N   23
Benjamin Av. N&S .25W—35N   23
Bergan St. NE&SW
..............25W—34N   23
Beverly Dr. N&S ...26W—35N 22,23
Boesch Pl. E&W ...26W—36N 14,15
Blackhawk N&S
..............26W—35N 22,23
Brandenberg Rd. NE&SW
..............28W—33N   22
Broadway E&W ....28W—37N   14
Brodie Dr. NE&SW 25W—35N   23
Burkhart Ln. E&W .26W—34N 22,23
Camp Horner Rd. N&S
..............26W—34N 22,23

Page

Carol Ln. NE&SW .26W—34N 22,23
Catherine St. N&S 25W—34N   23
Central E&W ....28W—37N   14
Central Rd. NE&SW
..............26W—36N 14,15
Champion Hartigan Rd.
NE&SW ....27W—34N   22
Channel Dr. E&W ..28W—34N   22
Chicago Av. E&W .25W—35N   23
Chris Larkin Rd. N&S
..............27W—35N   22
Christa Dr. N&S ...25W—33N 22,23
Clara Dr. E&W ..25W—36N 15
Claredon Dr. E&W .27W—35N   22
Converse Ln. N&S .26W—34N 22,23
Cooney Island Rd. E&W
..............26W—36N 14,15
Creek Ln. NW&SE .26W—33N 22,23
David Ct. N&S .....26W—34N 22,23
Decora Av. N&S ...25W—34N   23
Dewey St. NE&SW 28W—37N   14
Dolores Ct. NE&SW
..............26W—33N 22,23
Donald Ct. E&W ...25W—35N   23
East End Av. N&S .26W—36N 14,15
Elm Av. N&S ....25W—35N   23
Elm St. N&S ....26W—34N 22,23
Elmwood Av. E&W 26W—35N 22,23
Edgewater Ln. N&S
..............27W—35N   22
Edward Av. E&W ..26W—34N 22,23
Everett Av. N&S ...25W—35N   23
Faith Ct. E&W .....26W—35N 22,23
Fischer Dr. NW&SE
..............26W—34N 22,23
Fish Lake Rd. N&S 26W—32N 22,23
Forest Dr. N&S ....26W—34N 22,23
Fox Lake Rd. NE&SW
..............27W—32N   22
Francis Av. N&S ...26W—36N 14,15
Frank Ct. E&W .....28W—37N   14
Franklin Av. N&S ..25W—35N   23
Fredheim Av. E&W 25W—34N   23
Glenaybee St. E&W
..............25W—34N   23
Graham Ct. E&W ..25W—34N   23
Grand Av. E&W 25,26W—36N 14,15
Grant Av. N&S .....26W—36N   15
Great Bear Tr. E&W
..............28W—34N   22
Green Av. N&S ....25W—35N   23
Haiwatha Tr. N&S .28W—34N   22
Hawthorne Dr. N&S
..............25W—36N   15
Helen Ct. E&W ....26W—35N 22,23
Helen Ct. N&S .....28W—34N   23
Helendale Rd. N&S
..............26W—35N 22,23
Hickory Av. N&S ...25W—35N   23
Hickory Ct. N&S
..............25W—35,36N 15,23
Hickory Ct. N&S ...26W—34N 22,23
Hickory St. E&W ...25W—35N   23
Hickory Tr. NW&SE
..............26W—36N 14,15
High Point St. E&W, N&S
..............25W—35N   23
High Rd. NW&SE ..28W—35N   22
Hill Ln. N&S ....26W—36N 14,15
Hilldale Dr. N&S ...27W—35N   22
Hillside Av. N&S
..............25W—35N   23
Hill Top Rd. N&S ..28W—35N   22
Hillwood Dr. E&W .26W—35N 22,23
Holman N&S ....25W—34N   23
Hudson Av. N&S ..26W—35N 22,23
Hunt Av. N&S .....26W—35N 22,23
Indian Ln. N&S ....26W—35N 22,23
Indian Trail NE&SW
..............28W—35N   22
Ingleside Dr. N&S, E&W
..............26W—35N 22,23
Ingleside Rd. E&W 26W—36N 14,15
Iola Av. N&S ....25W—36N   15
Iroquois Tr. N&S ...28W—34N   22
Jackson Av. N&S ..25W—36N   15
James Av. N&S ....25W—35N   23
James Ct. N&S ....26W—36N 14,15
Jennette Pl. NE&SW
..............28W—37N   14
Karen Ct. NW&SE 28W—37N   14
Kerwin Ct. N&S ...25W—36N   15
Knollwood Dr. N&S 26W—35N 22,23
Lake Av. N&S .....25W—35N   23
Lake St. N&S ......26W—36N 14,15
Lake Mathews Tr. N&S
..............28W—34N   22
Lake Shore Dr. E&W
..............25W—34N   23
Lake Shore Rd. NE&SW
..............28W—35N   22
Lake Shore Woods Dr. N&S
..............26W—35N 22,23
Lakeview Av. E&W 26W—35N 22,23
Lakeview Av. N&S .28W—34N   22
Lake Vista Terr. NE&SW
..............28W—37N   14
Larkin Ln. E&W ....25W—34N   23
Laughing Water Tr. N&S
..............28W—35N   22

Page

Laurel Av. N&S ....25W—34N   23
Lee Ct. E&W ....26W—35N 22,23
Leonard Rd. N&S ..28W—34N   22
Levi Waite Rd. E&W
..............26W—33N 22,23
Lincoln Av. N&S ...25W—34N   23
Lincoln Ct. E&W ...26W—36N 14,15
Linder Rd. E&W ...25W—35N   23
Long Av. N&S .....25W—34N   23
Long Beach Dr. NW&SE
..............25W—34N   23
Long Lake Rd. E&W
..............25W—34N   22
Longwood Av. N&S 26W—35N 22,23
Louise Pl. N&S ....25W—35N   23
Lovers Tr. NW&SE
..............25W—34N   22
Luana Dr. E&W ....27W—35N   22
Luby Ct. E&W .....26W—35N 22,23
Madison St. E&W ..25W—34N   23
Mall Rd. NW&SE ..28W—35N   22
Malmquist Dr. N&S 28W—34N   22
Manitou Tr. NE&SW
..............25W—34N   22
Maple Av. E&W ....26W—35N 22,23
Maple Rd. N&S ....26W—36N 14,15
Maple St. N&S .....26W—35N 22,23
Marquette Dr. E&W
..............26W—35N   15
Margie Pl. NW&SE 28W—37N   14
Marian Av. NW&SE
..............25W—34N   23
Marie Ln. E&W ....26W—35N 22,23
Marine Dr. NW&SE 27W—35N   22
Marion Ct. NE&SW
..............26W—35N 22,23
Marshall Av. E&W .26W—36N 14,15
Mary N&S ....26W—36N 14,15
McHenry Rd. N&S .28W—37N   14
Meadow Ln. N&S ..25W—35N   23
Michael Rd. N&S ..28W—34N   22
Milwaukee St. E&W
..............25W—35N   23
Mishtenana Tr. E&W
..............28W—34N   22
Mitchell Ct. NW&SE
..............25W—35N   23
Molidor Dr. E&W ..27W—33N   22
Moody St. N&S ....27W—35N   22
Morraine Dr. E&W .27W—35N   22
Mudjekeewis Tr. N&S
..............28W—34N   22
Muskego Av. NW&SE
..............25W—35N   23
Myrtle Ln. E&W ....26W—35N 22,23
Nakomis Tr. N&S ..28W—34N   22
Navajo RR. E&W ..28W—34N   22
Nippersink Pl. NW&SE
..............28W—37N   14
Nippersink Rd. NW&SE
..............26W—34N 22,23
Nora Pl. NE&SW ..28W—37N   14
North Ct. E&W ....27W—35N   22
Northlake Dr. N&S 25W—35N   23
Oak Cir. Dr. E&W ..26W—36N 14,15
Oak Ct. N&S ....25W—35N   23
Oak Dr. N&S ....26W—33N 22,23
Oak Ln. E&W ......25W—35N   23
Oak St. E&W ......25W—36N   15
Oakland Dr. E&W ..25W—34N   23
Oakside St. N&S ..26W—34N 22,23
Oakwood Av. E&W 26W—35N 22,23
Oakwood Av. N&S 25W—35N   23
O'Kelly Ln. N&S ...28W—34N   22
Old Grand Av. E&W
..............25W—36N   15
Olive Ct. N&S .....25W—34N   23
Ooen Av. N&S .....25W—34N   23
Orchard Av. E&W ..25W—36N   15
Orchard Dr. N&S ..27W—35N   22
Park Dr. N&S ..26,28W—34N 14,15
Park View Pl. E&W 28W—37N   14
Patricia Ln. N&S
..............28W—37N   14
Pleasant Rd. E&W 26W—36N 14,15
Polk St. N&S ....26W—34N 22,23
Poplar Av. N&S ....25W—35N   23
Randhill Dr. N&S ..27W—35N   22
Reed St. E&W .....26W—34N 22,23
Ridge Rd. E&W ....27W—35N   22
Ridge Rd. N&S ....26W—36N 14,15
Robin Rd. N&S ....26W—35N 22,23
Rockford St. E&W .25W—35N   23
Rock Island Av. NW&SE
..............25W—34N   23
Rollins Rd. E&W ...26W—36N 14,15
Roseland Ct. E&W 26W—36N 14,15
Rosewood Dr. N&S 26W—35N 22,23
Sequoia Tr. N&S ..28W—34N   22
Sheridan Dr. N&S .27W—35N   22
Shore Rd. N&S ....26W—36N 14,15
Snowshoe Tr. E&W
..............28W—34N   22
South Av. E&W ....28W—37N   14
South Ct. E&W ....27W—35N   22
South Ct. E&W ....28W—34N   22
South St. E&W ....28W—34N   22
Squaw Rd. E&W ..26W—36N 14,15
Stanley Rd. N&S ..27W—34N   22
Stanton Bay Rd. E&W
..............26W—36N 14,15

Page

St. Olaf Av. NE&SW ....25W—34N 23
Stockholm Dr. E&W ....26W—33N 22,23
Stone Ct. E&W ......26W—33N 22,23
Stroughton Av. E&W ....25W—34N 23
Sullivan Lake Rd. E&W ....28W—33N 22
Sunnybrook Rd. E&W ....26W—34N 22,23
Sunnyside Av. N&S ....25W—35N 23
Sunset Dr. N&S .....25W—34N 23
Sunset Terr. NW&SE ....25W—34N 23
Tamarack Dr. N&S 25W—36N 15
Tam Ln. N&S ....25W—35N 23
Tara Ct. N&S ....25W—36N 15
Tarvin Ln. E&W .....26W—35N 22,23
Terrace Ln. NE&SW ....28W—37N 14
Thomas Ct. E&W ..28W—34N 22
Tree Top Rd. NW&SE ....28W—35N 22
Tyrone Pl. NE&SW 28W—37N 14
Valley Rd. NW&SE 28W—35N 22
VanBuren St. E&W 26W—34N 22,23
Venetian Dr. NW&SE ....25W—34N 23
Vincent Ct. E&W ...26W—36N 14,15
Watts Av. NE&SW .28W—37N 14
Watson Av. N&S ....26W—35N 22,23
Waterside Ln. N&S 25W—36N 15
Ward Ln. N&S ....25W—35N 23
Wesley Rd. N&S ...26W—36N 14,15
West Lake Av. E&W ....28W—37N 14
West Lake Vista Terr. E&W ....28W—37N 14
West St. N&S ....28W—37N 14
Wenona Tr. E&W ...28W—34N 22
White Rabbit Tr. E&W ....28W—34N 22
Wildwood Av. E&W 26W—35N 22,23
William Pl. NW&SE ....28W—37N 14
Wilson Rd. N&S 26W—34,36N 15,23
Wilson Rd.NW&SE 25W—32N 23
Wind Hill Rd. N&S 26W—36N 14,15
Wooster Ln. E&W .26W—34N 22,23
Woosterlake Dr. E&W ....26W—34N 22,23
2nd St. N&S ....27W—35N 22
3rd St. N&S ....27W—35N 22

Lake Villa Twp.

Academy Blvd. N&S ....25W—37N 15
Academy Ct. NW&SE ....25W—38N 15
Academy Dr. NE&SW ....25W—38N 15
Alberta Av. N&S ....24W—36N 15,16
Alice Ln. N&S ....21W—36N 17
Alpine Ct. E&W ......24W—37N 15,16
Alpine Ln. NE&SW 24W—37N 15,16
Antonio Av. N&S ....21W—37N 17
Apollo Ct. E&W .....23W—39N 8,16
Arcade Dr. E&W .....23W—39N 8,16
Arcade Dr. N. E&W 25W—37N 15
Arcade Dr. S. E&W 25W—37N 15
Armore Ln. N&S ....23W—38N 15,16
Aoon Dr. N&S ....25W—37N 15
Aztec Cr. E&W ......24W—39N 15,16
Balboa Dr. N&S .....24W—39N 15,16
Bald Eagle Rd. E&W ....25W—37N 15
Beck Rd. N&S ....19W—38N 17
Belmoral Park N&S ....23W—38N 15,16
Bernice Dr. N&S ....22W—36N 16
Big Oak Dr. E&W ..24W—37N 15,16
Birch St. NE&SW ..21W—38N 17
Blackcherry Ln. E&W ....24W—36N 15,16
Blackstone Dr. E&W ....25W—37N 15
Brentwood Ln. E&W ....21W—39N 9,17
Buena Av. E&W .....25W—37N 15
Caine Rd. E&W .....24W—36N 15,16
Capill Av. N&S ....20W—37N 17
Carol Ln. N&S ....21W—36N 17
Carson Dr. E&W ....25W—37N 15
Cedar Av. N&S ......23W—38N 15,16
Cedar Crest Ln. N&S ....25W—38N 15
Cedar Lake Rd. E&W ....24W—38N 15,16
Cedar Lake Rd. N&S ....23W—37N 15,16
Cedarwood Ln. E&W ....24W—36N 15,16
Central Av. NE&SW ....23W—38N 15,16
Cheshey St. E&W .25W—37N 15
Christianson Av. E&W ....21W—38N 17

Cobona Av. NW&SE ....20W—36N 17
Columbia Bay Dr. E&W ....25W—37N 15
Columbus Av. N&S 20W—37N 17
Cortez Dr. N&S .....24W—39N 15,16
Crabapple Dr. N&S 24W—39N 7,8
Crabtree Ln. E&W ....24,25W—36N 15,16
Cremana Av. N&S .20W—37N 17
Danny Ln. E&W ....21W—36N 17
Deep Lake Rd. N&S ....22W—39N 8,16
Dering Ln. E&W ....25W—38N 15
Diana Av. E&W ......24W—38N 15,16
Douglas Ln. N&S ..21W—37N 17
Eagle Ct. NW&SE .24W—36N 15,16
Eastmore Av. E&W 24W—36N 15,16
Edgewood Av. N&S ....21W—38N 17
Edward Av. N&S ....21W—36N 17
Elizabeth Ct. N&S .21W—36N 17
Elizabeth Dr. N&S .21W—36N 17
Elm St. E&W ....21W—39N 9,17
Engle Rd. E&W .....21W—36N 17
Fairfield Rd. N&S ....24W—36,38N 15,16
Fairview Cir. E&W .25W—37N 15
Fairview Ln. NE&SW ....25W—37N 15
Fairway Dr. N&S,E&W ....24W—39N 7,8
Fox Terr. E&W ....24W—36N 15,16
Garcia Av. E&W ....21W—39N 9,17
Genoa Av. NE&SW 20W—36N 17
George Ct. N&S ....22W—37N 16
Gillian Rd. NE&SW 24W—38N 15,16
Glade St. E&W ......25W—37N 15
Glen Lake Pl. N&S 23W—38N 15,16
Granada Blvd. N&S ....20W—37N 17
Grand Av. NE&SW ....25W—37,38N 15
Grand Av. E&W .....24W—38N 15,16
Grand Av. E&W .....18W—36N 18
Grand Blvd. N&S ...25W—37N 15
Grand Cir. NE&SW 19W—37N 17
Grafton Av. N&S ....22W—38N 16
Grafton Av. N&S ....22W—38N 16
Haidi Ln. E&W ....24W—37N 15,16
Half St. E&W ....25W—37N 15
Hampshire Dr. N&S ....25W—37N 15
Harbor Ridge Dr. NE&SW ....24W—39,40N 7,8
Harold Ln. E&W 21,22W—36N 16,17
Harding Av. N&S ...25W—37N 15
Hazelwood Dr. N&S ....24W—36N 15,16
Helen Ct. N&S ....21W—36N 17
Helen Dr. N&S ....21W—36N 17
Hickory St. N&S ....21W—38N 17
Hilda Ln. N&S ....21W—36N 17
Hillside Av. N&S ....25W—37N 15
Honey Av. E&W .....21W—36N 17
Inca Ln. E&W ....24W—39N 15,16
Ironwood Dr. N&S .19W—37N 17
Isola Av. E&W ....20W—37N 17
James Ct. N&S .....22W—36N 16
James Dr. N&S .....22W—36N 16
Lake Av. N&S ....23W—38N 15,16
Lake Av. NE&SW ..21W—38N 17
Lake St. E&W ....20W—36N 17
Lake Shore Dr. N&S ....25W—37N 15
Lakeview Av. NE&SW ....25W—38N 15
Lakeview Av. NW&SE ....20W—36N 17
Lakeview Dr. E&W 25W—37N 15
Lakewood Av. N&S 23W—38N 15,16
Laurel St. E&W .....21W—39N 9,17
Lawrence Ct. N&S 21W—36N 17
Lawrence Dr. N&S 21W—36N 17
Lehmann Blvd. E&W ....25W—37N 15
Liberty Dr. E&W ....23W—38N 15,16
Lincoln Blvd. E&W 25W—37N 15
Linden Ln. E&W ....21W—39N 9,17
Loretto Av. N&S ....20W—37N 17
Loon Lake Rd. E&W ....21W—39N 9,17
Maple Av. E&W .....25W—37N 15
Maple Av. N&S ......21W—38N 17
Marilyn Av. N&S ....21W—36N 17
Marshfield Rd. E&W ....25W—37N 15
Mary Ct. N&S ....21W—36N 17
Mary Dr. N&S ....21W—36N 17
Maurine Dr. E&W ..21W—36N 17
Milburn Rd. NW&SE ....19W—39N 9,17
Miller Rd. NW&SE .19W—39N 9,17
Mobey Ln. E&W ....24W—36N 15,16
Monaville Rd. E&W ....23,24W—36,37N 15,16
Morton Dr. E&W ....20W—36,37N 17
Morton Dr. E&W ....21W—36N 17
Morton Dr. E&W ....22W—37N 16

Munn Ln. N&S ....21W—38N 17
Newberry Ln. E&W 25W—37N 15
Nielson Av. E&W ...21W—36N 17
Nielson Dr. E&W ...21W—36N 17
Normandy Av. N&S ....21W—36N 17
North Av. NE&SW .23W—38N 15,16
North Columbia Dr. E&W ....25W—38N 15
North Entrance Dr. NW&SE ....25W—37N 15
North Nathan Hale Dr. N&S ....21W—36N 17
Northway Av. E&W 23W—38N 15,16
Oak Av. NW&SE ...21W—38N 17
Oakwood Dr. N&S .21W—36N 17
Orchard Pl. NE&SW ....25W—37N 15
Paradise Ct. E&W .21W—36N 17
Park Av. E&W ....21W—36N 17
Park Dr. E&W ....21W—36N 17
Park Pl. N&S ....25W—38N 15
Park St. NW&SE ...25W—38N 15
Park Forest Av. N&S ....20W—36N 17
Parma Av. N&S .....20W—37N 17
Peninsula Av. N&S 25W—37N 15
Petite Lake Rd. E&W ....24W—39N 15,16
Pine St. NE&SW ...21W—38N 17
Piper Ln. N&S ....25W—37N 15
Ponce Av. NW&SE 20W—37N 17
Poplar St. N&S ......21W—39N 9,17
Prairieview Dr. N&S ....20W—36N 17
Richard Dr. N&S ....22W—36N 16
Rivera Av. NE&SW 20W—37N 17
Romero Av. E&W ..20W—37N 17
Rose Av. N&S ....24W—38N 15,16
Rose Ct. E&W ....22W—36N 16
Rustic Dr. N&S ......21W—39N 9,17
San Rem Rd. E&W 20W—37N 17
Sand Lake Rd. E&W ....19W—37N 17
Sarah Dr. E&W ......21W—36N 17
Saxony Dr. NW&SE ....24W—37N 15,16
Shore St. N&S ......25W—37N 15
Siena Dr. E&W ......20W—37N 17
Sistina Av. NW&SE 20W—37N 17
South Av. E&W .....24W—36N 15,16
S. Nathan Hale Dr. NE&SW ....21W—36N 17
Spruce St. N&S .....21W—39N 9,17
Stonebridge Dr. NW&SE ....24W—40N 7,8
Sunnyside Rd. E&W ....25W—38N 15
Sunset Ln. E&W ....25W—37N 15
Sunshine Av. N&S .21W—36N 17
Terry Av. E&W ......22W—37N 16
Terry Dr. NW&SE ..22W—36N 16
Thorndale Pl. N&S 23W—38N 15,16
Timber Ln. E&W ....25W—37N 15
Valina Av. N&S ......25W—38N 15
Verona Av. E&W ...20W—37N 17
Villa Av. N&S ....23W—38N 15,16
Villa Ct. N&S ....22W—38N 16
Wacker Dr. E&W ...25W—37N 15
Wall St. E&W ....23W—39N 15,16
Walnut Av. N&S .....21W—39N 9,17
Washington Av. E&W ....24W—38N 15,16
Wayside Pl. E&W ..25W—37N 15
West Av. N&S ....23W—38N 15,16
Westmore Av. N&S 24W—36N 15,16
W. Park Av. N&S ...23W—38N 15,16
Wildwood Av. N&S 21W—36N 17
Willow St. NE&SW 21W—38N 17
Willow Way NW&SE ....23W—38N 15,16
Wilson Rd. E&W ....25W—38N 15
Winthrop Pl. E&W .24W—38N 15,16
Wittenburg Rd. N&S ....21W—39N 9,17
Woodland Av. NW&SE ....20W—36N 17
Woodland Terr. E&W ....25W—37N 15
Woods Av. E&W ....21W—38N 17
1st St. E&W ....21W—38N 17
2nd St. E&W ....21W—38N 17
3rd St. E&W ....21W—38N 17
4th St. E&W ....21W—38N 17
5th St. E&W ....21W—38N 17
7th St. E&W ....21W—38N 17
8th St. E&W ....21W—38N 17

Libertyville Twp. Unicorp. Streets

Adler Dr. NE&SW ...16W—30N 34
Allyson Ct. N&S ...15W—29N 35,36
Almond Rd. N&S ...17W—31N 34
Arcadia Rd. N&S ...13W—28N 35,36
Arlington Dr. E&W .16W—30N 34
Atkinson Av. E&W .13W—29N 35,36
Baker Rd. N&S ......13W—28N 35,36
Ballard Dr. N&S, E&W ....13W—28N 35,36

Bayonne Av. N&S ....13W—28,29N 35,36
Bell Ln. N&S ....17W—30N 34
Birchwood Ln. E&W ....15W—30N 35,36
Bradley Rd. N&S ...14W—28N 35,36
Brookhill Rd. E&W 17W—30N 34
Brookside Ct. E&W 17W—30N 34
Bruce Ct. NE&SW .15W—29N 35,36
Borde Ct. NE&SW .15W—29N 35,36
Bull Creek Dr. E&W ....18W—30N 34
Casey Rd. E&W ....18W—31N 34
Center Av. NW&SE 16W—30N 34
Cherrywood Ln. E&W ....15W—30N 35,36
Clover Ln. E&W .....15W—30N 35,36
Countryside Rd. N&S ....18W—30N 34
Country Ct. E&W ..18W—30N 34
Des Plaines Dr. NW&SE ....16W—30N 34
East End Av. N&S .15W—30N 35,36
Egidi Rd. NW&SE .16W—31N 34
Ellen Way E&W .....15W—29N 35,36
Elmwood Av. N&S .14W—26N 43,44
Elm Rd. E&W ....13W—28N 35,36
Energy Dr. N&S ....13W—28N 35,36
Fairhill Rd. E&W ....17W—30N 34
Fair Ln. E&W ....15W—30N 35,36
Fair Way E&W ....15W—29N 35,36
Forest Dr. E&W .....14W—27N 43 44
Foster Av. E&W .....13W—29N 35 36
Foster Knoll Rd. N&S ....13W—29N 35,36
Greenacre Dr. E&W ....17W—30N 34
Gurin Rd. E&W ......15W—31N 35,36
Harris Rd. N&S .....19W—30N 33
Hawthorne Av. E&W ....14W—27N 43,44
Hawthorne Ln. NW&SE ....15W—29N 35,36
Hawthorne Rd. N&S ....15W—29N 35,36
Herky Dr. N&S ......13W—28N 35,36
Idlewood Ln. E&W 15W—30N 35,36
Imperial Dr. E&W ...14W—26N 43,44
Ivy Ln. N&S ....15W—28N 35,36
Keith Dr. N&S ....13W—28N 35,36
Kildare Av. E&W .....17W—30N 34
Laurel Dr. E&W .....13W—28N 35,36
Leesley Ct. E&W ...18W—30N 34
Leola Dr. E&W ....13W—28N 35,36
Liberty Rd. N&S .....18W—31N 34
Linden Ln. E&W .....14W—28N 35,36
Lingwood Dr. N&S .14W—26N 43,44
Melody Ln. N&S ....14W—26N 43,44
Muir Av. E&W ....13W—29N 35,36
Nagel Ct. N&S ......13W—28N 35,36
Neils Rd. N&S ....15W—29N 35,36
N. Terre Dr. E&W ..15W—29N 35,36
Oak Av. E&W ....14W—26N 43,44
Oak Ln. N&S ....15W—28,29N 35,36
Oak Grove Av. N&S ....15W—30N 35,36
Oak Pond Ln. E&W ....15W—29N 35,36
Oak Springs Ln. N&S ....15W—29N 35,36
Old Hickory Ln. N&S ....15W—29N 35,36
Park Ln. N&S ....15W—30N 35,36
Peterson Rd. E&W 18W—30N 34
Petronella Dr. E&W ....14W—28N 35,36
Pinehurst Ct. N&S .18W—30N 34
Pinewood Ln. NW&SE ....15W—30N 35,36
Prairie View Ln. E&W ....13W—25N 43,44
Print-O-Tade Rd. N&S ....13W—28N 35,36
Quassey Av. E&W .13W—29N 35,36
Ranch Rd. N&S .....18W—31N 34
Redwood Ln. NW&SE ....15W—30N 35,36
Revere Dr. N&S .....16W—30N 34
River Dr. N&S ....15W—29N 35,36
River Rd. N&S ....16W—30N 34
Rockland Ln. N&S 15W—28N 35,36
Rocktop Rd. N&S ..14W—28N 35,36
Shagbark Ln. N&S 15W—28N 35,36
Sprucewood Ln. E&W ....15W—30N 35,36
St. Andrew's Dr. N&S ....18W—30N 34
Steger Rd. E&W ....18W—31N 34
St. Mary'S Rd. N&S ....15W—29N 35,36
Sunnyview Rd. N&S ....17W—30N 34
Tanglewood Ct. N&S ....15W—28N 35,36
Terre Dr. S. E&W ..15W—29N 35,36
Timber Ln. E&W ....15W—29N 35,36
Valley Ct. E&W ......18W—30N 34
Vernon Ct. N&S .....15W—28N 35,36
Victor Ln. E&W ......15W—31N 35,36

Whitman Ct. NE&SW ....15W—29N 35,36
Wildwood Ct. E&W 15W—30N 35,36
Woodale Ln. N&S .15W—28N 35,36
Woodhollow Ln. E&W ....18W—31N 34

Newport Twp. Streets

Bayonne Av. N&S ..13W—38N 19,20
Bayonne Av. N&S ..13W—40N 11,12
Beach Rd. E&W ....13W—38N 19,20
Belle Plaine Av. N&S ....13W—38N 19,20
Bonnis Sch. Rd. N&S ....16W—39N 10
Boulevard View Av. N&S ....13W—38N 19,20
Bryn Mawr N&S ....13W—38N 19,20
Crawford Rd. N&S ....18W—38,41N 10,18
Dale Av. N&S ....13W—38N 19,20
Delany Rd. N&S ....14W—38N 19,20
Delany Rd. N&S ....14W—40,42N 11,12
Edwards Rd. E&W 18W—42N 10
Forestview Rd. N&S ....13W—40N 11,12
Green Bay Rd. N&S ....12W—42N 12
Greenview Dr. E&W ....13W—40N 11,12
Hart St. E&W ....13W—38N 19,20
Hickory Rd. E&W ..14W—42N 11,12
Hunt Club Rd. N&S ....17W—42N 10
Ingram Dr. E&W ....14W—43N 11,12
Kaiser Rd. E&W ....14W—40N 11,12
Kazmer Rd. E&W ..14W—40N 11,12
Kelly Rd. E&W .16,18W—40N 10
Killbourne Rd. N&S ....14W—42N 11,12
Lester Ln. N&S .....13W—40N 11,12
Magnolia Av. N&S .13W—38N 19,20
Main St. E&W ....12W—38N 20
Martin St. E&W .....13W—39N 12,20
Mill Creek Rd. N&S ....16W—38,40,41N 10,18
Northwestern Av. N&S ....13W—38N 19,20
Pine Grove Av. N&S ....13W—38N 19,20
Rosecrans Rd. E&W ....18W—41N 10
Rosedale Av. N&S 13W—38N 19,20
Russell Rd. E&W ..15W—43N 11
Sharon St. E&W ....13W—39N 12,20
Sheridan Oaks Dr. N&S ....18W—43N 10
Stier Rd. E&W ....13W—40N 11,12
Stonegate Rd. E&W ....13W—40N 11,12
Sunset Rd. N&S ....13W—40N 11,12
Sylvan Av. N&S .....13W—38N 19,20
Timberland Tr. N&S ....13W—40N 11,20
Town Line Rd. E&W ....13W—38N 19,20
Tri-State North Tollway NW&SE ....16W—40N 10
Wadsworth Rd. E&W ....13W—39N 12,20
Waveland Av. N&S 13W—38N 19,20
Waverly St. E&W ...13W—40N 11,12
Winthrop Harbor Rd. E&W ....14W—42N 11,12
Woodland Av. N&S 13W—38N 19,20
Yorkhouse Rd. E&W 15W 38N 19
21st St. N&S ....15W—41N 11
21st St. E&W .....13,15W—41N 11,12

Nunda & Wauconda Twps. Slocum Lake Streets

Ada St. N&S ....28W—26N 38
Ash St. N&S ....28W—26N 38
Beech St. E&W ......29W—27N 38
Bernice St. N&S ....28W—26N 38
Brooks N&S ....28W—26N 38
Catalpa St. E&W ....29W—27N 38
Cedar St. E&W ......29W—27N 38
Channel St. NW&SE ....28W—27N 38
Clark St. N&S ....28W—26N 38
Darrell Rd. N&S .....28W—27N 38
Division St. N&S ....28W—27N 38
East Park Av. E&W 28W—26N 38
Ellen St. N&S ....28W—26N 38
Elm St. N&S ....28W—26N 38
Fairview Rd. E&W .28W—26N 38
Forest Blvd. N&S ..29W—27N 38
Gennesse St. N&S ....28W—26,27N 38
Geraldine Ln. N&S 28W—26N 38
Grace St. N&S ......28W—26N 38
Hickory St. E&W ....28W—27N 38
Huston Av. N&S ....28W—26N 38
Lake Dr. N&S ....28W—26N 38
Lakeview Ct. E&W 28W—26N 38
Lake View Dr. NW&SE ....28W—27N 38

	Page
Lamphere St. E&W 28W—27N	38
Langley St. ..28W—27N	38
Lexington Ct. 28W—27N	38
Leyte Ct. N&S ....28W—27N	38
Lindy Ln. E&W ......28W—26N	38
Locust Dr. N&S ....28W—26N	38
Main St. E&W ....28W—26N	38
Maple Av. E&W ..28W—26N	38
Maple Dr. E&W ...29W—27N	38
Maple Dr. E&W ...29W—27N	38
Maple St. N&S ....28W—27N	38
Marion St. N&S ...28W—26N	38
Meadow St. N&S ..29W—26N	38
Morey St. ......28W—26N	38
Mylith Rd. E&W ..28W—26N	38
North St. E&W ....28W—27N	38
Oak St. E&W ....29W—27N	38
Orchard Dr. N&S ..28W—26N	38
Palm St. N&S ..29W—26,27N	38
Park Av. E&W ......28W—26N	38
Pine St. N&S ....29W—26,27N	38
Polpar St. N&S ....28W—26N	38
Polpar St. N&S ...28W—26N	38
River St. N&S ..29W—26,27N	38
Roberts Rd. N&S ..29W—27N	38
Shady St. NE&SW 28W—27N	38
South Av. E&W ....28W—26N	38
Walnut St. N&S ....28W—27N	38
Wild St. N&S ....28W—26N	38
Willow Rd. N&S ....28W—26N	38
Willow St. E&W ...29W—26N	38

Shields Twp. Streets

	Page
Adelphia Av ......12W—28,29N	37
Atkinson Av. .12W—29N	37
Basil Rd. E&W ....12W—28N	37
Bayshore Dr. NE&SW ....11W—29N	37
Birch Av. N&S ....12W—28N	37
Birchwood Av. E&W ....12W—30N	37
Bittersweet Av. E&W ....12W—30N	37
Blodgett Av. .12W—29N	37
Bonaparte Av. E&W ....12W—30N	37
Brompton Av. E&W 12W—30N	37
Burris Av. E&W ..12W—29N	37
Clover Ln. N&S ....12W—28N	37
Fairbank Av. N&S ..12W—30N	37
Farwell Av. E&W ..12W—29N	37
Forest View Dr. NE&SW ....11W—29N	37
Foster Av. NE&SW 12W—29N	37
Glendell Av. N&S ..11W—29N	37
Green Av. N&S .12W—28,29N	37
Greenwood Av. N&S ....12W—31N	37
Hillcrest Av. N&S ..12W—31N	37
Hillside Av. N&S ...11W—29N	37
Jenkisson Av. NE&SW ....12W—29N	37
Juneway Terr. E&W ....11W—29N	37
Kohl Av. N&S ......11W—29N	37
Lawn Av. N&S ....12W—30N	37
Louis St. N&S ......11W—29N	37
Mawman Blvd. N&S ....11W—29N	37
Meadow Av. N&S ..12W—31N	37
Melvin Dr. NE&SW 11W—29N	37
Muir Av. E&W ......12W—29N	37
North Av. E&W ....12W—28N	37
Northern Av. .12W—28N	37
North Shore Dr. N&S ....11W—29N	37
Plaister Av. E&W ...12W—29N	37
Quassey Av. E&W .12W—29N	37
Rivers Dr. N&S ....11W—29N	37
Rockland Rd. E&W 12W—28N	37
Shagbark Rd. N&S 12W—29N	37
Skokie Blvd. N&S ..12W—28N	37
Skokie Hwy. N&S ..12W—31N	37
Smith Av. E&W ....12W—29N	37
Spring Ln. N&S ....11W—29N	37
Stafford Av. E&W ..12W—29N	37
Talbot Av. E&W ...12W—29N	37
Washington Av. E&W ....12W—28N	37
Woodland Rd. E&W ....12W—28N	37
22nd St. E&W ......12W—31N	37
23rd St. E&W ......12W—31N	37

Vernon Twp. Streets

	Page
Apple Hill Ln. N&S 16W—23N	50
Arlyd Rd. E&W ....16W—22N	50
Ash St. N&S ......14W—20N	51
Aspen Ct. NW&SE 14W—20N	51
Birchwood Terr. E&W ....14W—20N	51
Birch St. N&S ....14W—20N	51
Briar Terr. E&W ...14W—20N	51
Bridle Trail Rd. N&S ....14W—24N	43,44
Brockman Av. E&W ....16W—23N	50
Brockman Ct. N&S 16W—23N	50
Busch Rd. E&W ...17W—21N	50
Calvin Ct. N&S ...13W—22N	51

	Page
Carmen Av. N&S ...15W—20N	50,51
Catalpa St. N&S ...14W—20N	50
Celia Av. N&S ......16W—20N	50
Cemetery Rd. E&W ....15W—23N	50,51
Clarice Av. N&S ...16W—20N	50
Columbus Pkwy. E&W ....14W—20N	51
Conway Rd. NW&SE ....13W—25N	43,44
Country Side Ln. N&S ....18W—20N	50
Depot Pl. E&W .....16W—21N	50
Diamond Lake Rd. E&W ....19W—24N	41
Dogwood St. N&S .15W—20N	50,51
Dover Pl. NW&SE .15W—20N	50,51
Driftwood Pl. N&S .16W—20N	50
East Chevy Chase Dr. NE&SW ....14W—20N	51
Easton Av. E&W ...16W—23N	50
Estonian Ln. E&W .14W—21N	51
Elizabeth Av. N&S .15W—20N	51
Elm Rd. N&S ....14W—23,24N	43,51
Elmwood Av. N&S .14W—20N	51
Falmouth Terr. E&W ....15W—20N	50,51
Farmer Ct. N&S ...13W—22N	51
Florence Av. N&S .15W—20N	50,51
Forest Av. N&S ....15W—20N	51
Frank Av. N&S ....15W—20N	50,51
Frontenac Pl. E&W 14W—20N	51
Garden Ct. N&S ..15W—20N	50,51
G K Line N&S ....15W—22N	50,51
Gregg Rd. E&W ...14W—22N	51
Hawthorne Ln. E&W ....13W—25N	43,44
Hilgers Ct. N&S ...18W—25N	42
Holtz Rd. N&S ....15W—23N	50,51
Horatio Blvd. N&S .16W—20N	50
Indian Creek Rd. N&S ....15W—20N	50,51
Inverrary Ln. E&W 15W—20N	50,51
James Cir. N&S ...14W—20N	51
Juneway Av. NW&SE ....15W—20N	50,51
Kingston Ct. NE&SW ....16W—23N	50
Kingston Row N&S 16W—23N	50
Lancaster Rd. N&S 15W—20N	50,51
Lee Ln. E&W ......16W—23N	50
Lincoln Dr. NW&SE ....15W—20N	50,51
Linden Av. E&W 14,15W—20N	50,51
Lita Av. E&W ....15W—20N	50,51
Longwood Dr. E&W ....14W—20N	51
Long Beach Dr. N&S ....14W—20N	51
Long Grove Aptakistic Rd E&W ......15,18W—22N	50,51
Loyola Av. NW&SE 14W—20N	51
Main St. N&S .....16W—22N	50
Maple Ct. N&S ....15W—20N	50,51
Maple Pl. N&S ....15W—22N	51
Maplewood Dr. N&S ....14W—20N	51
Marie Av. E&W ...16W—20N	50
Margaret Av. N&S .16W—20N	50
Marquette Pl. E&W 16W—20N	50
Meadow Ln. E&W .13W—25N	43,44
Meadow Ln. E&W .18W—25N	41,42
Meadowlark Dr. E&W ....18W—20N	50
Menna Ct. N&S ...16W—23N	50
Mercier Av. NW&SE ....15W—20N	50,51
Michael Av. N&S ..15W—20N	50,51
Milwaukee Av. NW&SE ....14,15W—21,23N	50,51
Myville Dr. N&S ...14W—21N	51
Newman St. E&W .15W—20N	51
Norfolk Terr. E&W .15W—20N	50,51
North Woodbine Cir. ....15W—24N	43
Oak Ln. N&S ....14W—24N	43,44
Oakwood Terr. E&W ....14W—20N	51
Old Mill Rd. N&S ..13W—23N	51
Olsen Ct. N&S ....13W—23N	50,51
Orchard Hill Rd. NE&SW ....13W—25N	43,44
Osage Rd. NW&SE ....18W—25N	41,42
Park Av. N&S .....16W—23N	50
Pauline Av. E&W ..16W—20N	50
Pekara Av. N&S ...16W—20N	50
Pinehurst Dr. N&S 14W—20N	51
Port Clinton Rd. E&W ....16W—23N	50
Pope Blvd. E&W ..16W—20N	50
Prague Av. N&S ...16W—20N	51
Prairie Ln. N&S ...16W—23N	50
Prairie Rd. N&S 16W—22,23N	50
Private Rd. N&S ..16W—20N	50
Public Rd. N&S ...16W—20N	50
Public St. N&S ....16W—22N	51
Public St. NE&SW .15W—20N	50,51
Rabbe Ln. N&S ...15W—22N	50,51

	Page
Raleigh Dr. N&S ....16W—23N	50
Raphael Av. N&S ..15W—20N	50,51
Richard Ct. N&S ...16W—23N	50
Riverside Rd. N&S .14W—20N	51
Riverside Rd. E&W 14W—21N	51
Roosevelt Pl. E&W ....15W—20N	50,51
Rose Terr. N&S ....13W—22N	51
Saunders Rd. N&S 13W—25N	43,44
Schaffer Rd. N&S ..18W—20N	50
S. Chevy Chase Dr. ....14W—20N	51
S. Woodbine Cir. E&W ....15W—24N	43
Story Book Ln. N&S ....13W—23N	51
Strenger Ln. N&S ..13W—22N	51
Terril Pl. E&W .....15W—20N	50,51
Valdon Rd. E&W ...14W—23N	51
Walnut Dr. N&S ...15W—20N	50,51
Warwick Terr. E&W 15W—20N	50,51
Washington Dr. E&W ....15W—20N	50,51
Weiland Rd. NE&SW ....16W—20N	50
West Dr. E&W .....15W—20N	50,51
West Lake Terr. E&W ....15W—20N	50,51
William Av. N&S ...15W—20N	50,51
Willow Spring Rd. N&S ....18W—25N	41,42
Woodbine Dr. N&S 15W—24N	43
Woodland Ln. E&W ....13W—25N	43,44
1st St. N&S ....16W—22N	50
2nd St. N&S ......16W—23N	50

Warren Twp. Streets

	Page
Adelade Av. E&W ..12W—37N	20
Adelaide Av. E&W .13W—37N	19,20
Adelphi Av. N&S ...12W—35N	28
Almond Rd. N&S ....17W—32,33N	26
Apple Ln. E&W ....16W—35N	26,27
Applewood Ct. N&S ....16W—35N	26,27
Arbor Blvd. E&W ..18W—32N	26
Arizonia Av. E&W ..12W—36N	20
Ash Dr. E&W ......18W—36N	18
Atlantic Av. E&W ....12,13W—37N	27,28
Audrey Av. E&W ....13W—37N	19,20
Bairstow Av. E&W .10W—37N	21
Bairstow St. E&W ....12,13W—37N	19,20
Barberry Ln. NE&SW ....14W—35N	27,28
Bayonne Av. N&S .13W—36N	19,20
Beechnut Av. N&S 12W—33N	28,29
Belle Plaine N&S ..13W—37N	19,20
Elle Plaine Av. N&S ....13W—35,36N	20,28
Beverly Av. N&S ...18W—36N	18
Birch Av. N&S ....12W—33N	28,29
Blanchard Rd. E&W ....12,13W—37N	19,20
Blossom St. E&W ....12,13W—37N	19,20
Bough Ct. N&S ...15W—35N	19,27
Boulevard View Av. N&S ....13W—35,36N	20,28
Branch Rd. N&S ..15W—35N	19,27
Brooke Av. E&W ..18W—32N	26
Carvis Dr. N&S ....18W—34N	26
Cemetery Rd. E&W 16W—34N	26,27
Center Dr. N&S ...18W—36N	18
Cheyenne Rd. E&W ....12,13W—36N	19,20
Circle East SE&NW ....17W—34N	26
Clearview Av. E&W ....13W—36N	19,20
Colorado Av. E&W 12W—36N	20
Cottage Av. E&W ..18W—34N	26
Country Club Av. E&W ....12,13W—36N	19,20
Crescent Av. E&W 12W—35N	28,29
Dartmoor Dr. E&W 17W—33N	26
Delany Rd. N&S ..14W—35N	27,28
Dillys Rd. N&S ....15W—36N	19
Dorothy St. N&S ..12W—37N	20
Dromey Av. N&S ..12W—33N	28,29
Douglas Terr. N&S 18W—36N	18
Duggalo Av. E&W .12W—35N	28,29
Eastwood Av. E&W 14W—33N	27,28
Eastwood Pl. E&W 14W—33N	27,28
Eastwood Rd. E&W ....11,12W—37N	20,21
Edgewood Dr. E&W ....16W—35N	18,26
Edgewood Dr N&S ....16,18W—35N	26,27
Elizabeth St. E&W .13W—37N	19,20
E. McArthur Dr. E&W ....10W—37N	21
Everett Pl. N&S ...14W—33N	27,28
Florida Av. E&W ....12W—36N	19,20
Forest Av. E&W ...14W—33N	27,28

	Page
Forest Dr. NW&SE 18W—32N	26
Frolic Av. N&S ..12W—35,37N	21,28
Gages Lake Rd. E&W ....16,17,18W—33N	26,27
Ganster Rd. N&S ..9W—37N	21
Garnett Av. N&S ..10W—37N	21
Garrick Av. N&S 12W—35,36N	21,28
Geier Rd. E&W ....18W—36N	18
Geraughty Av. N&S ....10W—37N	21
Glen Flora Av. E&W ....12,13W—35N	28,29
Grand Av. E&W 17,18W—36N	18
Grandmore Av. E&W ....12W—35N	28,29
Grandview Av. E&W ....12W—35N	28,29
Grandville Av. E&W ....12W—35N	28,29
Grandwood Dr. NE&SW ....18W—36N	18
Grant Av. N&S ....18W—34N	26
Graves Av. E&W ..12W—37N	20
Green Av. N&S .12W—35,37N	21,28
Greenwood Av. E&W ....12,13W—36N	19,20
Greenleaf St. N&S ....13W—33,34N	27,28
Grove Av. E&W 12,13W—35N	28,29
Hanlon Rd. N&S ..15W—32N	27
Harrison Av. E&W .12W—35N	28,29
Hendee Av. E&W ..10W—37N	21
Hendee St. E&W ....12,13W—37N	19,20
Highland Av. E&W ....12,13W—36N	19,20
Highland Av. E&W ....12,13W—36N	19,20
Highfield Dr. West E&W ....18W—36N	18
Highfield Dr. North N&S ....18W—36N	18
Hill Av. E&W ......14W—33N	27,28
Holdridge Av. N&S 10W—37N	21
Hunt Club Rd. N&S ....17W—33,36N	18,26
Hutchins Rd. N&S .18W—37N	18
Hyatt Ln. N&S ....14W—33N	27,28
Ingleside Pl. E&W .14W—33N	27,28
Johns Manville Av. E&W ....13W—35N	27,28
Jonathan Rd. E&W 16W—35N	26,27
Judy Dr. E&W .....18W—36N	18
Juniper St. N&S ...15W—35N	27
Karelia Rd. N&S ...16W—34N	26,27
Karen Ln. E&W ...18W—36N	18
Keith Av. E&W ..12,13W—35N	28,29
Kennedy Dr. E&W .14W—33N	27,28
Knight Av. N&S ...12W—33N	28,29
Knowles Rd. NE&SW ....18W—35N	18,26
Lake St. N&S .....18W—34N	26
Lake Crest Av. N&S ....10W—37N	21
Lakeview Terr. E&W ....18W—36N	18
Lakewood Av. N&S 12W—34N	28,29
Lawn Av. E&W ....14W—33N	27,28
Lee Av. E&W ..12,13W—35N	28,29
Lee Cir. E&W .....18W—36N	18
Limb Ct. N&S ....15W—35N	27
Lincoln Av. NW&SE ....18W—34N	26
Linda Ln. E&W ....18W—36N	18
Loyola Av. N&S ...10W—37N	21
Magnolia Av. N&S ....13W—35,36N	20,28
Manor Av. N&S ...10W—37N	21
Maple Av. E&W ...18W—32N	26
Marian Dr. E&W ..18W—35N	18,26
Mawman Av. E&W 10W—37N	21
Mawman St. E&W ....12,13W—37N	19,20
Meadowbrook Dr. E&W ....17W—33N	26
Meadow Ln. E&W .18W—36N	18
Melody Rd. N&S ..14W—33N	27,28
Meyer Rd. E&W ...14W—37N	19,20
Mill Ct. E&W ......18W—36N	18
Milwaukee Av. N&S ....14W—36N	19,20
Milwaukee Av. NE&SW ....16W—32N	26,27
Morton Av. E&W ..10W—37N	21
N. Bonnie Brook Ln. E&W ....12W—37N	20
Nemesis Av. E&W ....12,13W—36N	19,20
Northern Av. N&S ....12W—35,36N	20,28
North Shore Av. N&S ....10W—37N	21
Northwestern Av. N&S ....13W—37N	19,20
Northwoods Av. N&S ....14W—33N	27,28
Oak Av. N&S .....12W—37N	20
Oak Knoll SE&NW 17W—34N	26
Oakwood Av. N&S 12W—35N	28,29
Oakwood Dr. .18W—36N	18

	Page
O'Plaine Rd. N&S .14W—32N	27,28
Orchard Rd. N&S ..11W—37N	20,21
Orchard Valley Dr. ....16W—35N	26,27
Pacific Av. E&W ...13W—35N	27,28
Paddock St. E&W ....12,13W—37N	19,20
Pamela Pl. E&W ..18W—36N	18
Park Cres. E&W ...18W—34N	26
Park Dr. E&W .....18W—36N	18
Park Pl. E&W .....18W—36N	18
Parkway Av. E&W .14W—33N	27,28
Pine Av. N&S ..12,18W—32N	26,29
Pleasant Pl. E&W .18W—34N	26
Polo Av. E&W .....18W—36N	20
Public Service Av. N&S ....12W—35N	28,29
Rae Ln. E&W .....18W—36N	18
Red Oak Dr. N&S .17W—34N	26
River Rd. N&S ....15W—32N	27
Rosedale Av. N&S 13W—36N	19,20
Royal Oak Ln. N&S ....18W—33N	26
Sallmon Av. N&S ..13W—37N	19,20
Sallmon Rd. E&W .12W—37N	20
Sand Lake Rd. E&W ....18W—37N	18
Sheridan Av. E&W 18W—34N	26
Sherman Av. E&W ....12,13W—35N	28,29
Shirley Dr. N&S ...14W—37N	19,20
Sibelius Ln. E&W ..16W—35N	26,27
Skokie Hwy. N&S ....13,14W—32,36N	20,28
Southview Av. E&W ....12W—35N	28,29
Staben Av. N&S ..12W—33N	28,29
Stratton Av. N&S ..9W—37N	21
Summit Dr. E&W ..17W—33N	26
Spruce St. N&S ..15W—35N	19,27
Streamwood Ct. E&W ....18W—36N	18
Streamwood Dr. N&S ....18W—36N	18
Stearns School Rd. NW&SE ....17W—36N	18
Telegraph Rd. N&S 13W—32N	27,28
Town Line Rd. E&W ....13W—38N	19,20
Treaer Terr. E&W ....18W—36N	18
Tri-State North Tollway N&S,NW&SE ..16W—36,37N	18
Tyler Av. E&W ..12,13W—36N	19,20
Verco Av. E&W ...13W—37N	19,20
Vercoll Av. E&W ..12W—37N	20
Vermont Av. E&W ....12,13W—36N	19,20
Wall Av. E&W ..12,13W—36N	19,20
Walnut Av. N&S ..12W—32N	28,29
Warner Av. E&W ..12W—37N	20
Washington St. E&W ....18,19W—34N	25,26
West Av. N&S ....13W—33N	27,28
Westwood Pl. E&W ....18W—36N	18
Wilson Av. N&S ...13W—33N	27,28
Windslow Dr. E&W 17W—33N	26
Woodhill Dr. E&W .15W—35N	19,27
Woodland Dr. E&W 17W—33N	26
Woodland Terr. E&W ....18W—36N	18
Yorkhouse Rd. E&W ....13,15W—37,38N	19,20
11th St. E&W .....12W—32N	28,29
12th St. E&W .....12W—32N	28,29

Wauconda Twp. Streets

	Page
Alvinia St. N&S ...25W—27N	39
Anderson Rd. N&S ....27W—26,27N	38
Ann Ct. N&S ....26W—26N	38,39
Ash St. N&S ......25W—27N	39
Belvidere Rd. E&W ....26,28W—31N	30,31
Berke Ct. N&S ....25W—28N	31
Blakley Pkwy. E&W ....25W—26N	39
Bluff St. N&S .....25W—27N	39
Bonner Rd. E&W ....26,27W—28N	30,31
Burnett Rd. E&W ..28W—29N	30
Callahan Rd. N&S ....26W—29,30N	30
Cary Plaza NE&SW ....25W—28N	31
Case Rd. E&W ...27W—29N	30
Cook St. N&S ....25W—28N	31
Crest Rd. E&W ...28W—28N	30
Darrell Rd. E&W 28W—29,31N	30
Dowell Rd. NE&SW ....28W—30N	30
East Lake Shore Dr. NW&SE ....25W—26N	39
Elmwood Av. NE&SW ....26W—27N	38,39
Fisher Rd. N&S ...28W—30N	30
Fish Lake Rd. N&S 26W—31N	30,31
Gardner Rd. E&W .25W—29N	31
Garland Rd. E&W .26W—28N	30,31

Page

Garland Rd. N&S ..25W—29N   31
Gilmer Rd. NW&SE
.....................26W—31N 30,31
Gossell Rd. NW&SE
.....................25W—29N   31
Grace St. N&S ....27W—27N   39
Greenbriar Ct. N&S
.....................27W—26N   38
Harrison Av. N&S ..25W—29N   31
Hermosa Av. E&W 25W—26N   39
Hickory Av. N&S ...25W—28N   31
High Rd. N&S ....28W—28N   30
Hill Av. N&S ....25W—26N   39
Hill St. E&W ....25W—27N   39
Hillside Av. E&W ..25W—26N   39
Ivanhoe Rd. E&W
.............25,26W—26N 38,39
Karen Dr. E&W .....26W—26N   39
Knollwood Dr. N&S 25W—26N   39
Lake Dr. N&S ....25W—28N   31
Lake Pkwy. E&W ..25W—29N   31
Lake St. E&W ....25W—27N   39
Lakeland Dr. N&S .26W—26N   39
Lake Shore Ct. N&S
.....................25W—26N   39
Lakeview Cir. N&S 28W—28N   30
Laurel Av. E&W ....26W—26N   39
Laurel Ct. N&S .....26W—26N   39
Legion Ct. N&S .....25W—26N   39
Lemon St. N&S .....20W—28N   33
Liberty St. E&W ...26W—27N 38,39
Locust Dr. E&W ....28W—26N   38
Mac St. N&S ....27W—27N   38
Madison Av. NE&SW
.....................25W—29N   31
May St. E&W ....27W—27N   38
Mead Av. NE&SW .25W—26N   39
Meadow Ln. N&S ..25W—26N   39
Meadow Lane Rd. E&W
.....................28W—28N   30
Meeker Ct. E&W ...28W—27N   38

Page

Monroe Av. NE&SW
.....................25W—29N   31
Myrtle St. N&S ....25W—27N   39
Neville Rd. E&W ...28W—30N   30
North Lakeview Dr. E&W
.....................27W—26N   38
Oak Dr. N&S ....25W—26N   39
Oak Knoll Dr. N&S 28W—28N   30
Old Rand Rd. N&S 26W—28N 30,31
Orchard Dr. NE&SW
.....................28W—27N   38
Pleasant View Av. E&W
.....................25W—28N   31
Rand Rd. NW&SE 25W—26N   39
Ridge Rd. E&W ....28W—28N   30
Ridge St. N&S ....25W—27N   39
S. Lakeview Dr. E&W
.....................28W—26N   38
Slocum Lake Rd. E&W
.....................27W—27N   38
Sunset Dr. E&W ...28W—31N   30
Swift Ct. N&S ....26W—26N 38,39
Tamarack Dr. E&W 25W—26N   39
Valentine Rd. N&S 25W—27N   39
Valleyview Dr. NW&SE
.....................28W—31N   30
Wade St. N&S ....25W—29N   31
Washington Av. NE&SW
.....................25W—28N   31
Wellis Dr. N&S ....25W—28N   31
Werden Av. N&S ...25W—28N   31
West Dr. E&W ....25W—28N   31
West End Rd. N&S 26W—28N 30,31
Williams Park Rd. N&S
.....................27W—27N   38
Wilson Av. E&W ...25W—27N   39
Wilton Rd. N&S ....25W—26N   39
Winding Lane Dr. N&S
.....................25W—28N   31
York Dr. N&S ....25W—26N   39

Page

Waukegan Twp. Streets
Adelaide Av. E&W .12W—37N   20
Adelphi Av. N&S ....12W—35N 28,29
Arizonia Av. E&W ..12W—36N   20
Atlantic Av. E&W ...12W—35N 28,29
Audrey Av. E&W ....12W—37N   20
Bairstow Av. E&W .10W—37N   21
Bairstow St. E&W .12W—37N   20
Blanchard Rd. E&W
.....................12W—37N   20
Blossom St. E&W
.............12,13W—37N 19,20
Brooke Av. E&W ...12W—36N   20
Charleston Rd. N&S
.....................11W—37N 20,21
Cheyenne Rd. E&W
.....................12W—36N   20
Clearview Av. ....12W—36N   20
Colorado Av. E&W 12W—36N   20
Country Club Av. N&S
.....................12W—36N   20
Crescent Av. E&W 12W—35N 28,29
Dorothy St. E&W ...12W—37N   20
Duggale Av. E&W .12W—35N 28,29
Eastwood Rd. E&W
.............10,12W—37N 20,21
Elizabeth St. E&W 13W—37N 19,20
E. McArthur Dr. E&W
.....................10W—37N   21
Evergreen Av. N&S 12W—37N   20
Florida Av. E&W ....12W—36N   20
Frolic Av. N&S
.............12W—35,36,37N 19,28
Ganster Rd. N&S ...9W—37N   21
Garnett Av. N&S ....10W—37N   21
Garrick Av. N&S 12W—35,36N 19,28
Geraughty Av. N&S
.....................10W—37N   21
Glen Flora Av. E&W
.....................12W—35N 28,29

Page

Grandmore Av. E&W
.....................12W—35N 28,29
Grandview Av. E&W
.....................12W—35N   20
Grandville Av. E&W
.....................12W—35N 28,29
Graves Av. ...12W—37N   20
Green Av. N&S .12W—35,37N 19,28
Green Bay Rd. NE&SW
.....................12W—36,37N   20
Greenwood Av. E&W
.....................12W—36N   20
Grove Av. E&W ...12W—35N 28,29
Harrison Av. E&W .12W—35N 28,29
Hendee Av. E&W ..10W—37N   21
Hendee St. E&W ..12W—37N   20
Highland Av. E&W .12W—36N   20
Holdridge Av. N&S 10W—37N   21
Johns Manville Av. E&W
.....................12W—35N 28,29
Keith Av. E&W .....12W—35N 28,29
Lake Crest Av. N&S
.....................10W—37N   21
Lee Av. E&W ....12W—35N 28,29
Loyola Av. N&S .....10W—37N   21
Manor Av. N&S .....10W—37N   21
Mawman Av. E&W 10W—37N   21
Mawman St. E&W .12W—37N   20
Metropolitan Av. N&S
.....................12W—37N   20
Morton Av. E&W ...10W—37N   21
N. Bonnie Brook Ln. E&W
.....................12W—37N   20
Nemesis Av. E&W .12W—36N   20
Northern Av. N&S
.............12W—35,36N 20,28
Northfield Av. E&W 12W—35N 28,29
North Shore Av. N&S
.....................10W—37N   21
Orchard Rd. N&S ..11W—37N 20,21

Page

Pacific Av. E&W ....12W—35N 28,29
Paddock Av. E&W .10W—37N 20,21
Paddock St. E&W .12W—37N   20
Polo Av. E&W ....12W—36N   20
Public Service Av. N&S
.....................12W—35N 28,29
Sallmon Rd. N&S .12W—37N   20
Sherman Av. E&W .12W—35N 28,29
Southview Av. E&W
.....................12W—35N 28,29
Stratton Av. N&S ....9W—37N   21
Tyler Av. E&W ....12W—36N   20
Vercoe Av. E&W ...12W—37N   20
Vermont Av. E&W .12W—36N   20
Wall Av. E&W ....12W—36N   20
Warner Av. E&W ..12W—37N   20
Wilson Av. N&S .....10W—37N   21
Yorkhouse Rd. E&W
.............10,13W—37N 20,21

West Deerfield Twp. Streets
Birchwood Ln. N&S
.....................11W—23N   52
Cris Ct. E&W ....12W—21N   52
Dawson Ct. E&W ..12W—22N   52
Deer Run Dr. N&S 12W—20N   52
Elmwood Pl. N&S ..11W—23N   52
Forest Ct. N&S ......11W—23N   52
Half Day Rd. E&W 12W—23N   52
Hawthorne Ln. E&W
.....................12W—20N   52
Hickory Knoll Ln. E&W
Montgomery Rd. N&S
.....................12W—21N   52
Oakwood Pl. E&W 11W—23N   52
Riverwoods Rd. N&S
.....................12W—20N   52
Tri-State Tollway NW&SE
Wildwood Ln. N&S 11W—23N   52
Woodland Ln. N&S 12W—22N   52
Woodview Ln. N&S 12W—20N   52